Republican Paradoxes and Liberal Anxieties

Republican Paradoxes and Liberal Anxieties

Retrieving Neglected Fragments
of Political Theory

Ronald J. Terchek

ROWMAN & LITTLEFIELD PUBLISHERS, INC.
Lanham · Boulder · New York · London

ROWMAN & LITTLEFIELD PUBLISHERS, INC.

Published in the United States of America
by Rowman & Littlefield Publishers, Inc.
4720 Boston Way, Lanham, Maryland 20706
3 Henrietta Street
London, WC2E 8LU, England

Copyright © 1997 by Rowman & Littlefield Publishers, Inc.

All rights reserved. No part of this publication may be reproduced, stored in a retrieval system, or transmitted in any form or by any means, electronic, mechanical, photocopying, recording, or otherwise, without the prior permission of the publisher.

British Cataloging in Publication Information Available

Library of Congress Cataloging-in-Publication Data

Terchek, Ronald, 1936–
Republic paradoxes and liberal anxieties : retrieving neglected fragments of political theory / Ronald J. Terchek.
p. cm.
Includes bibliographical references and index.
1. Liberalism. 2. Republicanism. 3. Political science—Philosophy.
I. Title.
JC574.T47 1997   320.5'1—dc20   96–17917   CIP

ISBN 0–8476–8373–7 (cloth : alk. paper)
ISBN 0–8476–8374–5 (pbk. : alk. paper)

Printed in the United States of America

 The paper used in this publication meets the minimum requirements of American National Standard for Information Sciences—Permanence of Paper for Printed Library Materials, ANSI Z39.48-1984.

To
Mary

Contents

Acknowledgments	xi
Introduction	1
The Center Does Not Hold	2
The Players: Old and New	3
Strong Republicans	6
Anxious Liberals	8
The Multiple Languages of American Political Discourse	11
Politics and Political Theory	11
1 Debates between and about Traditions	15
Politics and Particularities	19
Constructing Traditions and Critiquing Society	21
How Distinctive Are the Languages of Republicanism and Liberalism?	25
Rich Commentaries and Rigid Commentaries	30
Theory and Practice	34
Moving Fragments across Time	35
2 The Stakes of Citizenship and the Citizen's Stakes	47
Thinking about Stakes	48
Property and Citizenship	51
Aristotle, the Household, and Money	54
Machiavelli's Citizens and Householders	64
Rousseau, Property, and Liberty	70
Economic Contingencies and Republican Politics	77
Self and Society, Not Self or Society	79

3 Noisy Republicans: Mythologizing the Founding and Justifying Conflict   95
Differences, Disagreements, and Agreements   96
Foundations, Ambition, and Equilibrium: The Case of Machiavelli   99
Passivity, Agitation, and the Longevity of Rousseau's Republic   107
Another Republican Paradox   113

4 Anxious Liberals I: The Moral Individualism of John Locke   121
Liberal Choice and Responsibilities   122
Abstracted vs. Busy Liberals   123
Liberal Imperfections: Autonomy and the Good Life   125
Radical Individualism and the Problem of Subjectivity   127
Making Freedom an Opportunity and a Burden: John Locke's Anxious Liberalism   128
Locke's Liberalism and Ours   137

5 Anxious Liberals II: J. S. Mill on Overcoming the Natural Self   147
J. S. Mill and the Renewal of Tradition   153
The Participatory Mill   155
Is Mill a Genuine Liberal?   159
The Status of Culture in Mill   162
Anxious Liberals: Do We Need Them?   164

6 Interest-Group Liberals and Libertarians: The Critique of Adam Smith   171
Interest-Group Liberals   172
Libertarian Debts   173
Adam Smith's Secular and Moral Agents   174
Dependence and Independence   179
Interests and Markets   183
The Deception of Wealth   185
Internalizing Limits: The Deception of Deference   187
The Dangers of a Demythologized Politics   189
Politics and the Corruption of Interests   190
Taxes and the New Civic Duty   191
Reading Smith Today   193

7 The Languages of American Politics — 205
Continental Republicanism: A Reprise — 206
The American Version of Republicanism — 207
Recovering Liberalism — 208
Republican Deference and American Egalitarianism — 211
Republican Fragments and Reformulations: Stable
  Property or the Opportunity Society — 214
Reconstituting the Founding and Lincoln's Moral
  Impatience — 216
American Rhetorics — 225

8 Paradoxes and Anxieties for Politics Today — 231
Reconsidering the Two-Language Paradigm — 232
Returning to Republican Roots — 233
The Lives of Ordinary Liberals — 236
Enlarging the Debate for Communitarians — 239
Enlarging the Debate for Contemporary Liberals — 241
Welcoming Politics Back to Theory — 245

Bibliography — 251
Index — 267
About the Author — 277

Acknowledgments

Debts are easy to accumulate but hard to repay. In thinking and writing about republicanism and liberalism, I have amassed substantial debts. Some are to the authors, both ancient and modern, I have read and reread. Even when I disagreed with them, I continue to find them exciting and important in their efforts to engage theory and politics. Although I am frequently critical of some contemporary theorists today, I continue to learn much from them.

I particularly want to acknowledge the help that Alfonso Damico and Charles Helms have given over the years, both as forthright critics and generous readers. Suzanne Jacobitti, Kenneth Deutsch, Emily Gill, John Nelson, William Galston, George Graham, Jane Mansbridge, Patricia Wrightson, Eldon Eisenach, Richard Flathman, and Fred Alford have been especially helpful in their comments and suggestions. My colleagues at College Park have been constant sources of stimulation and support, particularly Don Piper and my fellow theorists.

Several of the ideas that appear in *Republican Paradoxes and Liberal Anxieties* were initially presented at various conferences here and abroad, and the many comments and suggestions have been welcome and useful. Particularly stimulating have been the participants of the Roundtable on Political Myth, Rhetoric, and Symbolism of the Foundations of Political Theory.

The arguments in this book were tried, tested, and revised in my undergraduate course on the history of political theory as well as my graduate seminars on democratic theory and the liberal-communitarian debate. My students showed they could be simultaneously civil and demanding and that as important as the content of an argument is its clarity of expression. Stephen Wrinn and Julie Kuzneski at Rowman & Littlefield have been patient in helping me in many ways see this manuscript to press.

In their very different ways, Kristin and Daniel have eased the routines of scholarship with their good humor. My greatest debt is to my wife, not only because she proved to be an invaluable editor, a helpful critic, and a patient listener, but most especially because of her encouragement and love over our years together. I dedicate this book to her.

Introduction

All is not well in modern liberal-democratic society. We seem unable to speak to a common good, present a coherent view of citizenship, reconcile valid but competing demands, address the issue of community while respecting diversity, harness materialism and self-interest, and confront the needs of society's most vulnerable citizens. In the debate about the responsibility for what ails us, we continually return to the liberal tradition. Communitarians lament the liberalism we have inherited[1]; libertarians endeavor to recover the liberalism we have discarded[2]; and liberals seek to improve our liberal legacy.[3]

These critiques not only address contemporary practices in the liberal democratic regime but also provide particular readings of the republican and liberal traditions. Communitarians, who are the latest expression of republicanism, find that the fundamental flaws in early liberal thinking continue to haunt contemporary liberalism, with Alasdair MacIntyre pointing to the emotivism of Hume, and Michael Sandel to the abstractness of Kant. In their discussion of our present discontents, communitarians frequently look back to earlier republican texts to provide an ennobling reading of a politics that aims for what is common and seeks both liberty and civic virtue.[4] Libertarian critics find a much different problem, namely, an abandonment of what they take to be the foundational principles of liberalism. Libertarians argue that modern liberal democracies have strayed from their liberal origins and urge us to rejuvenate Adam Smith's negative state and robust market[5] or protect a revised Lockean conception of private property.[6] For their part, liberals emphasize the rights-based features of their tradition, frequently reaching back to Kant or Locke to establish the inviolability of the person and to deny that individual rights must first pass a morals-means test.[7] They refuse to endorse libertarian claims to return to a past that they read as restrictive to autonomy and blind to nonpolitical forms of power. They fear that communitarian solutions neglect diversity, threaten or ignore basic rights, and freeze current inequities.[8]

In asking us to restore earlier civic republics, return to Adam Smith's markets, or be guided by Kantian or Lockean conceptions of the person, each position ignores important parts of its own tradition. One of the purposes of this book is to renew discussion about some of the elements of early republicanism and early liberalism that have been neglected or discounted in recent discussions.[9] I also pose questions about the rigid way the debate is framed today and seek to locate alternative ways of facing some of the issues that continually follow us.

The Center Does Not Hold

An important part of the debate about the status of contemporary democracy concerns the relationship of the parts to the whole. Sometimes this is expressed in communitarian terms which challenge an assertive, materialistic individualism and introduce us to liberals who are largely left to their own devices to understand who they are and what is important to them. Without a consensus about what constitutes the good, liberals are said to be preoccupied with their immediate situations, not realizing how they are connected to one another and to the institutions of the republic. Bound only by the thinnest of threads to other citizens, they share no deep understandings of civic responsibilities or common projects, and politics becomes a place where the strongest groups dominate and the weaker pay the costs of defeat or neglect. We are left with fragmented political practices that are characterized by a disintegrating legitimacy, language, and direction. If only the center can be reestablished, community renewed, and understandings shared, many communitarians argue, we can proceed with our common tasks of politics and uncover a general good.[10]

For their part, many contemporary liberals also see fragmentation but find it in the deep, undeserved inequalities that were historically generated and are now reinforced by contemporary institutional practices. These liberals cannot understand how we can talk about a vital center that is exclusionary and find that the major task of contemporary politics is to include those who are only partially incorporated into the political community. In this account, inclusion cannot mean returning to a fixed past or stable practices that ignore historic disabilities or continue past patterns of subordination. Rather, we are told, we require a set of rules or procedures sharp enough to dismantle obstacles to rights.

The Players: Old and New

Today's debate between liberals and communitarians is not an orderly standoff between two well-delineated positions. Rather, we find a vast variety of communitarians and an even larger panoply of liberals in the fray. We can conceptualize each of these two broad positions as two extended families with many branches, some supportive of one another and others hardly on speaking terms except when they shout at each other. Rather than setting out precise definitions of liberalism and communitarianism, I want to consider them as general persuasions, or positions whose supporters agree about some general priorities as well as share similar views about what is most menacing in the world.[11]

Before doing so, it is important to emphasize that both liberals and communitarians prize liberty. For liberals, the greatest threat comes from external efforts to restrict individual choice; communitarians see the primary danger residing in a culture that is fragmented and narrowly individualistic. In many ways, the contest between liberals and communitarians is about what subverts autonomy. However differently various liberals conceptualize autonomy, they are particularly concerned about obstacles to choice: some are concerned about the disabilities associated with particular background attributes, such as race and gender; others about state intrusions into the market; and still others about blockages to pluralist politics. Communitarians, however, cannot understand how liberals can consider people to be autonomous if they are abstracted from their everyday settings when they make choices. For this reason, communitarians look to a strong, coherent moral foundation for society, which provides agents with meaning and direction.

We encounter an immediate problem in determining just who contemporary liberals and communitarians are. The way they describe each other is very different from the way they understand themselves. For their part, liberals think of themselves as generous and optimistic, insisting that ordinary people ought to be able to make fundamental choices for themselves. Communitarians see these same liberals leaving agents lonely, rudderless individualists who do not know what to make of their freedom except to advance economically. For the most part, communitarians hold that they want to provide a coherent foundation for free men and women who are socially and morally extended in the life of their community. This emphasis on coherence, connectedness, and civic direction troubles many liberals who find such commitments stifle choices, particularly for those who are not part of the normative consensus.

In what follows, I will be talking about three different branches of contemporary liberalism to distinguish them from what I call the anxious liberalism of John Locke, Adam Smith, and John Stuart Mill. I also consider contemporary communitarians to show how they differ from the strong republicanism of Aristotle, Machiavelli, and Rousseau. I do not mean to suggest that any particular branch of liberalism or republicanism is the embodiment of its tradition. Each tradition is too internally argumentative to assign priority to one branch as its real embodiment. Rather, I mean to show that most current constructions of the two traditions are rigid and would be enriched by retrieving some of the concerns of earlier writers.

The Republican Family Today

In academic debates today, republicanism is generally understood as celebrating a robust, coherent community which provides citizens with the moral materials to make choices and to resist corruption. The strong republicans I discuss, Aristotle, Machiavelli, and Rousseau, seek ways for citizens to enjoy their liberty and be civically virtuous. Unlike contemporary republicans, who generally go by the name "communitarians," strong republicans see that the very things that are required for a strong republic serve to undermine it. For them, republican politics is paradoxical and fluid, and they resist efforts to freeze the good and reach for rigid formula.

For all their differences, there are two sorts of agreements that join communitarians together. One is a shared reading of contemporary liberal society as morally empty and populated by materialistic, lonely, and fragmented individuals. Another is that individuals cannot be understood apart from their community, which should play a central role in grounding choice. Rather than finding individual entitlements in a liberal society a reason for celebration, they see them as damaging and alienating. As they survey contemporary liberal-democratic society, communitarians find a landscape disfigured with shattered liberal dreams.

Many communitarians find the liberal language of rights undermines its own best commitments to choice because it forgets that choice is the end of a process that begins in a community. Some, such as Charles

Taylor and Benjamin Barber, want to reconstitute contemporary liberal society to make it into a thriving community.[12] Other communitarians place much less emphasis on institutional practices and focus on arguments about the importance of community in general; about the need to find a way of incorporating moral knowledge into contemporary society, particularly in the family and in schools; and about the need to recapture earlier ideals in the nation's history and make them our own today.[13] However, there is no communitarian consensus about what is the character of the good community. Some look to ancient texts for inspiration and some to religious foundations. For other communitarians, the pressing need is to restore past traditions, particularly those they find at the American founding, which is said to be a time when citizens were civically virtuous, politics aimed at the general good, and citizens shared a common outlook. When we survey their writings today, we find communitarians occupying positions on the left, center, and right of the political spectrum in their search for the good community, and notice sharp disagreements among them about the way republican principles should be incorporated into contemporary politics.[14]

The Liberal Family Today

In addition to the anxious liberalism of John Locke, Adam Smith, and John Stuart Mill, I also consider three branches of contemporary liberalism: procedural, libertarian, and interest groups liberals. Procedural liberals are associated with the work of John Rawls, Ronald Dworkin, and Bruce Ackerman in their quest to find rules that overcome narrow interests and that aim at neutrality and impartiality. For them, the most ominous threats come from the institutional practices of both the state and civil society, which have historically disabled particular groups from fully participating in society. Libertarian liberals also seek to defend a set of rules they take to be impartial; in their case, they focus on rules that protect an unrestricted market and a negative state. Interest-group liberals believe they have found neutral rules, such as political competition and bargaining, for a pluralist democracy.

However much these three branches of liberalism differ from one another, they nevertheless share important characteristics as members of the liberal family. For each, individual choice is paramount. All three branches privilege freedom even though they differ as to what this means, what gets in its way, and how best to achieve it. Rawls and Dworkin, for example, are concerned as procedural liberals about the disabilities attached to individuals because of background characteristics, such as parental income or education, gender, or race. For them, we need to find rules sharp enough to cut through conventional practices that disable some and construct a polity that is impartial and fair. Such a solution, however, troubles libertarian liberals because it calls on the state to rearrange the opportunities supplied by chance, thereby converting the negative state into an active one and regulating the market for social purposes. Friedrich Hayek and Robert Nozick find procedural liberals misunderstanding choice, which they take to mean freedom from the supervisory and regulatory policies of the state. Working with the free-choice assumptions of other liberals, interest-group liberals see democratic politics ideally as open and competitive, with no one group controlling the system. At the normative level, interest-group liberals hold that citizens should be free to form their own preferences and act on them politically with others who share their interests.

In each of these three branches of liberalism, community plays a background role, and the analytical and normative foci are the choices available or denied to individuals. The good community that emerges for procedural liberals is one that is open to diverse identities; libertarian liberals seek a culture whose members do not seek favors from the government and oppose those who do; interest-group liberals look to a culture that respects the "democratic creed" with its commitment to free speech and assembly and representative government.

Strong Republicans

As strong republicans, Aristotle, Machiavelli, and Rousseau are concerned not only with a common good and the dangers of a corrupt society but also with the institutions, practices, and experiences that inform the lives of ordinary citizens.[15] For them, republican politics does not continually require ordinary citizens to make hard choices between the security of their own households and the common good. Strong republicans are strong in comparison to most communitarians who avoid the hard work of thinking about how ordinary people face their daily routines, how they earn a living, and whether they are secure.

Strong republicans hold that citizens, regardless of the character of their regime, care about themselves, not in a narrow, selfish way but in ways that acknowledge that people want to attend to their many needs, including their needs for a livelihood and security. Consequently, they find that any effort to build a politics for a free people that emphasizes citizenship, patriotism, and duty but disregards the ways ordinary citizens live from day to day is bound to fail. For this reason, strong republicans want the institutional arrangements of the republic to validate its foundational commitment to the liberty and security of every citizen.

In contrast, most contemporary approaches to community devote attention to a civic education as a way of achieving patriotism and civic virtue, a position they share with Cicero.[16] In this version of republicanism, all citizens are thought capable of practicing civic virtue and meeting their civic duties regardless of their personal security or well-being. Although strong republicans recognize a civic education is essential to the vitality of the republic, they also know that civic commitments are closely tied to the experiences of citizens and to the deep structures of their society and that moral axioms that stand apart from the way ordinary citizens lead their daily lives have no purchase.

Aristotle, Machiavelli, and Rousseau hold that good republican citizens require not only coherent foundational principles (as most communitarians argue today) but also a secure household (as most communitarians ignore today). Strong republicans want citizens to know that their own well-being and the security of their households give them an enduring, substantive stake in the vitality of their republic. The issue I explore is why, in these strong republicans, stakes are considered absolutely necessary for the good republic and why individuals without stakes will be hostile or apathetic citizens, seeing either no relationship between their own well-being and the common good or a conflict between the two. In stressing the importance of stakes, I argue that strong republicans expect the citizens of the good republic to be concerned about themselves, and the issue is how they frame that concern.

Strong republicans require citizens to be property owners not just for exclusionary reasons or even to enable citizens to confront necessity and have the leisure to devote to politics, as important as these latter goods are. Strong republicans also believe that property ownership gives citizens a concrete investment in maintaining the vitality and strength of their republic. For compelling reasons, we have emphasized the restrictive nature of a property qualification requirement for full citizenship and we have impatiently worked to dismantle barriers to full civic participation. But in advancing claims for political equality, we have ignored why strong republicans claim that full citizenship requires concrete stakes and why they believe citizens are concerned with their own well-being. That the self and society are different is obvious enough, and as contemporary communitarians helpfully remind us, the self cannot be understood outside of society.[17] However, the idea that citizens should routinely place the republic before themselves seems counterintuitive, and not merely to liberals.[18]

Nor do strong republicans make the kind of mistake that characterizes some communitarians who confuse political theory with moral philosophy or theology. The former tell us what is good independent of setting or of personal costs: Christians, for example, are expected to remain steadfast to their faith in a coliseum filled with lions. Strong republicans assume the task of avoiding not only the coliseum but any political regime that forces men and women to choose between their moral standards and elementary concerns about themselves. This hardly means strong republicans never expect citizens to confront situations where they are called to make personal sacrifices. In ordinary times, however, strong republicans want us to be free from severe hardships and enjoy the kinds of goods that Aristotle thinks are important, namely our households and our friends.

Beside the dangers that come from external adversaries, republics are also vulnerable to the ambitions of their closet friends and beneficiaries: their own citizens. For strong republicans, political discourse must challenge the proclivity of even the best citizens to become self-involved and politically lethargic. The very property that gives citizens a stake in supporting and defending the republic can become converted into narrow interests and contribute to the politics of faction, and this danger reveals the paradox that resides in strong republicanism. For strong republicans, politics must challenge the tendency of people to become preoccupied with themselves. Stressing agreement and harmony in the good republic becomes an impediment when the maintenance of the republic requires patriotic citizens to confront ambition, including their own. It turns out that the republican settlement is fragile and problematic, and intense controversy is often necessary to restore its health.[19]

Anxious Liberals

John Locke, Adam Smith, and John Stuart Mill are familiar liberals and have conventionally been read as champions of individual rights and tolerance, topics that remain important to liberals. In what follows, I read them with a different emphasis than is usually the case in the liberal-communitarian debate. Rather than concentrating on the reason why people are due rights and what these rights are, I take rights as given even though I acknowledge their precise nature and content are often disputable. In turning to Locke, Smith, and Mill, I show them as anxious liberals who hold that everyone is entitled to rights but our very rights impose an inescapable and profound burden on us. Our rights, from this perspective, enable us not only to become flourishing agents but also to fail miserably as human beings. To achieve the former and avoid the latter, anxious liberals argue that free men and women require a moral grounding for their choices.[20] In this way, Locke, Smith, and Mill exhibit an anxiety about freedom that seldom concerns contemporary liberals who seem to think that if people have rights and are treated fairly they will use their liberty wisely and develop morally.

Anxious liberals hold that rights are necessary for all persons but, unlike procedural liberals, they recognize that rights have problematic outcomes for rights-carriers. This is usually taken to mean that some rights-carriers might harm others. But what also emerges persistently and clearly in Locke, Smith, and Mill, making them anxious liberals, is the theme that freedom is both essential and dangerous to the good life of rights-carriers who may harm themselves through their free choices. That anxious liberals reject efforts by the state or monopoly churches to "save" people from their own moral mistakes hardly means that they are content to see people making errors simply because individuals are now free. In this way, anxious liberals separate themselves from contemporary ones who tend to avoid the problematic nature of freedom and the need for moral standards for choice.

Locke, Smith, and Mill see a free society extending the choices available to men and women. People are free to become better; but their rights open the possibility to become worse as well and to succumb to the temptations housed in their society. Indeed, one of the arresting features of anxious liberals is their critique of the dangers that reside in a society of rights, and the hazards are not just political but also moral. When anxious liberals compare the status of rights in their generation with earlier generations, they are optimistic and buoyant; when they gaze at behavior in their own society, they are often dour and always cautionary. Their writings are replete with stories about temptations and examples of moral failure. To be free, in their accounts, means that people are in charge of themselves as moral persons. As Mill put it, it means that we have the opportunity to forge a plan of life for ourselves, and in doing so, to be honest to our deepest aspirations and to our conception of who we are and what we are becoming. In embracing the opportunities provided by freedom, anxious liberals assign us an extraordinary responsibility for what we are becoming. For this reason, freedom is simultaneously an extraordinary good and a heavy burden.

Procedural liberals focus on a critically important factor that received little attention from such anxious liberals as Locke and Smith, namely the inequities and disabilities that are housed in civil society and that diminish the autonomy of some persons. Given their expansive requirements for autonomy, procedural liberals seek to regulate various aspects of civil society in order to promote liberty or to design just institutions.[21] In expanding our understanding of how agents can be disabled in civil society, contemporary liberals miss the anxious liberal view that civil society is also the locale where we become morally socialized or corrupted and form our deepest attachments or become alienated. Writers such as Locke, Smith, and Mill appreciate that conventional standards of material and social success frequently collide with moral principles. For anxious liberals, the dangers that confront liberal agents are not limited to monopoly churches or the arbitrary state—even though these represent formidable threats; great moral peril also comes from civil society with its confusions about what constitutes happiness. To take advantage of the enabling opportunities that reside in civil society while knowing its dangers and having the courage to confront them, anxious liberals rely on a robust moral character and supportive localized settings to meet the challenge of freedom.

Much that follows about the anxious liberalism of Locke and Mill applies to Smith; however, I join his concerns as an anxious liberal with his theory of economic markets in order to engage him in a debate with libertarians and interest-group liberals.[22] I mean to show that many contemporary uses of Smith are contrary to his own intentions, particularly his commitments to justice and moral autonomy. For Smith, markets are an important means to these goals, not themselves the ends. In their preoccupation with markets, both libertarians and interest-group liberals leave behind Smith's expectations and requirements for the moral personality and his reliance on particular cultural standards and social practices to act as gatekeepers on self-interests. I ask why Smith fears a society where restraint is weak, where the market mentality penetrates noneconomic practices and institutions, and where people deceive themselves that more wealth will make them happy.

The Multiple Languages of American Political Discourse

At various times in our history, Americans have employed the languages of republicanism and liberalism, particularly during the founding period and the Civil War. Finding republicanism robust during these earlier periods, many communitarians hold out the promise that if we return to our earlier civic language, we can reconceptualize politics and, therefore, be able to think about our problems and possible solutions more clearly than we do now. When the founding generation speaks in the language of republicanism, it has its own distinctive accent, often contradicting basic principles of continental republicanism. In both versions of republicanism, we hear about civic virtue, duty, and the general good. However, in continental republicanism, we also hear about the importance of stability and contentment, something that is missing when Americans employ republican rhetoric. For them, the ideal of equality of opportunity, with its accompanying mobility and change, embodies the good of their republic. However, these goods, so important to Americans, undermine the continental requirement of steadiness if not fixity. I take up the American founding and the Civil War to show that although we can locate a republican presence in the country, its dominant language is liberal. Americans employ a republican rhetoric to challenge an exaggerated individualism, insularity, and materialism that continually follow liberalism and threaten to disfigure what is important in liberalism.

Politics and Political Theory

In what follows in this book, I discuss what strong republicans and anxious liberals consider to be open, fluid, and paradoxical in their own projects.[23] Strong republicans, for example, call attention to the problems that attend political success in the good republic and the dangers inherent in an uncritical citizen body. Anxious liberals celebrate freedom, see ominous dangers in it, and fear that freedom can be self-destructive. Discussing the irony embedded in these texts is meant to extend the space for politics in political theory. Epistemology, ontology, deontology, and psychology are helpful to political theory in many ways, but the focus of much recent political theory has been noticeably apolitical.[24]

In considering earlier texts, I rely heavily on a reading that emphasizes the indeterminate nature of politics and that simultaneously works with and attempts to supersede the personal and the conventional in order to move toward the good regime and the morally autonomous person. At the same time, I seek to enlarge both liberal and communitarian discourse to include arguments and visions that were once robust in their respective traditions but are generally dormant today. I do not seek to convert one side to the other or show how the two traditions can be merged into one. Rather I show that, historically, these traditions frequently used comparable vocabularies, shared common aspirations, and detected similar dangers to the liberty of a free people. In arguing that strong republicans and anxious liberals have multiple concerns and a vocabulary to express them, I do not mean to make them interchangeable or blend the two into one comprehensive language.

In what follows, I take up several themes in strong republicanism and anxious liberalism that speak to these issues. Their texts do not provide us with simple solutions to our problems but offer ways of thinking about our discontents and invite us to move beyond the rigid boundaries that block discourse today.

Notes

1. Alasdair MacIntyre, *After Virtue* (Notre Dame, Ind.: Notre Dame University Press, 1981), and Michael Sandel, *Liberalism and the Limits of Justice* (New York: Cambridge University Press, 1982).

2. Friedrich A. Hayek, *The Political Order of a Free People* (Chicago: University of Chicago Press, 1979), and Robert Nozick, *Anarchy, State and Utopia* (New York: Basic Books, 1974).

3. Ronald Dworkin, *Taking Rights Seriously* (Cambridge: Harvard University Press, 1978), and John Rawls, *A Theory of Justice* (Cambridge: Harvard University Press, 1971).

4. MacIntyre, *After Virtue*, and William Sullivan, *Reconstructing Political Philosophy* (Berkeley: University of California Press, 1982).

5. Hayek, *Political Order*.

6. Nozick, *Anarchy*.

7. Dworkin, *Taking Rights Seriously*; Rawls, *Theory of Justice*. Many liberals talk about rights and others about liberty or equal respect and dignity; all work with the same commitment to the premise that individuals carry properties as human beings that ought not be trumped by cultural, utilitarian, or other considerations.

8. Many communitarians would reject this reading of their project, particularly one such as Charles Taylor who has been attentive to many of these

issues. See his *Multiculturalism and the Politics of Recognition* (Princeton: Princeton University Press, 1992).

9. Although liberalism and libertarianism are distinct in several important ways, I will often be joining them for purposes of discussion because of what they share, namely a rights-based orientation to politics that distinguishes each of them from communitarians.

10. To say "the center does not hold" does not mean there cannot be serious political disagreements in the good republic, something many communitarians forget. Machiavelli and Rousseau, for example, not only celebrate what is common among citizens, but also acknowledge that there can and sometimes should be deep disagreements among citizens, and that political conflict acknowledges these disagreements. But these disagreements are not necessarily thought to injure the democratic community. Rather, they return it to its original principles. For a further discussion of domestic conflict, see chapter 3 of this volume.

11. Marvin Meyers wrote about *The Jacksonian Persuasion* in 1957 and, more recently, J. David Greenstone used the term "persuasion" as an organizing principle to understand Lincoln. (See J. David Greenstone. *The Lincoln Persuasion: Remaking American Liberalism* [Princeton: Princeton University Press, 1993]).

12. For some, such as Taylor and Benjamin Barber (*Strong Democracy* [Berkeley: University of California Press, 1984]), contemporary liberal society needs to be shaken institutionally to recognize the claims of minorities or unseen and unheard citizens.

13. Gordon Wood, *Creation of the American Republic* (New York: Norton, 1969), and Bernard Bailyn, *Ideological Origins of the American Revolution* (Cambridge: Harvard University Press, 1967).

14. For an informative review of the many different kinds of communitarians, see Robert Fowler, *Dance with Community* (Lawrence: University Press of Kansas, 1991).

15. Richard Sinopoli uses the term "strong republicanism" to refer to his reading of Pocock where property ownership "enables freeholders to participate in politics independent of others' wills" (*The Foundations of American Citizenship* [New York: Oxford University Press, 1992], 10). On this reading, "civic participation is an authoritative good" and the "moral and rational faculties are perfected . . . only by civic participation." As helpful as he is, Sinopoli offers no sustained discussion about the importance or role of property in republicanism.

16. Skinner lays out the "Ciceronian concept of *virtus*: first that it is in fact possible for men to attain this highest kind of excellence, next that the right process of education is essential for the achievement of this goal; and finally, that the contents of such an education must be centered on the linked study of rhetoric and ancient philosophy" (Quentin Skinner, *The Foundations of Modern Political Thought* [Cambridge: Cambridge University Press, 1978], vol. 1, 88).

17. For two recent but very different efforts to join the two, see Jack Crittenden, *Beyond Individualism: Reconstituting the Self* (New York: Oxford University Press, 1992), and Philip Pettit, *The Common Mind* (New York: Oxford University Press, 1993).

18. Strong republicans expect that in times of crisis, citizens are willing to sacrifice their own personal goods for the good of the whole because they see the relationship between themselves and their republic, but that is not the same as arguing that everyone is constantly prepared to sacrifice personal considerations for civic ones.

19. Today neither contemporary communitarians nor liberals are very good at warning their own constituents that they are becoming self-righteous; each is much more adept at calling attention to the deficiencies of its opponents.

20. In contrast to anxious liberals, many other liberals, such as Thomas Malthus and Jeremy Bentham assume that people can take care of themselves morally, assume morality is a highly personal affair, or are confident that moral issues do not matter. Such liberals are not necessarily unconcerned about an individual's moral development but are not preoccupied with the issue.

21. Rawls, *Theory of Justice*.

22. Locke has been seen by Nozick as a contributor to the libertarian literature, and the early Mill provides arguments against social and economic regulation.

23. For a recent effort to problematize texts, see Michael Shapiro's reading of Adam Smith (*Reading Adam Smith: Desire, History, and Value* [Newbury Park, Calif.: Sage, 1993]). My concern is different: I want to see how Smith and the other authors I discuss problematize their own texts.

24. See Deborah Baumgold. "Political Commentary on the History of Political Theory," *American Political Science Review* 75 (1981): 928–940; John Gunnell, *Between Philosophy and Politics* (Amherst: University of Massachusetts Press, 1986); John Wallach, "Liberals, Communitarians, and the Task of Political Theory," *Political Theory* 15 (1987): 581–611; Sheldon Wolin, "The Liberal/Democratic Divide," *Political Theory* 24 (1996): 996.

Chapter One

Debates between and about Traditions

The story is familiar by now: communitarian critics find liberalism morally vacuous, socially empty, and psychologically unsatisfying, leaving individuals without a sense of purpose or direction and isolating them from one another except for their market relations.[1] For their part, liberals fear that the communitarian emphasis on a strong community united around a common moral life is not only anachronistic and insensitive to a world filled with acknowledged diversities and inequalities, but also dangerous to the freedom required for autonomous persons and the good society.[2]

Communitarians see liberals working with abstracted rights carriers who are then planted in a world crowded with desires and contingencies but without any prior understanding of what is good or of their social and civic responsibilities.[3] In this confusing and lonely world, liberal agents are said to be detached and unable to make consistent commitments. The individual rights at the core of liberalism are seen to invite liberals to pursue their interests, indeed to make their interests the center of their identity and activity. This liberal permission to pursue interests has more recently been taken as a justification for interest-group politics which emphasizes the particular over the general and which places a premium on individual goods rather than common ones and provides a rationale for neglecting moral obligations and social duties.[4] In short, our present malaise is sometimes understood as the natural consequence of the assumptions and axioms of liberalism.[5]

One reason liberals take us down this road, according to many communitarians, is that liberalism personalizes conceptions of the good and deprives citizens of a coherent, shared moral standard.[6] They further argue that the special status given to rights or a fair, neutral proceduralism[7] in liberal theory allows rights to trump everything in its way, including community, tradition, justice, civic virtue, and obligation. For Michael Walzer, rights are critically important but problematic when the language of rights denies standing to these other considerations.[8] The issue for him is not that rights-claims are merely desires made manifest or that other goods, such as tradition, virtue, or civic obligations are superior to rights. Walzer argues that when such goods are not given standing, there are important substantive and normative losses and democratic politics is deprived of its openness and contestability.

There is no single communitarian position, or for that matter, no single liberal or libertarian position. One internal debate among communitarians centers on what their tradition is and what it should be called. For their part, Quentine Skinner, Gordon Wood, and William Sullivan prefer to talk about a republican tradition; John Pocock favors the term "civic humanism" to discuss Aristotle, Machiavelli, and James Harrington; and Alasdair MacIntyre avoids both terms. For someone such as Quentin Skinner, Aristotle muddies the republican waters with a telos that, Skinner holds, adds fixity to what should be fluid in republican politics.[9] John Pocock wants to show a continuity running from Aristotle through Machiavelli through Harrington through the American founders.[10] MacIntyre wants to avoid Machiavelli on all counts and emphasizes the importance of a tradition embodying standards of excellence, something he finds the Florentine cannot offer.[11]

Some communitarians try to retrieve lost or neglected communities they find are morally coherent. MacIntyre and Allan Bloom return to the classics, Robert Bellah to the American founding, Pocock and Skinner to Machiavelli.[12] Other communitarians are primarily interested in extending community today, with Charles Taylor looking to issues of diversity, Ronald Beiner to economic equity, and Benjamin Barber to participation.[13] For all of their differences, communitarians agree about several important matters. They see a crisis spawned by liberalism and the need to (re)construct a vibrant community that is not subverted by liberal proceduralism and material self-interest. They also believe that with its preference for neutrality-based solutions, liberalism spawns relativistism, is unable to talk about duties, and is subversive of the good community. In addition, most communitarians favor something like liberty or autonomy, which they decline to equate with the liberal conception of rights because they see such claims separating persons from a sense of duties and from one another as well as trumping other conceptions of the good.[14] From the communitarian perspective, liberals have lost their moral coherence and are unable to embark on any intelligible quest. The liberal who emerges from the pages of critics is a person without a strong moral character, civic ties, or social responsibilities. Sandel finds a "solitary self," Taylor the "atomistic person," MacIntyre discovers the "emotivist," Bloom, the "nihilist," Bellah the "adolescent," Vaughan, the "hedonist," Lasch the "narcissist," and Nisbet, the "loose individual."[15]

Contemporary liberals do not accept these assessments, and see themselves respecting the dignity of all persons and securing basic liberties for everyone, regardless of background. When they speak, they employ a language of rights and proceduralism.[16] What this means can be seen in Dworkin's arguments on behalf of procedural liberalism. We need rules, he tells us, that protect the dignity of individuals, even if that conflicts with other goods, such as tradition, efficiency, or social stability. While virtually all liberals agree about the importance of proceduralism, they not only disagree significantly about the nature of those procedures, but also whether they should be firmly fixed or contextualized in ways that take account of other goods.[17]

Just as there is no single reading of communitarianism, no single understanding of liberalism has gained general acceptance. We find a wide variety of emancipatory liberalisms stressing repair, inclusion and extension. Rawls, Dworkin, and Kymlicka deal with previously excluded categories of persons or include previously neglected spheres of conduct or identity. For their part, libertarian liberals concentrate on the protection of private property and markets, and interest-group liberals stress the rules of the game that assures openness, unrestricted interest aggregation, articulation, and bargaining.[18]

Concerned as they are about rights or fair procedures, liberals have been accused of neglecting moral issues. It turns out that liberals have two sorts of standards available to make moral decisions. One concerns the moral principles that individuals inherit as children from their parents, churches, and culture and which they retain, intensify, modify, revise, augment, or reject as adults. In this sense, liberals draw from myriad understandings of the good based on religion, philosophy, or tradition.[19] For their part, procedural liberals offer a second set of principled standards based on rules that address the dignity and equality of persons.[20] Rather than being relativistic, liberals such as Dworkin claim that a principled proceduralism enables us to stand away from our own particularities and interests to see what is just and unjust and understand what must be done. By his account, political theory can make no contribution to how we govern ourselves except by struggling, against all the impulses that drag us back into our own culture, toward generality and some reflective basis for deciding which of our traditional distinctions and discriminations are genuine and which are spurious.[21]

Dworkin finds that customary standards have often denied the equality or diminished the dignity of some in the name of a timeless verity. As standards become hallowed by continued practices and loyalties, they seem beyond the reach of revision or correction. What Dworkin and other procedural liberals offer are rules that are sharp enough to cut across custom and penetrate any particular standard to mount the necessary challenge on behalf of equal dignity and respect.

While the ensuing debate has not won many converts from one side to the other, it has demonstrated some of the vulnerabilities of each position and helped to clarify important issues. Liberals, for example, can no longer be confident that the principle of neutrality will settle disputes; neutrality, as the debate clearly demonstrates, is much more contestable than had been previously acknowledged, and the liberal commitment to state neutrality in deciding issues of the good cannot be sustained in a world where many conceptions of the good are simply incommensurable with others.[22] Some of our conceptions of the good not only depart from those of our fellow citizens but sometimes also turn out to be in direct conflict with some of our own understandings of the good.[23] As William Galston and many communitarians are eager to observe, contemporary liberals have relied on neutrality to avoid judging which claims to the good should supersede other claims.[24] Galston objects to liberal neutrality in order to force his fellow liberals to make choices; communitarians claim that liberals cannot make the choice that Galston demands.

The debate also reveals serious problems in the communitarian critique, which has continually called for renewed moral standards and a cohesive community. Beyond broad generalizations, most communitarians have failed to identify what those standards might be today or have tried to resuscitate ancient traditions without showing how classical ideals might be institutionalized in the late-modern world.[25] Others, such as Walzer, rely on the customs of ongoing communities to provide moral foundations for citizens, but Walzer has been accused of fostering relativism and ignoring the steep hierarchies and deep inequalities that characterize many traditional practices.[26]

Particularly troubling to many observers is the inability of communitarians to address pressing and persistent issues in the late-modern world such as the extension of equality, the pervasiveness of diversity, and the rise of democracy. The appearance of identities that had previously been masked frequently gives rise to socially unsettling self-understandings and self-assertions. It is not surprising that democratic politics should reflect the demystification of once sturdy authorities and the formation of new identities, and it is not clear how communitarians plan to deal with these issues in the late-modern world.

Politics and Particularities

What is ordinary about ordinary men and women, according to Plato's Socrates, is that they cannot consistently understand the good apart from their own particularities. Most of us rely on our attributes to discern not only what is important to us but also what is just. On Socrates' account, our preoccupation with our attributes corrupts the person and society in the deepest and most pervasive ways. Socrates makes this point by looking at the household where people become deeply attached to their families and their private property and use these materials to judge whether politics is or is not fostering their particular good. But Socrates denies that the particular can provide a basis for justice or the harmony of the city, and he turns to the philosopher-king to provide a just rule.

In addition to what Socrates takes to be their natural endowments and their superior education, philosopher-kings are set apart from ordinary people by their ability to do without the personal attachments of family and property. In this sense, they escape the weight of the household to understand the good and can, with the proper education, find what is best for the city. By releasing politics from the routine interests of ordinary people, Socrates expects no one part of the city, understanding the good primarily through its own particularities, will rule on its own behalf. Socrates' solution is not to abolish the pull of the particular or to teach ordinary people how to transcend their personal attachments but to create a politics that bypasses the gravitational pull of chance and interest.

Socrates thinks some people, namely philosopher-kings, can avoid the heavy draw our attributes command of us, but St. Augustine is not convinced that any human being can fully escape the interest that people invest in their own well-being. According to Augustine, each of us believes we are an "end to itself," and we become "self-pleasers" and try to be "self-sufficient."[27] We privilege ourselves over other human beings, and our pride brings us into inevitable and invariable conflict with others who are just as interested in themselves as we are in ourselves. However, Augustine finds no natural hierarchy and sees everyone as equal in the eyes of God. For him, our "pride in its perversity apes God. It abhors equality with other men under Him; but instead of His rule, it seeks to impose a rule of its own upon its equals."[28] Augustine argues that the pervasive preoccupation of people with their own welfare undermines the prospects for harmonious relations, even where we would expect security and affection.

> But who can enumerate all the great grievances with which human society abounds in the misery of this moral state? . . . Is not human life full of such things? Do they not often occur even in honorable friendships [of the family]? . . . If then, home, the natural refuge from the ills of life is itself not safe, what shall we say of the city which . . . is never free from fear?[29]

Even if the household is suspect and even though politics cannot avoid corruption, Augustine does not counsel that, as members of "the city of man," we turn away from the world, but his engagement is essentially private. This can be seen in his recommendation that, for all of its problems, each person should give "his own household . . . his care, for the law of nature and of society gives him readier access to them and greater opportunity of serving them."[30] The task for Augustine's ordinary men and women is spiritual and localized rather than political and expansive, reflecting his view of the limited capacities of individuals to discipline their pride and their almost unlimited capacity to deceive themselves and harm others.

Two other ways of responding to contingency come from the strong republicanism of Aristotle, Machiavelli, and Rousseau and the anxious liberalism of Locke, Smith, and Mill. Each approach seeks to confront the proclivity of people to be concerned about themselves. Strong republicans attempt to build on what is common among recognizably different people. For Aristotle, Machiavelli, and Rousseau, citizens share not only a common tradition but, just as importantly, also share institutions that enable them to practice their liberty and to attend to the well-being of their households.[31] Their argument on behalf of liberty and personal well-being builds on the assumption that some of our particularities need protection not only for the sake of individual citizens but also for the sake of the republic. Both strong republicans and communitarians want to provide citizens with a robust community that binds them to the republic rather than leaves civic attachments to random chance or dumb luck. But strong republicans also seek to construct institutions that assure citizens that their livelihoods are not contingent on their backgrounds, their cunning, or their strength but are secured by the free institutions of their republic against those with favored backgrounds, more cunning, or greater strength.

Anxious and procedural liberals agree that some of the attributes attached to persons ought not to count in the assignment of rights. A person's wisdom, virtue, wealth, background, or status are simply irrelevant from this perspective. Anxious liberals, however, go on to insist that the moral materials that agents require to construct their own moral life ought not be left to happenstance and they devote considerable attention to why moral knowledge is important and how agents acquire it.[32] Anxious liberals insist that freedom can be enabling but it becomes disabling when agents lack the moral materials to judge alternatives and injure themselves.[33] For anxious liberals, the standards that agents employ are too important to be left to chance.

Constructing Traditions and Critiquing Society

In their own highly distinctive ways, political philosophers from Socrates and Aristotle through the present see a conventional world that is often unreliable, and they attempt to sort out what is permanent from what is transient, what is common from what is particular, and what is good from what is not. In reading their texts, we find that some political philosophers share common themes, perspectives, or goals with one another, and we often assemble political philosophers whom we take to be similar under generic headings we call traditions. We speak of ancient and modern traditions, scholastic and Marxist traditions, or republican and liberal traditions. Such categories enable us to address regularities among texts and sharpen contrasts with texts outside of the tradition. Within these broad classifications, we talk about a telos in the classical tradition, civic virtue in the republican tradition, and individual rights in the liberal tradition.

Although much of the liberal-communitarian debate today does not reach further back than Rawls's *Theory of Justice* published in 1971, some of the most important contributors have looked to the history of political ideas for support.[34] There are Rawls' famous debt to Kant; Galston's debts to both Aristotle and Kant; Nozick's to Locke; Kymlicka's to Mill; and Hayek's to Smith. Communitarian debts include MacIntyre's to Aristotle, Augustine, and St. Thomas; Barber's and Sullivan's to Rousseau; Pocock's and Skinner's to Machiavelli;[35] Taylor's to Hegel; and Bellah's and Wood's to the republicanism they discover in the American founding. Others have turned to earlier texts to defend one or another position against their critics. Moon, for example, defends the liberal distinction between the private and public realms by defending Locke's position on the subject.[36] The current reliance on earlier texts in the liberal-communitarian debate serves to guide and illuminate arguments as well as mount criticisms against their opponents. When liberals critique communitarians today they respond not only to their contemporaries, such as MacIntyre, but also to Aristotle,[37] just as Rawls' critics take on both him and Kant.[38]

Our reliance on a tradition need not be self-conscious; it can reflect, as Michael Oakeshott observes, "the underlinings" every society "marks in the book of its history . . . and in which is hidden its own understanding of its politics."[39] In the United States, we underline rights, to protect or extend them or to criticize their pervasiveness or an exaggerated individualism. The nation's basic political vocabulary is the language of rights,[40] which can be read as expansive, ennobling, and generous or as egoistic, narrow, and materialistic. When critics reach for a language to criticize liberalism today, the primary language of challenge is communitarian, not, say, a language of class analysis.[41]

Commentaries as Critique

As vehicles for organizing similar textual themes and ignoring other textual topics, commentaries about traditions enable us to make parsimonious generalizations about recurring issues in political philosophy. We know, for example, that Socrates and Aristotle differ profoundly about some critical matters, but we also find that they share important outlooks that distinguish them from most modern political theorists, and for certain analytical purposes, we find it helpful to group Socrates, Plato, and Aristotle into the classical tradition. Which authors and texts should be included in a tradition is not always clear. Leo Strauss's commentary on the classical tradition, for example, emphasizes Plato (and to a lesser extent Aristotle) while Martha Nussbaum and Peter Euben cannot understand the classical tradition without including Homer or the tragic poets.[42] When communitarians offer commentaries on their tradition, they concentrate on Aristotle and Machiavelli with additional attention paid to James Harrington, Rousseau, Algernon Sidney, and Milton. What is culled from these authors is a strong sense of community, civic virtue, patriotism, and self-sacrifice. Contemporary liberals, for their part, turn to a wide array of writers including Locke, Smith, Kant, and J. S. Mill to talk about the moral equality of persons. However, efforts at including some texts but expunging others from a tradition come at a cost. By forcing some texts into a tradition regardless of the fit and expelling texts that do not conform to the categorizing paradigm, we can distort the rich thematics of a tradition, ignore the debates within a tradition, and hide the problematizing elements that reside in a tradition.

Deborah Baumgold reminds us what is involved when academic theorists offer commentaries on particular texts or traditions. For her, commentaries become substitutes for texts and refuse to "grant an inherent difference between" original texts and the commentary itself. Commentaries "make their own arguments" in their "choice of texts for interpretation, the approach taken to interpretation [and] the interpretative argument."[43] Not surprisingly, any text can give rise to a surprising variety of commentaries, some of which are highly discordant with one another.[44] Which reading of John Locke, for example, reveals the real Locke? Is it Dunn's Calvinist theologian, Macpherson's possessive individualist, Colman's moral philosopher, Tarcov's moral educator, Ashcraft's revolutionary, or Nozick's governmental minimalist?[45] In presenting themselves as they do, commentaries tell us something not only about the texts but also about the interpreters, particularly about what they think is important and what is not.

Today, commentaries on traditions are offered as guides to the good regime and as explanations of our discontents. We are told that a correct reading of tradition will help us through moral confusion. In many current commentaries, we read that contemporary society and politics are in trouble, and so is political theory.[46] As early as 1950, John Hallowell found that liberalism had contributed to the "crisis of Western civilization."[47] He was soon joined by several European emigres who were simultaneously horrified by the Nazism and Stalinism they found in Europe and deeply disappointed about what they saw in the United States. For Eric Voegelin, we faced a "spiritual disorder in an age of gnosticism," and Strauss complained of "decline" and "decay" in the modern age.[48] With Strauss, Voegelin and later MacIntyre, we are offered not only commentaries on the classics but also claims for their superiority over modernity. Or one can turn to Macpherson's reading of early liberalism as sowing the seeds for the fully developed "possessive individualism" we often encounter today. More recently, Pocock and Skinner summon Machiavelli, and Gordon Wood[49] and Bellah turn to the republican rhetoric prominent during the American revolution to reproach contemporary liberalism. For these critics, the deficiencies that many of us recognize in modern society come from the way we organize our ideas and think.

Thinking about Political Traditions Philosophically

In constructing their commentaries, political theorists frequently turn to philosophy to supply meaning and order for a disorderly world. This is the task writers such as Rawls and Sandel have undertaken in showing the importance of liberal justice and civic commitments. In the ensuing debate between communitarians and liberals, we are presented with arguments about how logic, consistency, and coherence can be restored to political theory, whether liberal or republican. But the next move, applying a logical, coherent, consistent theory to the real world of democratic politics, invites serious problems because the phenomena at hand are fluid and resistant to settled solutions.[50]

John Gunnell has criticized academic theorizing for becoming increasingly removed from the political world it purports to study. For him, what is "original and definitive" in contemporary commentary is the belief that a "solution to the philosophical problem would be a solution to the political problem or in some fundamental but usually unspecified way would provide the grounds for such a solution."[51] As Gunnell sees it, political theory speaks past the very political issues it claims to address because of the way it has conceived the issues.

> The myth of the tradition . . . estranged the discourse of political theory from actual political issues and the particularities of politics. Above all, it has distanced political theory from an authentic understanding and consideration of its relationship to politics. . . . Political issues were transformed into pseudophilosophical issues and solved accordingly. Real political events, and even crises, became devalued because they were only symptoms of the big underlying crisis.[52]

Gunnell's argument that philosophically derived procedures or standards deprive democratic politics of its open, contestable character parallels Oakeshott's position that unconditional theorizing drives us "far out of sight" of our original concerns in the real world.[53] He attacks efforts to flatten explanations in the name of science, philosophy, or efficiency. For Oakeshott, to be too philosophical is to deny politics, and he wants the serious student of politics to "foreswear metaphysics."[54] There is a fertile literature that denies that politics must be fixed and static in order to be guided by principled standards. Hannah Arendt, Reinhold Niebuhr, and Bernard Crick want the politics of a free people to occur among citizens who speak openly about matters that concern them. Arendt shudders at any political philosophy that stops speech and imposes solutions; Niebuhr celebrates the unsettled, problematic nature of the politics of a free people, and Crick resists efforts to provide formula to intractable issues among free men and women.[55]

Becoming highly dependent on philosophy, academic theorists risk not only avoiding politics but also overlooking the tensions and problematics that reside in their own traditions. When traditions are presented as coherent, internally logical, and goal driven (whether it is a telos, civic virtue, or rights), texts are forced to conform to an assigned paradigm and read from the framework provided by the paradigm. However, in emphasizing the coherence and continuity of a tradition, we risk muting discordant themes that reside in texts and ignoring the paradoxes and ironies housed within texts and among authors who purportedly belong to the same tradition. In the process, we run the risk of making political theory static, mechanical and apolitical.

How Distinctive Are the Languages of Republicanism and Liberalism?

We find two very different kinds of commentaries in the current liberal-communitarian debate. One is based on the premise that there are two discrete, nonoverlapping traditions, each with its own logic and language. From this perspective, participants speak in two highly distinctive, incompatible political grammars and each vies with the other to determine which will be the national language. The alternative to bipolar discourse comes from scholars who find that political languages frequently share vocabularies and address similar issues and needs and that linguistic boundaries are often porous and shifting. On these latter accounts, much is lost when political languages are made unnecessarily adversarial. Much of the communitarian-liberal debate has proceeded with the first assumption, forcefully advanced by John Pocock who finds "two vocabularies in which political thought has been conducted that are markedly discontinuous with one another because they premise different values, encounter different problems, and employ different strategies of speech and argument."[56]

In this view, one language is "civic humanist," or republican, and the other is liberal.[57] The former stresses participation, civic virtue, equality, and citizenship in the good republic. In Pocock's civic humanism, the citizen is "a participant in the authority by which he was ruled."[58] In ruling and being ruled, no republican citizen is inferior to another citizen as citizen, and all see themselves mutually tied together in their civic undertakings. Pocock finds the alternative language is legal and liberal and deemphasizes the participatory and political in favor of a sovereignty that is "extra-civic." In juristic language, the citizen is "defined not by his actions and virtues, but by his rights to and in things."[59] For Pocock, "the history of liberalism is a matter of law and rights" and not virtue.[60]

In various ways, the premise that there are two irreconcilable languages has been repeatedly employed in the current debate. MacIntyre holds that traditions provide a specific foundation for practical reasoning and the foundations cannot be mixed. For him, "All reasoning takes place within the context of some traditional mode of thought . . . and this is true of modern physics as of medieval logic."[61] Skinner argues that after Machiavelli, the language of community is corrupted by the language of rights, and modern liberals have no way of talking about virtue or duty.[62]

Accepting the two-language paradigm, Rawls restricts concepts of the good and morality to the realm of individual commitments and denies them a place in politics. Recently, he has asked "how it is possible for there to exist over time a just and stable society of free and equal citizens who remain profoundly divided by reason of religious, philosophical, and moral doctrines?"[63] In posing the question as he does, Rawls calls attention to the diverse moral principles that are important to different individuals but, because they are important, also serve to separate people. Rawls refuses to chose which moral standard should be favored and which rejected; instead he wants to give "special priority to [certain basic] rights, liberties, and opportunities, especially with respect to claims of the general good and perfectionism."[64]

As he delineates his theory of justice, Rawls seeks to keep it, "as far as possible, independent of opposing and conflicting philosophical and religious doctrines that citizens affirm."[65] By his account, "the comprehensive philosophical and moral doctrines" that are important to us as persons "should give way in public life." This leads him to a "political and not metaphysical conception" of public life where "each person has an equal claim to a fully adequate scheme of equal basic rights and liberties."[66] So long as individuals do not intrude on the principles of justice, how they use those rights should be beyond the scope of public controversy.[67] After several decades of debate with his critics and after several adjustments to his original argument, Rawls continues to work in the two language paradigm. Its boundaries are looser today than they were in his *Theory of Justice*, but Rawls and other procedural liberals can never accept Pocock's and MacIntyre's priorities.

Others deny there are two distinctive, incompatible languages. Some notice that writers assigned to different traditions often share common concerns and even vocabularies. Liberals often are preoccupied with virtue and participation and republicans frequently insist citizens own private property. Working from this perspective, Jeffrey Isaac detects several flaws in the claim that we speak in one of two conflictual languages and argues that Pocock fails to recognize how the ideal of citizenship is not at all incompatible with liberalism . . . and fails to see how the republican notion of virtue and the independence of the citizen can underwrite liberal individualism."[68]

Denying the idea that liberals and civic humanists have different genealogies, Isaac goes on to reject the proposition that they can only speak to each other in anger. Reflecting a theme that appears among other critics of Pocock's two-language paradigm, Isaac listens to authors appropriated by civic humanists as one of their own and hears them speaking a liberal language. By his account, liberalism is not "historically self-contained . . . . Liberalism incorporates Aristotelian, republican values of individual independence and patriotism in its understanding of the good life."[69] He adds, "These languages—the language of rights and the language of virtue—are both component parts of an integral liberal ideology which . . . serves to justify the practices of the liberal democratic state."[70]

Alan Houston is also troubled about the way languages have been placed in adversarial roles. In his close textual reading of Algernon Sidney, Houston does not find the writer that contemporary civic humanists present as an alternative to Lockean liberalism in England and North America in the seventeenth and eighteenth centuries.[71] The Locke and Sidney who emerge in Houston's analysis are not two oppositional figures speaking in radically different languages. They "drew on the same intellectual resources," but more important to his argument, Houston finds that Sidney and Locke are interested in many of the same issues, such as liberty and the abuse of power. At best, Sidney offers us fragments, that "may be used to criticize liberalism, [but] they do not constitute a distinct and coherent alternative to it."[72] Isaac's commentary on Harrington and Houston's commentary on Sidney reveal writers who rely on a porous and generous language to advance their cases for liberty.

The growing number of commentaries on individual liberal writers such as Locke, Smith, and Mill also pose an important challenge to the way communitarians understand liberalism within a rigid two-language paradigm. The readings of liberalism employed by Pocock, Skinner, Taylor, MacIntyre, Sullivan, and most other communitarians stem from their construction of liberalism as a theory of unbridled individualism, materialism, and atomism where terms such as virtue or community are foreign.[73] However, John Dunn, Nathan Tarcov, Ruth Grant, John Colman, D. D. Raphael, Alan Ryan, Bernard Semmel, and Wendy Donner offer us a Locke, Smith, and Mill who are deeply concerned about moral issues.[74] This scholarship demonstrates that the earlier, received readings of Locke, Smith, and Mill as possessive individualists and emotivists rest on textual fragments and not on the corpus of their texts, which shows a strong commitment to promoting both a free and moral life for ordinary men and women.[75] This research also demonstrates that liberalism is a more porous language than a rigid construction of the two language paradigm would allow and that many liberals share overlapping concerns with many republicans.

Another set of commentaries also challenge, even if only indirectly, the idea that we speak either in liberal or communitarian tongues. It comes from scholars who have reassigned the labels conventionally placed on particular writers. Gertrude Himmelfarb discovers a Mill who is dedicated to traditionalism, Donald Winch introduces us to a civic humanist Adam Smith, and Gary Wills finds Jefferson is not a Lockean liberal but a communitarian indebted to the Scottish-Enlightenment.[76] Sometimes these reassignments involve transporting authors from one of Pocock's two political languages to the other. Such reconstructions of texts and authors problematize the distinctions attributed to the two-language paradigm, showing the constructedness of academic political theory and illustrating that different fragments yield different results. This can be seen in the unlikely case of Aristotle who seems to offer communitarians one of their best historical sources. Indeed, both MacIntyre and Pocock rely heavily on his texts, particularly his attention to the common good and a civic personality. However, William Galston denies communitarians any exclusive appropriation, and Stephen Salkever repudiates the idea that Aristotle offers us a telos that covers all our needs and seeks to displace him from what he calls "the communitarian" camp.[77] Salkever and Galston seek to dislodge Aristotle from the communitarian position because they understand liberalism as something much different from a theory of possessive individualism or atomism and something more than what is offered by procedural liberals. The reading Galston and Salkever assign to liberalism speaks to moral purposes and recognizes the multidimensionality of human nature better than any rigid commentary can offer.

Another way of conceptualizing the relationship between liberalism and republicanism comes from scholars who find liberalism generates its own excesses. In this account, the language of rights does not carry effective internal properties to discipline itself and sometimes requires republican remonstrances to sober it up. Troubled by the same rootlessness and materialism that critics of liberalism detect in modern society, these scholars hold that the possessive individualism and relativism that are so rampant today are not the animating principles of liberalism but a by-product that can emerge at any time, needs to be challenged, and can be tethered.

One reason why liberalism gets itself into trouble follows from its proclivity to universalize. Locke, for one, speaks in global terms: "all men," have rights and "everyone" is rational. We all know that Locke's conception of rights is highly limited and that he had no intention of sponsoring many of the kinds of rights that have evolved in liberal theory. His language of rights is designed to cover a limited domain of liberties—such as religious freedom—for everyone. But there is nothing to preclude liberal speakers from advancing rights-claims to cover those who had been previously excluded or claims that had been ignored earlier. Where the language of rights is the official political language, disputes are argued out not with reference to justice, patriotism, the general welfare, or other goods but with reference to what a person is due as a person. Speaking in their absolutist accents, procedural liberals find it difficult to acknowledge that there are other languages that address important issues. Because rights do not come served as slices—either thin or thick ones—but as a whole loaf, it becomes difficult to fashion compromises that are attentive to alternative conceptions of the good.[78]

In universalizing rights-claims, procedural liberals continually jeopardize other important goods, including other rights-claims. William Connolly finds that liberalism "is . . . a destructive language, inadvertently sanctioning practices and policies which deplete the supply of civic virtue it needs."[79] With the liberal tendency to overreach itself, Walzer sees republicanism as a necessary remedy for its potential excesses because "liberalism is a self-subverting doctrine; . . . it really does require periodic communitarian correction."[80] From Walzer's perspective, republicanism makes its greatest contribution in its role as persistent, resident critic of liberalism, challenging liberals when they become obsessively individualistic and narrow. The republican critique of corruption, for example, carries greater bite than liberal appeals to moderation and temperance, and the republican conception of citizenship moves beyond the proceduralism and formalism characteristic of liberal theory today.

The debate between communitarians and liberals reminds us that individualism can become self-destructive and community can become frozen and unresponsive. For all of the problems associated with the rigidity of the way the two-language paradigm has been constructed, it is important to remember that liberalism and republicanism are different; Pocock's civic virtue and MacIntyre's moral agreements cannot fit harmoniously into Rawls's or Dworkin's efforts to achieve justice and equal respect through neutral procedures.[81] A looser construction of each language can build on the multiple needs of ordinary men and women, including their needs to care about themselves and to carry grounded moral standards. To move in this direction means each language must become less rigid and more expansive; it does not mean they ought to be merged into a single language.

Rich Commentaries and Rigid Commentaries

Some are suspicious about returning to any tradition because they find that its standards are anachronistic, its politics confining, its assumptions restrictive, and its teaching ill-suited to the late-modern world. For all of the problems associated with the way traditions are constructed in political theory, the concept is immensely fruitful if we distinguish rich commentaries of political theories from rigid ones. The former recognize the ambiguity, irony, and paradox of politics while the latter prize parsimony, logic, and coherence. Rich commentaries in political philosophy are first and foremost political and rest on the premise that even in the best regimes, unity is difficult to sustain, liberty can be self-destructive, and political participation can subvert the republic. In rich commentaries, we encounter theorists who are attentive to the problems that reside in their best efforts and who recognize that the good imbedded in their projects can undermine itself. They know their conception of the best regime, justice, or liberty is not sustained out of its own goodness.

Both rich and rigid commentaries are concerned with such issues as the nature of justice or the legitimacy of power, and each is heavily indebted to moral and analytical philosophy in this task. Moral philosophers worry about such issues as what it means to be good, what it means to be a person, and what is due to persons as persons. For their part, analytical philosophers emphasize that good arguments cannot be partial or emotive but must be logically grounded and developed. Working with these materials, most of the participants in the liberal-communitarian debate rely on moral or analytic philosophy as well as epistemology[82] to set directions and boundaries when they think about politics.

Constructing rich commentaries in political philosophy avoids the mistake of confusing political philosophy with moral and analytical philosophy. Today, however, some hold that if we get our moral philosophy "right," then politics can be expected to take care of itself. This is what MacIntyre offers in his argument that the way that we morally reason gives us either a fragmented community or a harmonious one.[83] Driven by the logic of simple, pure markets, the libertarian version claims that if we set economic markets free, then society, and ostensibly politics and morality, will take care of themselves. Procedural liberals argue that if we get our institutional or procedural arrangements "right," a good life will follow.[84] Such arguments, while instructive on many levels, avoid the fluid, contested world of democratic politics and ignore the multiple needs of men and women.

For their part, rich commentaries supply materials for self-criticism.[85] Because traditions are practiced by real men and women and, therefore, become vulnerable to pride and ambition, every tradition is subject to internal decay. Furnished with convincing standards about what is good and what is not, members of a tradition know when power is abused and when ritual or office masks private ambition and corruption. In this regard, Walzer talks about a church or state selling its offices to the highest bidders and finds that such behavior not merely ignores its own standards, it subverts them. For Walzer, robust traditions provide materials to critique actual practices, check power and pride, and delay their decay. Okin and others find the idea that traditions can *adequately* critique themselves untenable because any given tradition provides only a partial account of morality and omits much that is important.[86] The issue for her is that any tradition is incomplete and, therefore, unable to supply a reliable standard to challenge behavior that is not covered by its own principles. From this perspective, some traditions are already internally corrupt. Commentaries that extol or neglect issues such as racism, caste, or patriarchy cannot be used to censure such arrangements.

While Okin's point is undeniable and important, it is helpful to notice that there are many injustices and wrongs in the world and it would be a mistake to abandon the use of tradition to act as an internal monitor to confront corruption. More especially, it is important to notice that traditions are not static, particularly in the late modern world. Practiced traditions are always subject to revision, particularly today when the impenetrable walls that previously protected fixed principles have often become porous and transparent. In the process, new understandings of the good are often grafted to a tradition or new criticisms are often introduced within the context of the tradition. With these additions and critiques, traditions can be enlarged and vitalized. Today, this can mean that the equality and dignity of persons are recognized in ways not often included in previous understandings or practices of a tradition. Gandhi reflects the way a rich reading of tradition is helpful when he uses Hindu scripture to claim that untouchability is both alien and hostile to the core principles of Hinduism, and he spends considerable energy and effort to try to reconstitute Hinduism without the deep inequalities and indignities associated with untouchability.[87] A parallel move to enrich their religious traditions comes with the efforts of many women who seek to enlarge their role in their churches and synagogues. To advance their position, they rely on both emerging secular principles of equality as well as established religious teachings. In each of these cases, traditions are reconstructed in ways that attempt to maintain their core while responding to extended conceptions of the dignity owed to each person.

In this way, rich commentaries have considerable powers of inclusion and distinctiveness, enabling intertextual and countertextual interpretations within any tradition. In a rich reading of republicanism, for example, we find very different ways of thinking about the economy, with Rousseau relying on a one-class citizen body in contrast to Machiavelli's view of the inevitability and intractablity of a class-divided society. The issue here is not which republican position is correct but that strong republicans insist on paying serious attention to distributional issues even though they disagree among themselves about the best way of proceeding. A rich reading of liberalism could look at the highly divergent views of the relationship between the state and civil society with Locke and Smith favoring fairly restrictive boundaries and J. S. Mill and T. H. Green arguing for more porous ones. What is important about these debates among liberals is not that one or another of these writers gives us the "true" or "real" liberal position but that a rich commentary notices that liberals repeatedly negotiate the appropriate boundaries between the state and civil society.

Commentaries become rigid when they assign a coherent logic to the texts attributed to a tradition. For someone such as MacIntyre, each tradition contains its own distinctive conception of excellence as well as its own standards of rationality and justification and cannot contain different internal logics.[88] Armed with this kind of conclusion, critics commonly assign a specific logic or characteristic to cover all liberalism. MacIntyre defines liberalism by Humean rationality; for Sandel, Kant represents liberalism. Neither sees that liberals rely on very different epistemologies and a variety of psychologies and that they disagree among themselves about which is most appropriate. To reach conclusions about the autonomous person and the nature of the good liberal regime, Locke offers us a hedonistic psychology and grounded reason, Smith relies on a theory of the moral sentiments and stoicism, and Mill builds on a developmental psychology and utilitarianism. To talk about Kantian or Humean rationality and hedonism as the distinguishing marks of all liberalism is to miss the rich variety within the liberal tradition and to force nonconforming positions into inapplicable molds or to ignore them altogether. What is represented in a rigid reading of liberalism is a static caricature of what is actually internally argumentative and fluid.[89]

Rigid commentaries give rise to the cartel phenomenon where certain properties are appropriated into one tradition to the exclusion of other traditions. This can be seen in the pattern of most communitarian and liberal discourse today, which has assigned virtue and corruption to the republican grammars and private ownership and self-interests to the liberal vocabulary. However, such rigid readings ignore the ways that both earlier republican and liberal languages frequently employ these terms without respect to theoretical boundaries. One cannot understand Machiavelli any better than Locke if words such as virtue and corruption are appropriated exclusively to the former and words such as private ownership[90] and self-interest to the latter. Both strong republicans and anxious liberals promote virtue, require private property, fear the corrupt society, and attempt to tether narrow self-interest, even if they understand and respond to these terms very differently. Machiavelli's civic virtue, for example, requires social and economic security and political commitments in a way that Locke's treatment of moral virtue avoids. However, each writer associates virtue with freedom, each sees narrow self-indulgence undermining a moral life, and each is suspicious of the norms housed in a corrupt society. A rigid reading would have the common good always trumping concerns about the self in one tradition while liberty always has a veto in another tradition.

This kind of construction ignores the self-referencing features of strong republicanism and the anxious liberal suspicion of interests. A rigid reading forces writers or texts into a preassigned but often awkward fit and does not invite us to consider the multiple goals located in the texts. When texts are read rigidly and fragments of a text that do not neatly correspond to the paradigm are ignored, we need to ask, as Sherlock Holmes did in *The Hound of the Baskervilles*, why there is silence when there should be sound.

Theory and Practice

However we understand them, our moral standards mean something important to us not only because we take them to be good but also because we want to practice them. Appeals to a common good, for example, are not convincing if the exercise of such standards is penalized or ignored at the very time the pursuit of self-interests is widely rewarded. Practice depends not only on the character and credibility of moral standards but also on the institutional and distributional arrangements of society that advance or diminish the practice of those standards.[91] The validation of the good for Aristotle's ordinary citizens, for example, is found in their everyday experiences in both their households and city. Unlike philosophers and saints, ordinary citizens are not expected to leave the city or continually transcend their own particularities when they practice the good.[92]

MacIntyre takes up the relationship between moral standards and practices in his argument that standards of the good or of excellence presuppose "a sociology."[93] In his account, the good life can be understood only when "we have spelled out what its social embodiment would be."[94] If it is impossible to achieve a purported good in practice, then the theory fails to provide any reason to support it. We not only want to know what the good is but also that we can actually achieve it even if this is sometimes difficult and even costly. However, achieving the good in ordinary times ought not to be persistently difficult or costly, and we need to know what kinds of institutional arrangements promote its practice. In MacIntyre's reading, earlier traditions furnish us with both standards and practices that describe the good person in the good society. This is not what he finds in liberalism, which he believes is so fragmented and relativistic that it is impossible for citizens to practice their individual conceptions of the good.[95]

Even though I take MacIntyre's understanding of liberalism to be seriously flawed, his argument about the practice of moral standards is compelling. For this reason, it is appropriate to ask how he as one of the major contributors to the communitarian argument takes up this topic in his own work. Who is eligible to practice the goods of excellence embodied in MacIntyre's rendering of the classical tradition, and can those who are eligible, in fact, achieve the good? If it turns out the answer is that everyone is eligible, that means, in practice, some are flourishing (the Homeric hero and Athenian citizens) while others are languishing (their wives and slaves). But if citizenship is restrictive, we need to ask MacIntyre how he intends to address the issues of deep inequality and hierarchy in the traditions he explores since he claims that he wants to eliminate hierarchy.

It is not good enough to celebrate the Aristotelian telos with an aside that we should discard his defective "biology," MacIntyre's euphemism for Aristotle's claims about the natural inequality of persons. Reformulating Aristotle's "biology" requires more than adjustments in the ways we think. It requires a society that is organized differently than Aristotle imagined; to take the most obvious example, it requires one in which there is no slavery.[96] To transform large numbers of propertyless, subordinated individuals into flourishing citizens who find that their social practices cohere with commonly shared moral standards and who are virtuous depends on more than good intentions and good traditions. The issue is not that Aristotle cannot be helpful in confronting this problem but that MacIntyre offers no guidance in thinking through an Aristotelian response to the modern condition.[97] The problem in MacIntyre's commentary is not only that he does not speak to the equality of persons, as Okin complains, but also that he fails to talk about the political sociology essential to his project, namely the kinds of major institutional arrangements that promote a coherence between the good and its practice for all citizens in the late modern world.[98] And what is true of MacIntyre's neglect is characteristic of many other communitarians and liberals today. We want them to talk about how standards and practices can be linked not because we necessarily want to transport Aristotelian or Lockean solutions to the late modern world or because we expect political philosophers to become specialists in public policy. Rather, we want to explore how institutional arrangements are linked to the good community and the autonomous person and understand how such themes can enter into our own debate.

Moving Fragments across Time

As countless writers have forcefully argued, institutions in the late modern world are radically different from their historic predecessors, and these profound changes carry serious implications for the ways people organize their lives (or have them organized) and think about themselves.[99] Agrarian economies are succeeded by industrial ones, kinship gives way to bureaucracies, face-to-face relations fade before a distant impersonality, extended families are superseded by nuclear ones, and custom is replaced by markets. Modernization gives rise to unplanned, unexpected changes in the ways people work and raise families; where and how they live, pray, and learn; how they exchange goods and labor; the names they call themselves; and what they think they owe to others and what others owe to them. The changes attached to modernity and modernization presuppose a different set of institutional practices than was appropriate for earlier renderings of the good regime.

Communitarians have been very helpful in their discussion of some of the damaging effects of change in liberal democracies, pointing to fragmentation, incoherence, moral relativism, and civic lethargy.[100] And they have been useful in insisting that we are more than the sum of our attributes and that we seek a deeper meaning for ourselves than our material possessions. With some notable exceptions, such as Charles Taylor and Michael Walzer, most communitarians do not go beyond discussing these deleterious effects of change and, in important respects, many of them represent the cultural conservatives that Louis Hartz thought America lacked.[101] Having talked extensively about the effects of change in the modern world, nostalgic communitarians[102] seem to think we can repeal the consequences of change and introduce stasis by returning to earlier models of the good republic or classical standards of the good.[103]

Yearning for social, economic, and political stability (or coherence) in the late-modern world is neither tenable nor very interesting. Nostalgic communitarians, in their search for ties that would bind us and ways that repeal the seamy side of individualism, have been unable to show how they would address the issue of integrating diverse identities into a coherent community today. Any effort to build a vital community in the late modern world means, among other things, not confusing symptoms for causes.[104]

The pride of tradition cannot be that it has never changed. Its pride follows from its ability to maintain what is important in a changing environment. Its adherents modify their tradition, augment it, and eliminate or ignore certain parts in order to preserve what they take to be important in their tradition in a world of flux. But in the process of adjustment, important principles may be deleted or neglected, making its practice elusive.[105] How do we take and apply what we consider valuable in a tradition and make it our own in a world that is very different from when the principles were initially formulated? Our problems are compounded when we detach selected fragments of texts and expect them to do the work they had done when they were attached to a comprehensive argument and rested on very different sociological assumptions.[106] Inattention to the ways concepts are joined in their original presentations undermines our efforts to retrieve what Alan Houston calls "a usable past" and we risk making political theory "anachronistic and insensitive to the possibility of historical discontinuity."[107]

In transporting fragments across time, we want to know how texts can illuminate the way we politically respond to the opportunities, dangers, and disabilities of the late-modern world. Efforts to apply either a rigidly reconstituted liberalism or republicanism today will add to our problems, not solve them. Rigid constructions cannot adequately take account of the diversity, deep inequalities, and pervasive complexity that describe our condition today. In neglecting parts of their own traditions, contemporary liberals and communitarians make the solutions to our own predicaments more problematic than need be the case. We return to our traditions because they powerfully remind us what is important and good, what we are in danger of losing, and what requires our attention today. Strong republicans can remind contemporary communitarians and anxious liberals can remind contemporary liberals that they are neglecting important parts of their tradition. Moreover, strong republicans and anxious liberals can teach us about the complex needs of ordinary men and women. In this way, they warn contemporary liberals and communitarians that efforts to employ a rigid understanding of the world to put it right can be misleading and sometimes dangerous.

Notes

1. Liberalism as used in this section generally refers to procedural liberals. For the most part, these are the liberals most communitarians address directly. In attacking individualism and materialism, communitarians also take on libertarians and interest-group liberals. For a useful bibliography on communitarianism, see Michael Zilles, "Universalism and Communitarianism: A Bibliography," *Philosophy and Social Criticism* 14 (1988): 442–61.

2. For summaries of the debate, see John Wallach, "Liberals, Communitarians, and the Tasks of Political Theory," *Political Theory* 15 (1987): 581–611; Robert Fowler, *Dance with Community* (Lawrence: University Press of Kansas, 1991); Simon Carney, "Liberalism and Communitarianism: A Misconceived Debate," *Political Studies* 40 (1992): 273–89; and Will Kymlicka,

"Liberalism and Communitarianism," *Canadian Journal of Philosophy* 18 (1988): 181–203.

3. Michael Sandel offers a characteristic communitarian view of liberalism: it is an "individualistic, rights-based ethic" (*Liberalism and the Limits of Justice* [New York: Cambridge University Press, 1982], 66–67); also see Sandel, "The Procedural Republic and the Unencumbered Self," *Political Theory* 12 [1984], 81–96).

4. Theodore Lowi, *The End of Liberalism* (New York: Norton, 1969).

5. For his part, Will Kymlicka rejects such a reading of liberalism; we are, he writes, "dependent on a cultural community for our self-development and for our context of choice" (*Liberalism, Community, and Culture* [Oxford: Oxford University Press, 1989], 127).

6. This is why communitarian critics have found liberalism in general, and Rawlsian liberalism in particular, shallow, if not empty. For some critics, something like a prior good provides a standard that is applicable to everyone in a comprehensive community, unlike liberal conceptions of the good, which critics find to be abstract and procedural.

7. John Rawls searches for a "pure procedural justice as the basis of theory" (*Theory of Justice*, [Cambridge: Harvard University Press, 1971], 136; also see 88), and Bruce Ackerman seeks "a perfect technology of justice" in *Social Justice and the Liberal State* (New Haven: Yale University Press, 1980), 21. For Dworkin's proceduralism, see *Taking Rights Seriously* (Cambridge: Harvard University Press, 1978).

8. Michael Walzer, *Spheres of Justice* (New York: Basic Books, 1983).

9. Quentin Skinner, "On Justice, the Common Good, and the Priority of Liberty," in *Dimensions of Radical Democracy*, edited by Charles Mouffe (London: Verso, 1992).

10. John Pocock, *The Machiavellian Moment* (Princeton: Princeton University Press, 1975).

11. Alasdair MacIntyre, *After Virtue* (Notre Dame: Notre Dame University Press, 1981). In what follows in this book, I will not generally be involved in intramural debates, and the terms civic humanist and republican will be used interchangeably.

12. MacIntyre, *After Virtue,* and Allan Bloom, *The Closing of the American Mind* (New York: Simon and Schuster, 1987). Robert Bellah, et al., *Habits of the Heart* (Berkeley: University of California Press, 1985); Pocock, *Machiavellian Moment*. Skinner distinguishes his reading of republicanism with its strong emphasis on participation from MacIntyre's efforts to find an Aristotelian, "objective conception of the Good" ("On Justice," 222).

13. Charles Taylor, *Multiculturalism and the Politics of Recognition* (Princeton: Princeton University Press, 1992); Ronald Beiner, *What's the Matter with Liberalism?* (Berkeley: University of California Press, 1992); Benjamin Barber, *Strong Democracy* (Berkeley: University of California Press, 1984).

14. Sandel finds that "a person incapable of constitutive attachments . . . is not . . . an ideally free and rational agent, but . . . a person wholly . . . without moral depth" (*Liberalism*, 179).

15. Sandel, *Liberalism*; Taylor, *Sources of the Self* (Cambridge: Harvard University Press, 1989); MacIntyre, *After Virtue*; Bloom, *Closing of the American Mind*; Bellah, *Habits of the Heart*; Frederick Vaughan, *The Tradition of Political Hedonism from Hobbes to Mill* (New York: Fordham University Press, 1975); Christopher Lasch, *Culture of Narcissism* (New York: Warner Books, 1979); and Robert Nisbet, *The Present Age: Progress and Anarchy in Modern America* (New York: Harper and Row, 1988).

16. See Pocock's discussion of liberalism as a theory of law designed to protect rights (*Moment*, 43–46); also see Michael Sandel's discussion of the procedural republic in liberalism ("The Procedural Republic and the Unincumbered Self." For a discussion of the procedural rather than substantive character of the liberalism of Rawls, Dworkin, and Ackerman, see William Galston, "Defending Liberalism," *American Political Science Review* 76 (1982), 621–22 and Taylor, *Multiculturalism*, 62.

17. Dworkin, *Taking Rights Seriously*; Robert Nozick, *Anarchy, State, and Utopia* (New York: Basic Books, 1974); William Galston, *Liberal Purposes* (Cambridge: Cambridge University Press, 1991).

18. On the protection of private property, see Nozick, *Anarchy*, and Friedrich Hayek, *The Political Order of a Free People* (Chicago: University of Chicago Press, 1979). On the openness and bargaining of interest group liberalism, see Robert Dahl, *Who Governs?* (New Haven: Yale University Press, 1961) and William Riker, *Liberalism Against Populism* (San Francisco: W. H. Freeman, 1982).

19. Amy Gutmann holds that "communitarian values . . . are properly viewed as supplementary rather than supplanting basic liberal values" ("Communitarian Critics of Liberalism," *Philosophy and Public Affairs* 14 [1985]: 320).

20. Libertarian proceduralism focuses on protecting the market, and interest-group proceduralism concentrates on political competitiveness.

21. Ronald Dworkin, "Review of Michael Walzer's *Spheres of Justice*," *New York Review of Books*, (April 1983) 6.

22. See Galston, *Liberal Purposes*, and Steven Lukes, "Making Sense of Moral Conflict," in *Liberalism and the Moral Life*, edited by Nancy Rosenblum (Cambridge: Harvard University Press, 1989). Stephen Holmes helpfully reminds us that people may not be able to be completely neutral or "objective," but they can still avoid an excessive partiality (*Anatomy of Antiliberalism* [Cambridge: Harvard University Press, 1993]).

23. See Alasdair MacIntyre, *Whose Justice? Which Rationality?* (Notre Dame, Ind: University of Notre Dame Press, 1988).

24. The debate about liberal neutrality has also problematized liberal toleration by showing that liberals cannot readily assume that (almost) any morality can be accommodated with (almost) any other morality that reasonably decent people might hold.

25. This sort of generality can be seen in Taylor's view that "our highest and most complete moral existence is one we can only attain to as members of a community" (Charles Taylor, *Hegel* [New York: Cambridge University

Press, 1975], 197). However, Phillips observes that Taylor never tells us what community is (Derek Phillips, *Looking Backward: A Critical Appraisal of Communitarian Thought* [Princeton: Princeton University Press, 1993], 11). On resuscitating ancient traditions, see MacIntyre, *Whose Justice?* and Bloom, *Closing of the American Mind*. Also see Wallach, in "Liberals," and Kymlicka, in "Communitarianism," who have made strong critiques along these lines. Phillips, in *Looking Backward*, argues that the ideal republics never, in fact or practice, really existed.

26. See Susan Okin, *Justice, Gender, and the Family* (New York, Basic Books, 1989).

27. Augustine, *City of God* (New York: Random House, 1950), 460–61.

28. Augustine, *City of God*, 483.

29. Augustine, *City of God*, 681.

30. Augustine, *City of God*, 693.

31. This highlights one of the differences between strong republicanism and nostalgic renderings of republicanism, such as Cicero's. Writing at a time of republican decay, he summons standards of civic duty and restraint from ancient times to address a world that has been reconstituted in ways that are hostile, not supportive, to such principles. For a discussion of nostalgic communitarians, see Phillips, *Looking Backward*, 150.

32. For their part, libertarians want to organize politics in such a way as to preclude the chance that those with political power will determine how society will be organized.

33. The reason for this, and not only on the anxious liberal account, is that goodness rests on voluntary choice. People forced to conform to a moral standard can be called well-behaved but not necessarily good persons.

34. For two standard accounts of why the history of political ideas counts, see John Plamenatz, *Man and Society* (New York: McGraw-Hill, 1963), vol 1, vi, and Sheldon Wolin, *Politics and Vision* (Boston: Little Brown, 1960), 27.

35. Although Skinner finds that republicanism "was largely derived from Roman moral philosophy," particularly Cicero, he argues that "Machiavelli's *Discourses* [is] by far the most compelling presentation of the [republican] case" ("On Justice," 216).

36. J. Donald Moon, *Constructing Community* (Princeton: Princeton University Press, 1993), 151–52.

37. See Susan Okin, *Justice, Gender, and the Family*.

38. See Sandel, *Liberalism and the Limits of Justice*.

39. Michael Oakeshott, *Rationalism in Politics and Other Essays* (London: Methuen, 1962), 130.

40. Mary Glendon, *Rights Talk: The Impoverishment of Political Discourse* (New York: Free Press, 1991).

41. For Louis Hartz, Lockean liberalism crowds out competing languages such as socialism and conservatism (*The Liberal Tradition in America* [New York: Harcourt, Brace and World, 1955]). Wood claims that the American

Debates between and about Traditions 41

constitutional settlement, which he takes as a liberal document, forecloses further political debate in America and traps political discourse in the language of rights.

42. Leo Strauss, *Natural Right and History* (Chicago: University of Chicago Press, 1953); Martha Nussbaum, *The Fragility of Goodness, Luck and Ethics in Greek Tragedy and Philosophy* (New York: Cambridge University Press, 1986); and J. Peter Euben, *The Tragedy of Political Theory: The Road Not Taken* (Princeton: Princeton University Press, 1990).

43. "Political Commentary on the History of Political Theory," *American Political Science Review* 75 (1981): 929. On the constructedness of traditions, see Eric J. Hobsbawm, "Introduction, Inventing Traditions," in *The Invention of Tradition* edited by E. Hobsbawm and T. Ranger (Cambridge: Cambridge University Press, 1983) and Stephen Turner, *The Social Theory of Practices* (Chicago: University of Chicago Press, 1994), 92–93. For a discussion of Western constructions of Middle Eastern and Asian traditions as fatalistic and inferior, see Edward Said, *Orientalism* (New York: Pantheon Books, 1978).

44. Alan Ryan observes that "Once [a work] has been put before the public, it takes on a life of its own. . . . An author has only limited control over his own writings. What he writes will have implications which he did not see" (*Property and Political Theory* [London: Basil Blackwell, 1984], 3). And it is not only the reading public of the author's own generation that may alter the original intentions embodied in the text; later generations can be counted on to give their own varied glosses to the text.

45. John Dunn, *The Political Thought of John Locke* (Cambridge: Cambridge University Press, 1969); C. B. Macpherson, *The Political Theory of Possessive Individualism* (Oxford: Oxford University Press, 1962); Nathan Tarcov, *Locke's Education for Liberty* (Chicago: University of Chicago Press, 1984); Richard Ashcraft, *Revolutionary Politics and Locke's Two Treatises of Government* (Princeton: Princeton University Press, 1986); and Nozick, *Anarchy*.

46. John Gunnell forcefully emphasizes this point in *Between Philosophy and Politics* (Amherst: University of Massachusetts Press, 1986), 99.

47. *Main Currents in Modern Political Thought* (New York: Henry Holt, 1950).

48. Eric Voegelin, *Science, Politics, and Gnosticism* (Chicago: Regnery, 1968), 22, and Leo Strauss, *What Is Political Philosophy* (Glencoe, Ill.: Free Press, 1959), 17).

49. Gordon Wood, *The Creation of the American Republic* (New York: W. W. Norton, 1969).

50. Gunnell finds academic theorizing has usurped responsibilities that properly belong to democratic politics. He argues,

At this time in this place, political theory and politics are two symbolic forms that stand in an ambiguous relationship to one another. . . . What academic political theory has in various ways believed is that it

42   Chapter 1

could, through the avenue of certainty that philosophy professed to possess, gain a point of purchase by which it could with the hammer of knowledge persuade and coerce an intractable political reality. . . . [I]t found itself trapped within the dilemmas of philosophy and particularly within the circle of ideas that suggested that epistemology was theory (*Between Philosophy and Politics*, 219).

51. *Between Philosophy and Politics*, 110.

52. *Between Philosophy and Politics*, 114–15. For all of the power of Gunnell's position, particularly that the constructions we are given are heavily reliant on philosophical materials and questions rather than political ones, it is salutary to remember that political commentaries are not only constructions, they are also informed by principled standards that theorists think should count. Hayek takes us to civil society with its spontaneous practices, Bloom to great books, Bellah to our national origins, Rawls behind a veil of ignorance. Each of their arguments, in its own distinctive way, rests on assumptions about what should have priority, such as freedom, participation, or community. Looking at their own tradition, many theorists seek to invigorate, renew, or reform it. For his part, Charles Taylor argues that a robust tradition can enhance such modern conceptions as autonomy, John Rawls problematizes the once-central role of private property in liberalism in his search for liberal justice, and Richard Rorty (no friend of most traditions) insists that the way to tackle some of the pressing problems of the country is to appeal to what it means to be an American, a concept loaded with multiple moral principles (*Contingency, Irony, and Solidarity* [Cambridge: Cambridge University Press, 1989], 191).

53. Michael Oakeshott, *On Human Conduct* (Oxford: Oxford University Press, 1975), 30.

54. Oakeshott, *On Human Conduct*, 25, 33.

55. Hannah Arendt, *The Human Condition* (New York: Doubleday, 1958); Reinhold Niebuhr, *Moral Man and Immoral Society* (New York: Scribners, 1932); and Bernard Crick, *In Defense of Politics* (Chicago: University of Chicago Press, 1962). According to Crick, the "moral consensus of a free state is not something mysteriously prior to or above politics: it is the activity (the civilizing activity) of politics itself" (24).

56. Pocock, *Moment*, 39.

57. Pocock, *Moment*, 39.

58. Pocock, *Moment*, 43.

59. Pocock, *Moment*, 43.

60. *Moment*, 45. According to Pocock, "the languages of right and virtue are not readily interchangeable" (*Moment*, 46).

61. MacIntyre, *After Virtue*, 206.

62. In Skinner's reading, Rawls considers "the calls of social duty as so many 'interferences.'" ("On Justice," 215). Skinner wants to show that in republicanism, civic duties not only cohere with liberty but also reinforce one

another. He finds liberalism holds that it is "irrational to assign the common good a higher priority" than rights (216).

63. John Rawls, *Political Liberalism* (New York: Columbia University Press, 1993), 4.

64. *Political Liberalism*, 6. For an argument that Rawls introduces his own perfectionism, see Vinit Haksar, *Equality, Liberty, and Perfectionism* (Oxford: Oxford University Press, 1979).

65. *Political Liberalism*, 9.

66. *Political Liberalism*, 10.

67. *Theory of Justice*, 94. For a discussion of Rawls' avoidance of supervising the exercise of basic rights, see Ian Schapiro, *The Evolution of Rights in Liberal Theory* (Cambridge: Cambridge University Press, 1986), 276.

68. Jeffrey Isaac, "Republicanism vs Liberalism? A Reconsideration," *History of Political Thought* 9 (1988), 351.

69. Isaac, "Republicanism vs Liberalism?" 375.

70. Isaac, "Republicanism vs Liberalism?" 376.

71. Sidney figures prominently in Bernard Bailyn's republican revisionism of colonial America (*Ideological Origins of the American Revolution* [Cambridge: Harvard University Press, 1967]).

72. *Algernon Sidney and the Republican Heritage in England and America* (Princeton: Princeton University Press, 1991), 277. Houston concludes his work by challenging the idea that traditions can be transported through time to speak intelligently and coherently to us today. He writes, it "would be positively bizarre to imagine that the needs and aspirations of late-twentieth-century men and women are canonically expressed by a set of arguments intended to counter the principles and practices of seventeenth-century English Monarchs" (277-78).

73. Pocock, *Moment*; Skinner, *Foundations*; Taylor, *Sources of the Self*; MacIntyre, *After Virtue*; William Sullivan, *Reconstructing Political Philosophy* (Berkeley: University of California Press, 1982).

74. Dunn, *John Locke*; Tarcov, *Education*; John Colman, *John Locke's Moral Philosophy*; Ruth Grant, *John Locke's Liberalism* (Chicago: University of Chicago Press, 1987); D. D. Raphael, *Adam Smith* (Oxford: Oxford University Press, 1985), Alan Ryan, *J. S. Mill* (London: Routledge and Kegan Paul, 1974); Bernard Semmel, *John Stuart Mill and the Pursuit of Virtue* (New Haven: Yale University Press, 1984); and Wendy Donner, *The Liberal Self* (Ithaca: Cornell University Press, 1991).

75. The virtues found in anxious liberalism tend to be localized rather than civic and the domain of what constitutes public, participatory space has contracted in much liberal theory. That liberal virtues are not republican ones, however, does not mean that anxious liberals are without a commitment to a moral life.

76. Gertrude Himmelfarb, *On Liberty and Liberalism: The Case of John Stuart Mill* (New York: Knopf, 1974); Donald Winch, *Adam Smith's Politics* (Cambridge: Cambridge University Press, 1978); and Gary Wills, *Inventing America* (Garden City, N. Y.: Doubleday, 1978).

77. Galston, *Justice and the Human Good*; Salkever, *Finding the Mean*.

78. Mary Glendon shows that other countries have reached compromise positions on abortion policy by moving away from the language of rights to address competing concerns (*Abortion and Divorce in Western Law* [Cambridge: Harvard University Press, 1987]; see especially 112–42).

79. William Connelly, *Political Theory and Modernity* (London: Basil Blackwell, 1988), 102.

80. Michael Walzer, "The Communitarian Critique of Liberalism," *Political Theory* 18 (1990): 15. Walzer finds that "much of liberal political theory, from Locke to Rawls, is an effort to fix and stabilize the doctrine in order to end the endlessness of liberal liberation" (14).

81. Throughout his work, Rawls rejects claims that basic rights can be discounted in favor of particular claims to the good. His position is spelled out in "Priority of Right and Ideas of the Good," *Philosophy and Public Affairs* 17 (Fall, 1988): 251–76.

82. For an early and powerful critique of the role of epistemology in political theory, see Paul Kress, "Against Epistemology: Apostate Musings," *Journal of Politics* 41 (1979): 526–42. Kress forcefully rejects the idea that the troubles that confront us today are best explained by our epistemological inheritance.

83. See his *Whose Justice?*

84. Rawls makes much the same kind of argument about the status of envy and resentment in his just society in *Theory of Justice* (534–41).

85. For Beiner, "Theory is necessarily an exercise not only in criticism but in self-criticism. For a member of a liberal society, that means self-criticism of the shared way of life of liberal society" (*What's the Matter with Liberalism?*, 191).

86. *Justice, Gender, and the Family*.

87. Ronald Terchek, "Gandhi and Moral Autonomy," *Gandhi Marg* 13 (1992), 454–65.

88. See his *Whose Justice?* One of the difficulties with rigidly bound commentaries is that the problematic dimensions of politics are lost and politics looks mechanical rather than dynamic, moral standards become immutable, and the tensions resident in life are ignored. This can be seen in the fate that befell orthodox Marxism, which became highly dependent on a static, monolithic logic of philosophy and history and was unable to critique itself. And this is why someone such as Antonio Gramsci, who stretched tightly bound Marxism into something dynamic, became a breath of fresh air to non-orthodox Marxists who found that his writings explained historical change and stasis in ways that canonical Marxists could not. See his *Letters from Prison* (New York: Harper & Row, 1973).

89. John Gray argues that what we have is not a single theory called liberalism but rather liberalisms (*Liberalisms* [London: Routledge, 1989]).

90. Pocock in *Moment* and Skinner in *Foundations* acknowledge the importance of private property in republican thinking, but they hold that property is always subordinate to a common good.

91. For a discussion of how honor and shame, once central to traditional society, are replaced by new understandings of the good, notably personal integrity, see Peter Berger, "On the Obsolescence of the Concept of Honor," *European Journal of Sociology* 11 (1970): 339–47.

92. For the most part, moral philosophers and theologians are uninterested in myriad excuses about why it is difficult to be good. For them, the contingencies that buffet us are not valid excuses to ignore moral or religious principles. For their part, political philosophers fear certain contingencies can deflect persons from a principled life and seek to enhance what promotes the good life and challenge what undermines it.

93. *After Virtue*, 22–34.

94. *After Virtue*, 22.

95. In MacIntyre's account, there can be no coherent, broadly acceptable institutional solution in a society of extensive diversity because what satisfies some cannot satisfy others.

96. Feminist theorists have been particularly helpful in showing that much traditional political theory depends on patriarchal arrangements in the deepest way and that the goal of gender inclusion requires more than just opening formal or procedural rights. In other words, it is not good enough simply to "add women and stir." For feminists, it is necessary to address substantive institutional arrangements and practices as well. See Okin, *Gender*, and Carole Pateman, *Sexual Contract* (Stanford: Stanford University Press, 1988). See also Arendt's discussion in *The Human Condition* on why slavery is so critically important to the Athenian conception of citizenship.

97. See Salkever, *Finding the Mean*, for an effort to provide an Aristotelian approach in the modern world.

98. Accepting MacIntyre's advice to retreat from the late modern world may no longer be a sufficient way of escaping modernity and modernization simply because it has become so pervasive and intrusive.

99. In focusing on liberalism as the root cause of change, many communitarians talk as if nothing else of consequence intruded into the ways people once thought and acted. From this perspective, the causes of what ails us can be found in the epistemology, psychology, ontology, or moral philosophy of liberalism.

100. On fragmentation, see Sandel, *Liberalism;* on incoherence, see MacIntyre, *After Virtue*; on moral relativism, see Bloom, *Closing;* and on civic lethargy, see Barber, *Strong Democracy*.

101. But it is a curious cultural conservatism: MacIntyre's conservatism leads to despair and a sojourn into the desert because all is lost for almost everyone; Irving Kristol's leads to a blending of Aristotle and the market (*Two Cheers for Capitalism* [New York: Macmillan, 1977]).

102. Kymlicka finds most communitarians have "a romanticized view of earlier communities" (*Liberalism, Community, and Culture* [Oxford: Oxford University Press, 1989], 85). In *Looking Backward*, Phillips challenges the communitarian argument that there was once a harmonious past that can serve as a guide to us today by arguing that such a past never really existed.

103. For an important exception, see Wilson Carey McWilliams's discussion of the desirability of fraternity and its fleeting nature (*The Idea of Fraternity in America* [Berkeley: University of California Press, 1974]).

104. This is something that Ferdinand Toennies has in mind in his contrast between *Gesellschaft*, the materialistic, rationalistic, market, industrial society marked by conflict and loneliness, with *Gemeinschaft*, the stable, traditional, authentic, virtuous community characterized by spirituality and wholeness for late–nineteenth-century Germans. See his *Community and Society* (East Lansing: Michigan State University Press, 1957). Whatever one thinks of his argument, what is important for my purposes is his very adamant position that the modern problem is not solved by reorganizing the way we think when a reorganized world is resistant to such a move.

105. Hannah Arendt warns those who are "tempted to try their luck at the technique of dismantling, let them be careful not to destroy the 'rich and strange,' the 'coral' and the 'pearls' which can probably be saved only as fragments" (*On Revolution* [New York: Penguin Books, 1977], 212).

106. The need to reassess fragments can be seen in the role capitalism plays in the development of liberalism. Joyce Appleby argues that Jefferson favors markets because he believes it diffuses power and assures liberty (*Capitalism and a New Social Order* [New York: New York University Press, 1984]). In this reading, markets are not at the center of Jefferson's project; diffused power, open opportunity, and liberty are. If markets serve to concentrate private power and undermine autonomy, Jefferson is hardly committed to defending them. Also see Rawls's efforts to retain market capitalism in a highly regulated way (*Theory of Justice*).

107. "'A Way of Settlement': The Levellers, Monopolies, and Political Interest." Paper presented to the annual meeting of the American Political Science Association, 1993, 3–4. An effort to transport fragments into the present comes from Robert Bellah, who wants us to join religion and republican principles to provide us with a coherent standard that socially enlarges the self and creates the bonds of a strong community ("Civil Religion in America," *Daedalus* 96 [1967]: 1–21). If we take Hannah Arendt's claim seriously that the Roman trilogy of religion, tradition, and authority has been irreversibly shattered, Bellah reaches for fragments that fit awkwardly in the late-modern world (*Life of the Mind*, vol. 1 [New York: Harcourt, Brace, Jovanovich, 1978], 212).

Chapter Two

The Stakes of Citizenship and the Citizen's Stakes

Today, communitarians celebrate virtuous citizens who are patriotic, directed by civic duties, and tied to their tradition. When they look at liberals, communitarians discover individuals who are politically lethargic, preoccupied with their personal lives, indifferent to a common good, unconcerned about their civic obligations, and absorbed with their own rights-claims. In their critiques, communitarians capture an important part of the argument of strong republicans; but they generally neglect to notice, as Aristotle, Machiavelli, and Rousseau do, that the organization of civil society counts very much and that in the good republic, citizens care not only about their republic but also about themselves.

For strong republicans, the pattern of rewards, penalties, and indifference embedded in nonpolitical institutions is critical to the kinds of citizenship and politics that emerge. Arguing that no politics can escape the economic arrangements of civil society, strong republicans are particularly alert to the pattern of property ownership and the politically heavy costs to republican politics of deep inequalities among citizens.[1] They seek citizens who recognize that what is important to them depends on the free institutions of their republic and their support for those institutions. Sometimes, strong republicans relate property issues to justice, as with Aristotle, and sometimes there is no overt connection to justice, as with Rousseau; but in all of the strong republican literature, property arrangements never stand apart from politics and citizenship.

The strong republican approach to private property distinguishes its view of citizenship from those communitarians who draw a sharp distinction between the self and society. Many communitarians seem uninterested in the way citizens live their individual lives and are stuck on the argument that in the good polity, citizens are always ready to subordinate their own interests to the common good. Indeed, one of the puzzling features in the communitarian debate is that for all of the talk about situating, incumbering, and embedding citizens (primarily with duties and obligations), little attention is given to whether citizens have overcome necessity, are secure, and attend to the multiple needs that are important to them.

Thinking about Stakes

In taking up the issue of stakes, I want to inquire into the concrete investments citizens have in their republic. Two assumptions guide my exploration of stakes. First, patriotic citizens have normative or ideological investments in the vitality of their republic. They take it to be good and reach this conclusion on the basis of their civic education as well as from their experiences in society. Communitarians have been helpful in showing how tradition contributes to the attachments of citizens to republican politics but have not said much about the way everyday experiences tie citizens to their regime or separate them from it.

My second assumption is distinct from but related to the first. Citizens value their republic because it enables them to attend to their multiple needs, of which a civic life is only one.[2] Most citizens want to be caring parents, good friends, considerate neighbors, productive members of the economy, and patriotic citizens and they appreciate that the satisfactions they derive in their private life are closely related to the character of their republic. They care whether they are debased or respected; whether they are secure or defenseless; whether they can meet their basic needs or are continually threatened. To be able to lead respected, secure lives that have overcome acute scarcity gives people stakes in their republic, stakes that are normative, procedural, and substantive. Before taking up private property as a stake in strong republicanism, let me first briefly consider two alternative ways of conceptualizing stakes and show how each is inadequate to provide the close attachments Aristotle, Machiavelli, and Rousseau attribute to private property ownership.

At one level, simply being kept alive can count as a stake as Hobbes thought, but this is clearly an inadequate support for a government that depends on continued citizen support. It furnishes little incentive to care about the republic or invest one's time and identity in it. Moreover, citizens who can only claim their biological life as a stake are unlikely to heed calls for service and sacrifice during moments of civic crisis. In addition, such a flat conception of stakes is vulnerable to replacement by alternatives to anyone who wants to move beyond survival. The normative or ideological stakes communitarians want citizens to invest in a republic are also insufficient, by themselves, to stimulate commonality and patriotism if citizens are preoccupied about meeting necessity or find that many of their multiple needs are routinely neglected or jeopardized. Citizens absorbed with personal matters are not necessarily hostile to their republic or begrudge their civic obligations. They simply do not think much about political ideals, much less act on them, when they are distracted by pressing personal affairs.[3]

Strong republicans recognize that citizens care about themselves as they attend to their multiple needs. For Aristotle, Machiavelli, and Rousseau, the issue is how citizens frame their concerns and how they meet them. They know that citizens frequently pursue individualistic strategies and undermine the well-being of their republic but hold that this need not be the case. Their solution does not call for citizens to continually subordinate themselves but to see that their own well-being depends on the well-being of the republic.[4] To promote collective goods and patriotic citizens, ironically, requires citizens to be attached to their families and friends and to own property. Strong republicans believe these attachments and ownership give citizens a substantive investment in the republic and tie them to its normative standards. One of the tasks strong republicans set for themselves is to convert private property from an exclusively personal attachment to a stake citizens have in their republic.

Why, in particular, must republican citizens be property owners rather than propertyless? Strong republicans know that the propertyless discover that their well-being is only marginally tied to what happens to the republic. Property owners, however, find that their property enables them to overcome necessity and meet their multiple needs, giving them an investment in maintaining the strength and integrity of their republic. They understand that the republic is not only good in itself but also that their own good requires them to be civically committed. In this way, the fate of republican citizens is entangled in what is both personal and civic and both the private and the public realms are inexorably linked.

Private property has been disparaged in many quarters where it is seen as fostering individualism, engendering materialism and—in market economies—generating deep and persistent inequalities. For some, private property invites its owners to believe that they are responsible for their success, not social institutions or luck. Many who support private property have seen these possibilities, with de Tocqueville lamenting a narrow individualism in the United States and J. S. Mill castigating the "money-getting and money-having" of British society. Although strong republicans recognize these dangers, they seek to defeat the seamy side of private ownership rather than neglect it or reject property as essential to the politics of the good regime.

These strong republicans rely on a civic tradition to remind citizens that they are part of a community whose origins preceded them and, with their help, will survive them. Their membership in their political community is not merely defensive or utilitarian, although it is that. Their republic affords them a security that unattached men and women can never enjoy and shelters them against the arbitrariness of the stronger. But it does more, giving a civic identity to people who would otherwise be self-absorbed. The traditions of the republic remind citizens they are part of a continuing project that transcends their biological requirements. In contextualizing and anchoring the well-being of citizens in the vitality of the republic, property, ironically, can move citizens beyond their biological selves and extend them into a wider, normative project that they share with their fellow citizens.[5]

In offering a reading of Aristotle, Machiavelli, and Rousseau as strong republicans, I mean to challenge those communitarian accounts that make tradition serve as the foundation, superstructure, and glue of the good society. In their thick community, citizens lose their individuality in favor of a civic identity and politics is invariably coherent, consensual and stable. However robust their theory of community, Aristotle, Machiavelli, and Rousseau work with ordinary human beings who do not stop caring about themselves because they are good, patriotic citizens. These strong republicans offer a politics that builds on the personal attachments of citizens in order to achieve the good of the whole, and they do this by attempting to remove the basic economic concerns of citizens from the realm of political conflict. For Aristotle, Machiavelli, and Rousseau, property as a stake enables citizens to understand the relationship between their personal well-being and their civic responsibilities. But there is no assurance that such commitments will persist, particularly from one generation to the next, and the danger always looms that citizens believe they are the authors of their well-being and discard their civic commitments. At such times, people withdraw from politics or take their personal goods as the raw material for political interests and pursue the politics of faction. The strong republican argument for private property as a civic stake invariably introduces a paradox: the very goods required for full republican citizenship eventually threaten the republic because sooner or later citizens focus on their own prosperity and either neglect politics or use politics for their personal ends. To divert the unavoidable prospect of decay becomes the burden of republican politics.

Some recent discussions about the relationship between private property and democracy attends to how democracy should protect property, how it ought to redistribute property, how property should be subordinated to principles of justice, or how it needs to stimulate growth to insure general prosperity.[6] Other considerations of property and democracy emphasize the conflict between the wealthy few and the impoverished many and how the former must be protected or how the latter must be empowered. Finally, we have numerous discussions about why the regulation of private property by the welfare state and democracy are necessarily linked or why the former subverts the latter.[7] In talking about private property establishing stakes for democratic citizens, I ignore most of these issues in order to concentrate on the way concrete stakes are related to republican politics.[8] I am interested in showing that it is not enough to deplore the loss of what is common and call on citizens to rediscover the traditions they once shared when many citizens do not have substantive stakes in their own society.

In looking at the role of stakes proposed by Aristotle, Machiavelli, and Rousseau, I do not claim that such a reading gives us a comprehensive theory of citizenship. Nor do I claim that in understanding the issue of stakes in the writings of Aristotle, Machiavelli, and Rousseau, we know all we need to know about their theories of community or their broader theoretical projects. My argument is more modest: we cannot understand what constitutes a strong community or a thriving republic without recognizing the relationship between individual well-being and security with citizenship. Nor can we understand strong republican politics without acknowledging the ironic and paradoxical character of these requirements.

Property and Citizenship

Today, most communitarians pass over the economic well being of citizens and write as if a robust, coherent community is unrelated to the security of its citizens. When they look at private property, they see individualism, acquisitiveness, and materialism. A case in point can be found in *Sources of the Self* where Charles Taylor emphasizes the important and valuable ways a community can contribute to our identity but rarely discusses private property. When he does, he sees it contributing to our atomism.[9] Many others, such as Robert Bellah, find too much concern about material well-being in contemporary liberal society and offer us a solution where the common good supersedes self-interest.[10] To notice that many Americans are materialistic, that many measure their success as human beings by their income and consumption, or that many are socially and civically uninvolved does not supply us with sufficient material to build a robust community populated with other-regarding, active citizens. With most communitarians today, we find little discussion about what constitutes a good republic in practice. We search for an extended discussion about how people actually go about making a living and whether they see their households as secure or vulnerable.[11] The reason strong republicans find private property important to citizens has become a neglected fragment in most of the communitarian literature.

Two important exceptions to this general neglect of property ownership in the republican or civic-humanist tradition are J. G. A. Pocock and Quentin Skinner who have drawn a connection between property and republican citizenship in a way very few other commentators have.[12] In showing that private property is essential to republican citizenship, however, they argue that citizens are always ready to sacrifice and subordinate themselves whenever required by the republic. They reach their conclusions by way of their commentaries on Machiavelli's republican politics. Pocock makes the point that for Machiavelli, *virtu* "in the last analysis . . . rested on political, moral, and economic autonomy"[13] and he goes on to show that "economic independence" is a "prerequisite against corruption."[14] Pocock demonstrates that Machiavelli's citizen shares with Aristotle's citizen a "household of his own to govern so that he may not be another man's servant, so that he may be capable of attaining good in his own person, and so that he may apprehend the relation between his own good and that of the polis."[15] But the citizen-householder who emerges from Pocock's Machiavelli seems abstract except for his political commitments. With both Pocock and Skinner, we encounter arguments for civic virtue expressed in the constant readiness of citizens to submerge their own concerns in favor of the good of the republic. The "republican theorists" of Skinner "maintain that, if we wish to maximize our liberty, we must devote ourselves wholeheartedly to a life of public service, placing the ideal of the common good above all considerations of individual advantage."[16]

The republican citizens Skinner surveys desire to be free to determine how "to live together as they choose," to care for "their families without having to fear for their honour or welfare," and to own their own property.[17] How, then, do Pocock's and Skinner's republican citizens differ from liberal ones? Both appear self-referencing, value liberty, care most about those closest to them, and take their own private property to be a good. The difference, for both Skinner and Pocock, is that republican citizens are always ready to put themselves second when asked to do so by the republic. Patriotic citizens cannot think of themselves apart from their civic identities and always see themselves primarily as citizens. According to Skinner,

> The apparent paradox on which [republican] writers wish above all to insist is that we can only hope to enjoy a maximum of our own indiv-idual liberty if we do not place that value above the pursuit of the common good. To insist on doing so is—to adopt their terminology— to be a corrupt as opposed to a virtuous citizen; and the price of corruption is always slavery. The sole route to individual liberty is by way of public service.[18]

Although republican politics carries its own distinctive paradox, it is not that people to be free must continually sacrifice themselves. The paradox is that even the best politics in a free society requires the support and loyalty of citizens who never escape thinking about themselves. Strong republicans would find the claim of communitarians, including Skinner and Pocock, that good citizens always put the republic before themselves, to be overly optimistic if not utopian and would agree with Jeffrey Isaac's claim that communitarians have misunderstood "the individualist features of republicanism, particularly in regard to private property."[19]

Pocock and Skinner assign roles to private property that strong republicans never expected of it. For the latter, the task of good republican politics is to work with the view that people are never far removed from their own individual concerns. Their patriotic citizens do not continually deny their attachments and property and know how their security and well-being are intimately interwoven into the fabric of the good republic. On those rare occasions when strong republicans ask citizens to subordinate the personal for the public—as in time of war to use Machiavelli's persistent example—citizens accept their responsibilities and willingly suspend their private concerns. Their prior experiences in the republic have taught them that the goods they routinely enjoy are respected and protected by the free institutions of their republic. During times of crisis, citizens put their republic first not because they have no hesitations about sacrificing themselves but because their previous experiences validate its importance both as a good in itself and a necessity for their own continued well-being.

Rather than obliterate tensions between the personal and the civic, strong republicans appreciate that a politics for a free people that is devoid of tensions does not produce a continual sacrifice to the republic at the expense of the personal. A tension-free society for a free people is one where the personal dominates the civic for the simple reason that people are never far removed from considering their own well-being. Rather than requiring a free people to choose continually between their own good and that of the republic, strong republicans want to contexualize the personal in ways that show citizens how much they depend on the republic. For strong republicans, the issue is how a people's natural concern for themselves can invigorate republican politics, not undermine it.

Aristotle, the Household, and Money

Alasdair MacIntyre's Aristotle offers us a telos embodying a coherent standard of excellence, which, through practical reason, can be practiced in our daily lives. However, MacIntyre's Aristotle impresses many observers as confining. They see him mandating a prior good which restricts politics and emphasizes one particular good over others. This kind of reading leads Skinner to exclude Aristotle as a republican and explains why he turns to Cicero and the Roman stoics to inaugurate the republican tradition.

Recent scholarship introduces us to a different Aristotle, one who seeks to find ways in which different kinds of people can live together in harmony under the rules of justice and teaches that the virtuous life is not only preferable to other modes of existence but also possible.[20] This is an Aristotle whose political and moral projects blend in the comprehensive polity where citizens with complex, multiple needs work together to achieve their individual and collective needs. At the same time, this research emphasizes that both the individual and the civic are critically important to Aristotle, not because they are equivalent but because each depends on the other.

In Stephen Salkever's reading, Aristotle sets out to build the good regime that addresses the "multidimensionality of the problem of multiple needs." Because plurality, diversity, and complexity mark society, the "questions of practical choice cannot be resolved either by a single universal rule or by a series of rules." Salkever's Aristotle wants us to recognize and balance "competing needs or interests" intelligently and prudentially because the complexity of human needs "gives moral and political problems their indefiniteness."[21]

Working with the multiple needs of citizens, Salkever's Aristotle wants a politics that is open, tolerant, and fluid where no single understanding of the good automatically trumps alternative understandings of other citizens about their needs. We have needs for both liberty and order; for food, family, and friendship; for praxis and leisure; and for what is private and what is common. Salkever juxtaposes Aristotle's views on the multiplicity and complexity of human needs with modern arguments that "assign one particular interest . . . the role of the only one worth considering, and then deduce rules of justice and morality generally from that single dominant interest."[22] Such modern solutions delegitimize alternative arguments and depoliticize society, rejecting individual conceptions of the good that are not part of the preferred solution. Salkever's Aristotle does not ask us to reach for a fixed standard that can serve us anytime and in all situations but invites us to consider how different needs can be evaluated. To do so, we need to know how human needs are related to human nature, including its multidimensionality and complexity, if we are to understand what constitutes happiness and how people become happy.[23] Aristotle associates happiness with "success combined with virtue, or self-sufficiency in life or the pleasantest life accompanied with security or abundance of possession. . . . [H]appiness is pretty much one or more of these."[24]

Aristotle goes on to list some of the "parts" of happiness, mentioning numerous and worthy friendships, good children, economic well-being, a good old age, health, reputation, and virtue.[25] Whether we want to accept or modify his inventory of goods that it takes to become happy, it is clear that he thinks it consists of many things, and no single good, by itself, including virtue or a civic life, can lead to happiness. The Aristotle that follows builds on the understanding that people have multiple ends that deserve consideration and that it is mistaken to assume Aristotle is predisposed to have one standard determine how all our needs will be met.

A Note on Aristotle's Telos

Aristotle brings a cosmological outlook to his understanding of the telos, considering the ideal functions of both the whole and the parts and their relatedness. On Aristotle's account, the "whole must be prior to its parts"[26] and he goes on to argue that neither the whole nor the parts can be considered separately even though they are distinct from one another.[27] Because the parts are not free-standing, they ought not be pulled from the whole, isolated, and then treated independently of their surroundings and connections. From this perspective, neither the household nor the polity can be understood apart from each other. Even though the polity may be prior in nature to the household in Aristotle's account, he clearly expects it to maintain its integrity and perform its function—securing the well-being of its members—if the household is to make a solid contribution to the polity. Aristotle's cosmological perspective leads him to see the parts not as discrete fragments or unrelated moments but part of a broader harmony.

Aristotle's telos has two features that rob it of the fixity, universality, and scholastic transparency sometimes attributed to it. First of all, it can only be applied locally. The expression of the good regime for a simple agriculture community will not be the good we describe for a commercial society.[28] Aristotle also tells us that "as there are more kinds of constitution than one, there cannot be just one single and perfect virtue of a sound citizen."[29]

Second, Aristotle's telos must give room to its parts and recognize their own integrity as well as the contribution they make to the whole and to one another. This does not mean that the parts are always in harmony with one another, and they should not necessarily be. In looking at human beings, Aristotle finds persons who need both to be political and to be alone. To be only political is to neglect other goods, some of which require other people acting in their private capacities, such as with our families and friends, and some of which require us to escape our busy world in order to take stock of who we are and what we are becoming. Aristotle asks us to recognize that tensions among competing needs are an unavoidable part of any human life but are not necessarily debilitating, and he tries to show how we can combine the many dimensions of our lives to make a satisfying life.

The Naturalness of Caring about Oneself

Aristotle opens *The Politics* with a discussion of the household, then turns to villages and concludes with the political regime. While the household precedes the city temporally, Aristotle finds that the polity is prior to the household in nature.[30] This is sometimes taken to mean that the household has no independent status apart from the polity and that its concerns are invariably inferior to the polity's because this is a place where its members are self-referential in contrast to the civic concerns of public life.[31] Such a reading ignores the problematic dimensions of Aristotle's writings and overlooks the tensions and ambiguities Aristotle sees in even the best polity. For him, the household is characterized by the family and private property, and these individual attachments are important to ordinary people who think "for their own things above all, and less about things common, or only so much as falls to each individually."[32] Before becoming political, Aristotle's citizens first attend to the needs of their households.[33]

With Socrates, Aristotle believes that ordinary people are attached to their particular contingencies and their loyalty to the personal can never be completely defeated, even in the good regime. Both also see a deficiency of virtue in any society, not in the sense that individual citizens cannot practice virtues but that most people do not continually carry the highest virtues, even with the best education in the best republic. However, Aristotle departs from Socrates to show that ordinary people can become participants and flourish in the good republic. In his account, the outlooks and dispositions of individuals are sufficiently flexible and, in the good regime, ordinary people can move beyond their households to become civic and moral. For Aristotle, political philosophy works with both the opportunities and constraints such a view presents; in its philosophical aspects, it asks political philosophers to inquire about human nature and our quest for happiness; in its political aspects, it seeks to identify the most practical institutions for the good life.[34]

Aristotle's attention to the latter project separates his views from Socrates' concerning the possibilities of ordinary people governing themselves in a just polity. In his critique of Socrates, Aristotle distinguishes what is common or unified from what is individual or particular. We make a mistake, Aristotle claims, when we ignore what is important and natural to individual human beings and try to make everyone share in the same things or value the same goods. Someone who says that the "greatest good for cities" is a unified outlook and a common attachment "actually destroys them" because such a person forgets that "the good of each thing is surely what preserves it."[35] Aristotle holds that it is not unnatural to become more attached to our personal goods rather than those we share with all other citizens: people think about "their own things above all, and less about things common."[36] He goes on to argue that people "cherish and feel affection [for] what is one's own [private property] and what is dear [the family]; and neither of these can be available to those who" live in a regime that the denies the naturalness of caring for one's family and property.[37]

Holding that the city contains not only many persons, but different kinds of persons, Aristotle resists efforts to obliterate differences. He wants to preserve the integrity of both the individual parts and the whole. He assigns people a household and expects them to roam beyond their personal attachments and move into civic space. The move is never total; people always return to their homes; and politics ought never be totalizing: "To seek to unify the city excessively is not good."[38] Aristotle's argument about the naturalness of caring about oneself, one's family, and one's property is not merely a critique of Socratic politics but also represents his view of the substantive requirements for the good city. The purpose of Aristotle's politics, then, is not to deny or transcend personal attachments but to show how the multiple needs of every citizen can only be met within the good polity and that the good regime recognizes and builds on this understanding.[39] For this reason, he wants the citizens of the good regime to have "a minimum of property and work" but not to exaggerate the role that their own external goods contribute to their happiness.[40] Nor do they inflate their own contributions to their well-being but realize that the goods they enjoy depend on the health and strength of the city.

Aristotle's view of stakes and attachments associated with the household appear to deny Socrates' fear that property is inherently corrupting, but only to a point. For Aristotle, political and moral danger enters with the arrival of money and its ability to repeal the critical limits he believes are natural to agrarian households. In his argument about the unnaturalness of money, Aristotle claims that it changes the character of both the household and the city and can readily become an end in itself, corrupting what should contribute to the happiness of the individual and the justice of the city.[41] It gives a new meaning to property and threatens to destroy the attachments of the citizen to the city.[42] Before taking up Aristotle's arguments about money, it is helpful to say more about his view of the household.

Aristotle's Household

Aristotle's city is not a homogeneous collection of persons but a regime in which people who are different from one another in important respects live together under common laws that are just. Each citizen has a particular family, owns a particular piece of property, and carries a variety of other particularities. Even in the good polity where citizens share a common conception of the good, it is impossible to escape the pull of personal attachments, and Aristotle finds that "a city does not arise from persons who are similar." Within this vortex of differences, he attempts to find ways that subvert its centrifugal tendencies and encourage a politics that aims at the good of all. When Aristotle asks what principle guides different people when they come together in the good polity, he finds that it is "reciprocal equality which preserves cities."[43] Aristotle's "reciprocal equality" presupposes that citizens in the good republic are capable of "being ruled and ruling in turn," that is, that citizens participate in their own governance and live under common laws. They also recognize that the free institutions of the polity restrict certain behavior and, more important to them, the republic empowers them in ways that respect and protect the well-being of each of them.

Aristotle does not want to destroy the private in order to protect the public any more than he wants to destroy the public to protect the private. He knows that if the household is continually exposed to dangers, the polity will not be secure and he invests politics with a strong protective element that enables citizens to safeguard what is personal. As Booth emphasizes, the household is important to Aristotle because the "household with other associations . . . has a sovereign purpose that is something more than the satisfaction of material wants. That purpose is the well-being—the good life—of its free members."[44] Without a secure household, people are preoccupied with the elementary problems of physical necessity and revert to a prepolitical life. Under such conditions, there is not time, much less inclination, to cultivate virtues such as generosity and magnanimity.[45] More especially, a life of deprivation demands attention to the immediate issue of finding enough for oneself, not of extending oneself into the polity.

For Aristotle, the pursuit of virtue is not simply a matter of education or habit; it also most assuredly requires certain external goods to be in place. If Aristotle's citizens are constantly preoccupied with survival, they are tethered to the confines of physical necessity and unable to move to the self-sufficiency of the polis. In meeting the wants of its members and contributing to the good life, the household enables its free members to engage in public affairs.[46] Aristotle wants the polity to secure the liberty of its citizens; otherwise they will be "enslaved," and one reason some citizens might be "enslaved" comes from the ambitions of their fellow citizens who seize power for their own benefit.[47]

The society least likely to succumb to such a political calamity is the agrarian society. It provides the foundations for "the best democracy" because farmers "do not desire the things of others."[48] In agricultural societies, Aristotle detects little wealth,[49] and whatever a household possesses comes from the labor of its members rather than from the politics of redistribution.[50] In agrarian settings, Aristotle finds people who are moderate, industrious, prudent, and lacking envy and acquisitiveness. For him, an agrarian economy not only supplies people with the means of securing a livelihood for their household, it also shapes their satisfactions and their moral outlooks. With little incentive or opportunity to serve ambition, his agrarian citizens are satisfied with the marginal rewards that come from individual labor. In this simple economy and society, people are not tempted to increase their wealth or gain public power for themselves at the expense of others.[51]

Money and Civic Decay

Aristotle fears that the introduction of money tempts citizens into believing that their welfare is independent of their republic and they have no stakes in maintaining its constitutional integrity and civic vitality. Unsettling matters psychologically, socially, economically, and politically, money initiates a whole new set of problematics into both civic and moral life. One change comes with those citizens who find the well-being of their household is enhanced by commerce or money-lending. This creates a problem, as Aristotle understands it, because such people misunderstand the nature of external goods, believing they can substitute for the internal good of happiness. They are also apt to think their happiness stems exclusively from their personal exertions and is unconnected to the free institutions of their society.

The natural constraints that Aristotle attaches to an agrarian economy flee in the face of opportunities to acquire more and more. As a result, people increasingly get in one another's way as greed and envy intensify. The prospects for conflict also increase because of the new and widening inequalities that mark a money economy, with the very poor and the very rich seeing the world and what they are due in it in very different ways.[52] Sharing few experiences in societies with deep inequalities, individuals come to see politics as a means of assuring their own good, even at the expense of the rest. In this connection, Swanson observes that Aristotle finds the "chief cause of conflict is the desire for money and recognition. Men fight with one another even to the point of demanding constitutional change in order to gain or avoid losing either."[53]

Aristotle readily appreciates that money will remain an integral part of society and he takes its effects on the self-referencing proclivities of individuals into his account of politics. In addressing this issue, he acknowledges that good citizens care about themselves in even the best polity and denies that people who share a common citizenship will continually transcend their particularities because of their commonalities. Aristotle means to show that developing and sustaining virtue as well as the good regime take on a different dimension after the invention of money. The problem he encounters is not only that corrupt people desire money but also that everyone is vulnerable to its temptations.[54] For this reason, no regime is immune to decay. Unlike Socrates, whom he sees relating decay to the internal flaws of a particular regime, Aristotle finds there are innumerable reasons why a regime is transformed. For him, the most important ones pivot around changing conceptions of what various people think they are due. This alters the constitutional character of the regime and leads to its eventual replacement by a new regime that privileges the new rulers.

Although Aristotle offers no certain remedy to halt these destabilizing changes, he believes decay can be delayed and assigns the statesmen the task of forestalling such a calamity by devising constitutional arrangements that accord with the distributional character of civil society. For Aristotle, the best arrangement is found in the polity, a mixture of aristocracy and democracy where the few and the many are in a constitutional equilibrium. But if once-conscientious citizens become corrupt, even the statesman's best design is thwarted. For this reason, Aristotle turns to additional preventive measures to forestall decay, and an important one is a civic education "relative to that regime."[55] What he has in mind here is how people understand themselves within the context of their regime: they readily see its advantages, but they need to understand how such advantages can be abused.

Aristotle recognizes that the opportunities lodged in any particular regime can become the causes of its failure when citizens forget to be moderate and prudent and ignore the abiding interdependence between their personal goods and the good of the regime. The danger lodged in a republican regime is the assumption of ordinary citizens that each should "live as one wants."[56] A good civic education teaches republican citizens not to "define freedom badly" and to understand that freedom does not mean satisfying whatever the person craves. To remain one's own master, Aristotle's republican citizens must be free not only from a dependency on others but also from their own impulses and desires, and an education for republicans addresses what is most vulnerable in a free people. For him, both republican politics and civic education must show citizens that their private property gives them an investment in maintaining the continued strength of their republic and binds them to the polity rather than distances them from it.

Civic Time

The stakes citizens have in their republic depend on their robust civic dispositions and a readiness to respect the holdings of other citizens. Republican citizenship also requires civic time that comes from the leisure of citizens whose households are secure. For Aristotle and other strong republicans, civic time is a deep commitment, not some cognitive decision, to use an example from Robert Dahl, about determining whether to work in our garden, listen to the opera, or become involved in politics.[57] Civic time, for strong republicans, is not a segment in the life of citizens but one of their deep commitments that both extends their own lives as well as protects their liberty and vitalizes the polity.

For this reason, it is helpful to see how Aristotle draws stakes, leisure, and politics together. Once having overcome necessity, Aristotle's citizen has the time (or leisure) to devote to civic affairs. How does a citizen have the time necessary to attend to both the civic and the personal? For Aristotle, leisure depends on a well-functioning household which in turn rests on slavery.[58] In Booth's reading, "the servile person is without leisure. Leisure presupposes self-mastery, the freedom to use one's power and time as one wishes. That freedom is just what those who labor under compulsion lack. Their time belongs to the master."[59] Booth also notices that Aristotle finds that "those whose time is consumed in the mechanical occupations" cannot share in the good life and full citizenship.[60]

To the extent that either of these assessments is correct, we need to ask what this means for the robust community in the late modern world that has eliminated slavery but has hardly abolished servile labor that is psychologically and intellectually numbing. This is a pertinent issue because communitarians have been appalled by the way contemporary voters are notoriously uninformed and judge politics primarily on the basis of their individual interests. To move citizens away from this kind of narrow, reactive politics, many communitarians point to the importance of civic education. But unless we claim that Aristotle is wrong about both the importance of substantive stakes and leisure, we need to be suspicious that appeals to civic instruction, by itself, will be adequate to the tasks some assign to it today. The challenge for communitarians at this point is to ask what kinds of institutional arrangements speak to the essential equality of all persons and seek to diminish servility and increase security. We want them to tell us how citizens can be free and make a moral life for themselves, in Aristotle's sense.

That Aristotle works to assure republican citizens have the time for politics and a sense of their own self-worth when they enter the public realm should not lead us to conclude, as Pocock and Skinner do, the political life is the highest calling and we experience our autonomy most fully in our civic undertakings. Not only does Aristotle rank a philosophical life higher and friendship at least as important as politics, he cannot imagine fully flourishing persons inattentive to their other needs as persons. Politics is always important to Aristotle, but he never makes it the dominant feature of the lives of citizens, trumping our many other needs. By his reading, we also need to attend to our other attachments, such as our households and friendships. Aristotle's rendition of the best life is as skeptical of politics as it is of any other exclusive good that denies standing to the other goods that help to define the person. In this regard, Salkever argues that Aristotle holds that "anyone who takes politics too seriously will, like those who take commerce too seriously, overlook" what else is "important for human moral development."[61]

Aristotle goes on to insist that attention to property is vital to the success of the republic. For him, property and the economic well-being of citizens count for very much because he takes them to be absolutely necessary if human beings are to achieve the good. Aristotle can readily agree with the many commentators who have warned about the dangers of making economic success a person's touchstone. He knows that in such societies, economic standards of success act as a magnet which arranges and rearranges the other parts of our lives and of our society whenever it moves. For Aristotle, such a life or such a society is defective, not because it gives an important place to economic concerns but because it makes the economy central. In the process, it undermines other goods—such as the family or citizenship—and ignores the complexity and multidimensionality of human life.[62]

At the same time, Aristotle recognizes that a society that neglects economics is also defective. When he looks at the economy, he asks first and foremost how it contributes to the good of the household. It works best when it is organized in ways that enable citizens to meet their biological needs as well as address their other multiple needs.[63] If the economy is properly arranged, citizens are less likely to push economic issues into public space.[64] When civil society is crowded with scarcities and insecurities, Aristotle expects these concerns to invade the public realm. He would find the omission of any discussion about the importance of property by his communitarian commentators perplexing and would want to know why they have not insisted on the importance of something like substantive stakes for republican politics.

In Aristotle's reading, the dispositions of citizens, their multiple needs and concerns about their well-being, and the broad institutional framework of society are persistently linked. What always lurks in the background is the attraction of external goods, particularly money, which can undermine the best political institutions and corrupt once-dedicated citizens. The burden of Aristotle's politics is not only to address the institutional requirements for citizenship in the good republic but also to confront the problematic nature of republican politics with its unavoidable, self-destructive potential.

Machiavelli's Citizens and Householders

The burgeoning literature on Machiavelli's republicanism amply demonstrates his reliance on civic virtue and civic renewal to animate republican citizenship.[65] In the republican revisionist account, civic virtue is closely tied to patriotism, political participation, and the common good. Civically virtuous persons are said to be always ready to advance the good of the whole at their own personal expense. From this perspective, the citizen's identity, purpose and life itself are dedicated to the republic and its welfare.[66] I will be advancing a different conception of citizenship, one that gives the self greater independence than found in the revisionist version and that acknowledges the particular dispositions, outlooks, and activities of persons who share a common life and must live together in ways that respect their commonalities as well as their differences.

To arrive at what constitutes full citizenship in the good republic, Machiavelli first addresses the pervasiveness of self-interest and what he takes to be the natural desire of citizens to favor themselves, whatever the character of their regime. The issue for him is how they care about themselves and the extent to which their care includes a civic dimension. Accordingly, Machiavelli looks at the ways that tradition, religion, and civic virtue provide standards for identity and choice, even though he believes these organizing principles are exposed to the decay that invariably threatens any political community. Any account of the good republic, Machiavelli insists, must take account of the vulnerabilities that confront citizens, particularly the tendency of human beings to want more than they presently enjoy.[67] He argues that "nature has created men so that they desire everything, but [are] unable to attain it; desire being thus always greater than the faculty of acquiring, discontent with what they have and dissatisfaction with themselves result from it."[68]

Machiavelli does not find that nature has locked human beings into their own, raw self-centeredness. He believes that ordinary people desire liberty, by which he means that they want to be secure in their households, to speak and act freely, and to participate in the governance of their society.[69] Machiavelli's republican politics works with these goods while challenging the self-referential nature of individuals in order to provide the ideal medium for liberty.

Some commentators see Machiavelli's good citizens as always ready to subordinate their individual good to the public good and make this a mark of their patriotism. What is usually ignored is that Machiavelli's citizens are also closely tied to their families and private property. They do not lose themselves in the polity or continually sacrifice their own well-being for the sake of some mythic common good. The relationship Machiavelli draws between public and private goods can be seen in his discussion of the militia in *The Art of War*,[70] where he argues that citizen-soldiers must be ready to fight for the republic; when the battle ends, they should be "no less glad to return to their families" and "support themselves by their respective occupations." Machiavelli makes the same point in his discussion of the citizen-soldiers of Cincinnatus. They are patriotic not only because they express their loyalty by leaving their households and risking death on behalf of the republic, but also because they want to return to their farms and families: "If they had thought of enriching themselves by their wars, they would have cared little whether their fields were being spoiled or not" while they fought for the republic. When they "returned to private life, they were frugal, humble, and devoted to the care of their little properties."[71] The patriotism of Machiavelli's reliable citizens is nurtured and validated by their understanding that their personal goods are inexorably tied to the vitality of the free institutions of the republic.

The Good Citizen

What makes ordinary people into good citizens is the connection they see and experience between their personal well-being and the well-being of the whole, which means, in Machiavelli's account, a republic where liberty is protected and the households of citizens are secured.[72] According to Machiavelli, only in "cities and countries that are free" do people plan for the future.

> People will gladly have children when they know that they can support them and that they will not be deprived of their patrimony, and where they know that their children not only are born free and not slaves, but, if they possess talents and virtue, can arrive at the highest dignities of the state. In free countries we also see wealth increase more rapidly, both that which results from the culture of the soil and that which is produced by industry and art; for everybody gladly multiplies those things, and seeks to acquire those goods the possession of which he can tranquilly enjoy.[73]

The good citizen in the good republic, then, is someone who not only practices civic virtue but has personal hopes and dreams and works to achieve them.[74] Machiavelli's discussion about ordinary citizens who are concerned about their contingent interests must be read parallel to his arguments about the structure of republican politics, the reciprocal attachments he draws between citizens and their regime, and his emphasis on a virtuous citizen body upholding the good republic. In this reading, civic virtue not only assumes a disposition to move away from being stuck on the personal, but also expects people to be reasonably satisfied, not because they constantly discipline themselves and deprive themselves of personal goods, but because they find their actual situations are satisfying and secure. Machiavelli's citizens do not see politics as seeking "to deprive them of anything that is advantageous and useful to them."[75] If they live in a polity that undermines their security and threatens their personal goods, "the least occasion reminds them of it; and as these occur almost daily, their resentment is also daily revived."[76]

Machiavelli's Paradox

Machiavelli presents us with a paradox. The portrait he paints of a growing population and thriving economy reveals satisfied citizens and a city at peace. But these very goods lead to civic decay when citizens no longer see the relationship between their own personal well-being and the well-being of the whole. This occurs, Machiavelli fears, when the republic achieves what citizens want most: peace and prosperity. At such a time, citizens no longer understand their property as stakes and as dependent on the free institutions of their republic; they begin to view political participation as intrusive rather than liberating. To remind people they are not the exclusive or even major authors of their successes is woefully insufficient to the task of renewing their civic virtue at such times, as are efforts to kindle civic virtue through rhetorical appeals.

To forestall corruption, Machiavelli introduces the concept of "necessity" or crisis. During an acute crisis, he expects republican citizens to realize how deeply they depend on one another and how their free institutions secure their households.[77] Machiavelli is driven to accept crisis or necessity because he fears that "continued tranquillity would enervate [the republic] or provoke internal dissensions, which together or either of them separately, will be apt to prove her ruin."[78] During "normal" times, the danger lurks that people either use the polity to serve their own interests or think that politics makes no difference to them, thereby hastening the pace of corruption.

Corruption, a central theme in republicanism, signals the end of civic virtue and civic attachments.[79] In the corrupt society, the primary reference is personal and the issue for citizens is not how politics protects their well-being and security, therefore speaking to what is common, but how politics can be employed to enhance what is personal. In other words, it is about how public power can be used for private purposes. Because corruption initially infects only a few, Machiavelli holds that if the citizen body is vigilant, it can restore liberty and virtue to the republic. But if allowed to fester, corruption carries a powerful demonstration effect to the rest of the population. As more and more people see corruption spreading throughout their society, some become aggressively corrupt, seeking to gain more for themselves. But many, probably most, become defensively corrupt, finding that if they do not attend to their own good, others will employ public power at their expense.[80] At such a time, their daily experiences teach them that it pays to disregard republican politics and use political power to defend their own attachments. Citizens who had been patriotic find that when politics becomes corrupt, their civic duties and personal well-being no longer cohere and satisfy. What once was sheltered and even honored in the good republic becomes problematic, and civic virtue becomes self-defeating. Even if they wish to be patriotic and other regarding, they discover that rewards pass them by and their personal property and households are no longer protected by republican institutions that have now come under the control of those with power. From this perspective, civic virtue is not practiced by isolated individuals but by the citizen-body at large, and if civic-regarding conduct is spurned, people will quickly adopt to what, in fact, is rewarded in practice. "Men in their conduct . . . should well consider and conform to the times in which they live. And those who do not conform to the times in which they live, will in most instances live unhappily, and their undertakings will come to a bad end."[81]

To survive in a corrupt environment, Machiavelli finds that citizens use politics for their own personal benefit, thereby participating in their own corruption and the destruction of their own liberty. Whether factions contend with each other for public power or whether the more powerful invade the empty space of the polity vacated by citizens preoccupied with their private concerns, the process of decay intensifies. Particularly vulnerable is the republic's foundational principle of equity, the linchpin of Machiavelli's republic, and he devotes considerable attention to the issue.[82] In Machiavelli's ideal republic, equity takes many forms. For example, all citizens must be equal before the law without exception.[83]

Politically, Machiavelli's equity principle requires that the different forms of power remain within their proper domains, and he expects that the breach of this principle is likely to come from the wealthy. Moreover, he insists that the range of economic inequalities must be bounded in the good republic. At the minimum, every citizen is expected to have sufficient stakes to assure a livelihood.[84] At the upper level, no one should be able to "live idly upon the proceeds of their extensive possessions."[85] Machiavelli's concern about distributional issues is not about justice but about republican politics. Like Adam Smith later, he fears the very rich are tempted to use their surplus to make others dependent on them and, in the process, make loyalty to them, and not to the city and its free institutions, the requirement for satisfying their well-being.[86]

Moreover, those with great power seek to exempt themselves from the law or make laws that benefit themselves at the expense of the rest.[87] According to Machiavelli,

> republics which have thus preserved their political existence uncorrupted do not permit any of their citizens to be or to live in the manner of gentlemen, but rather maintain amongst them a perfect equality and are the most decided enemies of the lords and gentlemen that exist in the country . . . .
>
> Gentlemen . . . are pernicious to any country or republic; but more pernicious even than these are such as have besides their other possessions, castles which they command and subjects who obey them.[88]

Machiavelli sees that great personal wealth can be converted into political advantage, which subverts political equity, undermines equality before the law, introduces an offensive corruption, and ultimately stimulates a defensive corruption. The problem is compounded when some citizens believe their welfare depends more on pleasing those with great private power who direct their destiny than on the free institutions of the republic. If this situation spreads, the republic is lost; citizens are no longer invested in it but rather find their security dependent upon accommodating to the demands of independent centers of power.

For this reason, Machiavelli insists that "in well regulated republics the state ought to be rich and the citizens poor."[89] Later, he claims that a republic is wise to have laws that keep "her citizens poor" because wealth serves "only to ruin them."[90] Machiavelli's concept of poverty is not our own. For him, poverty means everyone must work for a living; no one has such wealth as to exempt the person from the concerns of ordinary citizens or enable the wealthy to use private fortunes for public gain or to make other citizens dependent on them.

The Causes of Decay: Corruption and Indolence

In his discussion of how the free institutions of the republic can be subverted and liberty destroyed, Pocock emphasizes the prior damage done to the moral foundations of the republic. By his account, Machiavelli's "constitutional order is rooted in the moral order, and it is the latter which corruption affects . . . . Institutions are dependent on the moral climate and laws which work well when people are not corrupt produce effects the reverse of those desires when they are."[91] Pocock's observation needs to be pushed further: Machiavelli's moral order is intimately tied to the attachments and treatment of republican citizens. True, if institutions favor one group at the expense of others, then Pocock's argument stands and the moral order is repealed. But that is only part of the story.

If citizens are prosperous and secure, they are tempted to devote more time to their own households and less to the public realm, not because they have already become corrupt but because they believe the good republic can sustain itself and continue to protect their goods without their own exertions. Machiavelli calls on the moral order to challenge the tendency of ordinary citizens to see political power as a burden, but he knows tradition and the founding cannot repeal this inclination.[92] Patriotic appeals to sustain Machiavelli's moral order are most likely to convince in times of crisis, not when everything seems to be going well. The proclivity of ordinary people to prefer to stay at home rather than crowd into public space, to laugh with friends rather than debate other citizens, and to attend to their personal household rather than the public household may stem from human weaknesses, but these are not the political sins of corruption. They are dispositions that can become dangerous not because they are vices in themselves (as depriving fellow citizens of their liberty would be) but because concern about one's self and a desire to be freed of the burdens of citizenship lead people to forget how much they depend on politics to preserve the positive goods ordinary people want. Their withdrawal from politics invites decay because it leaves republican institutions vulnerable to the conspiracies of ambitious citizens searching for ways to employ public power for private purposes. Because political passivity stems from innocence rather than corruption, Machiavelli's citizens have the capacity to shake their lethargy, return to civic space, and remember that the benefits they derive from their property come not only because of their own exertions but also because they are protected by the free institutions of their republic.

For Machiavelli, politics is unavoidable. Augustine's retreat into private virtue is unavailable to Machiavelli who finds that power follows all citizens, whether they decide to use or to avoid it. If some citizens decline to be political, politics does not disappear; others can be counted on to employ power for their own benefit, even if it costs lethargic citizens their liberty. Machiavelli requires civic involvement in the good republic to secure both the public and the private. Like Aristotle, he sees both the requirement of concrete stakes and their potentially corrupting effects. Machiavelli also appreciates that the more the republic succeeds in securing the well-being of citizens, the more they are apt to retreat from politics and thereby invite corruption and destroy their republic and eventually their own security.

Rousseau, Property, and Liberty

Recent accounts of Rousseau as a strong democrat[93] emphasize his participatory credentials in a world grown politically languid and economically preoccupied. However, I want to emphasize the way he links popular government with the concrete stakes of citizens. Although not denying the importance of the contradictions and tensions that others have found in Rousseau, I want to demonstrate that Rousseau expects good citizens to be concerned about both the republic and themselves.[94] His citizens not only are tied to the cultural, moral, and social standards of their community, as has repeatedly been demonstrated, but also are attached to something which has been taken by some to be antithetical to these standards, namely their individual households.

In pursuing his project, Rousseau treats citizens as equals and brings them together into a civic union where no person has inherent or natural jurisdiction over others. Each citizen is a member of a social order that embodies that "sacred right which is the basis of all other rights."[95] The "sacred right" of citizens is to live in a society that institutionally assures their civil liberties and challenges corruption and factionalism. To challenge these distortions of the "sacred right," Rousseau turns to civic virtue, patriotism, stability, and vigilant citizens whose private property give them concrete investments in the well-being of their republic.

In his account of the loss of innocence and the advent of civilization in *A Discourse on the Origin of Inequality*, Rousseau offers an extended argument about the way people historically accumulate constructed identities, needs, and attachments, how these accumulations assume moral meanings, and the ambiguous and sometimes contradictory ways human beings tie themselves to their accumulations.[96] Rousseau begins his historical narrative of the loss of innocence with the noble savage who is content, unalienated, and innocent.[97] Animated by passion, lacking a sense of time, compassionate but amoral, moving essentially among equals, the savage encounters no subordination. Rousseau finds the civilized person, however, is restless and miserable and directed by instrumental reason. Worst of all for Rousseau, as people become civilized, they consent to their own subordination and sacrifice their liberty for the sake of peace and order.[98] However, civilization enables people to construct, by Rousseau's telling, a polity that respects the essential equality of every citizen. Because the metamorphosis of the savage to the civilized person is complete and irreversible, Rousseau attempts to work with the civic opportunities that he sees characterizing the new human condition.[99]

Three features in Rousseau's narrative of the steady migration from the state of nature show the ambivalent character he attributes to these changes.[100] In each transformation, he finds the attachments we historically acquire annul the simple satisfactions and innocence of the noble savage. But Rousseau also holds we can reconstitute institutions and direct the moral effects of change in order to assure ourselves a politically secure and morally expansive life.

The first major change he detects is the acquisition of what he calls "conveniences," which begins with the invention of tools that make work less arduous and life more pleasant. Everyone desires to possess these "conveniences," but Rousseau finds they deliver no sustained contentment. We continually want more, only to find that our external goods do not deliver their promise, and disquiet again asserts itself. These "conveniences lost with use almost all their power to please, and even degenerated into real needs, till the want of them became far more disagreeable than the possession of them had been pleasant. Men would have been unhappy at the loss of them, though the possession did not make them happy."[101]

In discovering how to become marginally better off, a newly emergent self acquires "many conveniences unknown to his fathers, and this was the first yoke he inadvertently imposed on himself and the first source of evils he prepared for his descendants."[102] These new conveniences, according to Rousseau, are not inherently evil but they carry no compelling instructions on their limits. Yet he believes that under the proper conditions, people can voluntarily accept limits and he offers an idealized account of Geneva to demonstrate that people can know how to use the tools of their own trades to assure their livelihood and enjoy their liberty because of their republican institutions, practices, and dispositions.[103]

The second change Rousseau discusses is the early use of leisure, which he sees eroding innocence, fostering alienation, and introducing social conflict. With free time, people gather together to sing and dance, and a convention of good singing and dancing emerges according to which some are praised for their performances and others ridiculed. But these turn out to be more than aesthetic judgments; they signal the worth or worthlessness of the singer or dancer, not merely as a performer but especially as a person because, as Rousseau understands it, people internalize the assessments of others. "From these first distinctions arose on the one side vanity and contempt and on the other shame and envy: and the fermentation caused by these new leavens ended by producing combinations fatal to innocence and happiness."[104] By themselves, Rousseau claims, leisure and sociability do not initially lead to happiness but introduce discord and alienation. Like so many of the changes Rousseau detects, leisure has an enigmatic quality: it is clearly not a good in itself but becomes valuable or dangerous depending on its use, and in his good republic, he attempts to direct leisure to civic affairs.

More is involved here than the way people use their time. Rousseau is concerned with how social roles give us an identity and meaning: we encounter others and are encountered by others in our roles.[105] As we move in and out of different roles, we behave more or less according to the expectations others have conventionally attributed to the role. These assessments enable us to know what is expected of us in the role and what constitutes success in the role. But it turns out that not all roles are salutary to the individual, and Rousseau finds many of them alienating. Later in *The Social Contract*, he offers political and social arrangements that attempt to contextualize roles and provide us with a civic identity that does not require us to be dishonest to ourselves.

The third transformation of his narrative centers on how quasi-equal private property holdings give way to extensive inequalities of wealth. With new technologies in agriculture and metallurgy, Rousseau finds some people accumulate much more than others. The reason for unequal acquisitions originally might be traced to the physical or mental prowess of a person or it might be luck. In any event, what initially begins as small and largely undeserved individual differences becomes magnified and creates a gulf between the rich and poor. According to Rousseau, grossly uneven distributions of private property introduce greed and envy, intensify conflict, and sow the seeds for institutional inequality, alienation, and domination.[106] But this does not lead Rousseau to abandon private property in the good republic.

Property and Leisure

Rousseau tries to reconstitute the very factors that lead to the loss of innocence, equality, and freedom in ways that establish the basis of his harmonious, participatory society. He attempts to reinstitute a rough equality in his one-class society of property holders who have the means to assure their livelihood.[107] His patriotic citizens do not look to other individuals for their livelihood or security and recognize their good depends on a strong polity that establishes the conditions for their own well-being.[108]

Rousseau's arguments about the importance of private property can be found throughout his writings.[109] He assumes that people are entitled to the means to earn their own livelihood and ought not to be dependent on others in ways that subvert their autonomy.[110] This is one meaning of the "sacred right" of citizens who require the protection of "their lives, liberties, and property." If they do not enjoy such security but are "subjected to the duties of the state . . . they would be in the worst condition in which freemen could possibly find themselves."[111] He also pursues this topic in his dedication of *The Origins of Inequality* where he assumes a symmetry between the way the citizens of Geneva lead their lives and the requirements of the good republic. Praising their industry, frugality, and moderation as well as the pride they take both in their own accomplishments and the liberty of their city, Rousseau provides a lesson for all strong republicans about the relationship between private property and republican politics. One of Rousseau's most extensive claims on behalf of private ownership comes in his *Discourse on Political Economy*.

> It is certain that the right of property is the most sacred of all the rights of citizenship, and even more important in some respects than liberty itself; either because it more nearly affects the preservation of life or because property being more easily usurped and more difficult to defend than life, the law ought to pay a greater attention to what is most easily taken away, or finally because property is the true foundation of civil society, and the real guarantee of the undertakings of citizenship.[112]

For Rousseau, private property assures the autonomy of citizens by freeing them from dependency on others for their survival. Property-owning citizens need not ask for permission or wait for approval before they attend to the multiple needs. However, Rousseau also expects that citizens are basically satisfied with what they have and do not covet more. For this reason, he finds "that nothing is more fatal to morality and to the Republic than the continual shifting or rank and fortune among citizens; such changes are both the proof and the source of a thousand disorders, and overturn and confound everything."[113]

The private property of Rousseau's citizens is subverted not only by continual mobility and dissatisfaction but also by gross inequality. In his discussion of societies divided between the very rich and very poor, Rousseau offers us a series of calamities, ranging from alienation and conflict, jealously and avarice, and dishonesty and cruelty, to the disappearance of liberty.[114] For Rousseau, unequal distributions of property furnish resources to the few to advance their interests and make others dependent on them, leading him to insist that "liberty cannot exist without" equality. Rousseau does not require precise equality among citizens but rather depends on a range of differences identified by functional floors and ceilings to assure the independence of each citizen: "no citizen shall ever be wealthy enough to buy another, and none poor enough to be forced to sell himself."[115]

Leisure also assumes a new dimension in Rousseau's reconstituted politics where citizens extend themselves into the political world to assure their liberty. For Rousseau, participatory politics takes time and not only opens new opportunities but also imposes burdens on citizens. Rousseau's idealized participatory citizens do not consistently seek a general will but jealously protect the institutional arrangements that assure their liberty. However, the same leisure that can nourish political activity can be deflected to individual interests, including acquisitive ones.[116] In trying to defeat a certain kind of individualism, Rousseau does not want to deny the importance of personal attachments, as is clear in his discussions about the property-owning citizens of Geneva who are virtuous and patriotic. But he cannot escape the tensions resident in his theory of liberty that depends on a politically attentive and active citizen body who own private property. However, the very property that gives them stakes also provides Rousseau's citizens the incentives to become insular and individualistic.[117]

The ideal republic Rousseau constructs is defined, driven, and constrained by the general will, which is unconcerned with specific policies, particular cases, or routine administration but is said to aim at the good of all.[118] Rousseau is very careful to insist that citizens pronounce the general will only infrequently,[119] that its application is under the province of the people's government[120] and not of the sovereign people themselves, and that when the general will is determined by the people as sovereign, it reflects the small difference among them.[121] What subject matter does the general will address? First and foremost, it is concerned with protecting and vitalizing the free institutions of the republic which assure the liberty and security of each citizen. It is alert to efforts to exempt some from the obligations required of all other citizens; it rejects attempts to undermine political liberty, even in the name of some other good, such as national wealth or efficiency; and it defends the republic by rejecting efforts to establish private concentrations of wealth and power. The deliberations and decisions of citizens aimed at the general will are informed by both the tradition of the founding as well as the experiences of property-owning citizens who are invested in republican institutions.

Peace, Plenty, and the Decline of Politics

Peace and plenty are the very things we want for ourselves and our families. But their paradoxical relationship to the republic worries Rousseau who holds "the enjoyment of peace and plenty" is the time when the republic "is least capable of offering resistance and easiest to destroy."[122] With everything appearing secure, the imperatives to participate in politics no longer seem urgent and people become preoccupied with their own immediate concerns.[123] Rousseau dreads the day when politics becomes irrelevant, holding that "As soon as any man says of the affairs of the State, *What does it matter to me?* the State may be given up for lost."[124] If, as some commentators insist, Rousseau's citizens have no independent identity and lose themselves in the republic, then Rousseau would never have to worry about how once patriotic citizens come to ask, "*What does it matter to me?*"[125]

A preoccupation with peace and tranquility is a signal that corruption has established itself; indeed Rousseau thinks that in a thoroughly corrupt society, people "call a state of wretched servitude a state of peace" because their freedom is less important to them than the pursuit and enjoyment of their private successes.[126] Previously, people made this mistake when they consented to the defective contract offered to them in the late state of nature after their innocence, equality, and natural liberty were supplanted by suspicion, inequality, and conflict. Institutionalizing existing arrangements and distributions of property in civil society, the defective contract legitimized a government based on deep inequalities and favored the few at the expense of the many. It "bound new fetters on the poor, and gave new powers to the rich; which irretrievably destroyed natural liberty, eternally fixed the law of property and inequality; [and] converted clever usurpation into unalterable right."[127]

What occurred at the dawn of history, Rousseau holds, continually repeats itself when people choose stability over freedom. Even in the good republic, citizens do not escape thinking about their own well-being. When they become preoccupied with work and consumption and leave public affairs behind, they hasten their own subordination.

Whatever else Rousseau's elaborate theory of politics might involve, it is programmatically driven by his insistence that ordinary people care about themselves and this phenomena can serve to support or undermine the republic. In requiring stakes for every citizen, Rousseau attempts to lay the basis for equality and liberty. The Rousseau I am presenting appears to lose much of his pessimism and foreboding, and it might appear he leaves us with a middle-class society whose primary political orientations are to be law abiding, politically attentive, appropriately active, and ever ready to defend the regime and its free institutions when either its or their well-being is endangered. However, this can only be a partial view of Rousseau who sees the human psyche as constantly vulnerable and often pained; who detects dangers to happiness lurking everywhere; who acknowledges the weakness of reason but is unready to accept the adequacy of the passions in the modern world; and, most especially, who knows there is no stable way to establish a natural harmony between the capacities of individuals and their desires after we have lost our innocence.[128] Rousseau's political solution does not restore our innocence but gives us a way of framing our desires to secure our liberty and keep us from becoming dependent on others.

Rousseau does not offer a cure to all our cares, rather he wants to be sure that the inevitable agony that visits us all does not come from our political weakness or social inferiority. He also alerts us to the profound and persistent obstacles to a political perfectionism and warns us that even his ideal polity is bound to become unstable. The issue for Rousseau is how we prolong republican institutions which are, on his account, "only an ideal."[129] In pursuing his ideal, Rousseau calls for a politics that not only aims at political participation and equality but also requires substantive stakes in the form of private property that enable citizens simultaneously to care about themselves as well as to attach themselves patriotically to their community. But the very property required for republican politics can be its undoing.

Economic Contingencies and Republican Politics

There are many ways to identify the requirements for popular government. The one I wish to pursue here is driven by the way different strong republicans treat individual stakes and their implications for contemporary liberal democracies. For strong republicans, property provides citizens with stakes in maintaining the free institutions of their regime and frees them from necessity in order to participate in a robust civic life. Before proceeding to the implications of stakes for the current debate, it is helpful to talk about the role of property in two very different types of economy in order to show that although strong republicans differ about the way distributions should be cut, they agree that every citizen should have a substantive investment in the republic. According to them, political inattention to economic arrangements only serves to undermine the republican character of a regime that rests on the principles of liberty and political equality.

Most early theories of popular government deal with private property in a class-divided society. The story is well known how writers as diverse as Polybius, Machiavelli, Harrington, the early British Whigs, and finally John Adams attempt to separate discernibly unequal classes into distinct political entities that check and balance one another in a relatively static economy and stable society. Although there are clear differences in the ways they proceed, they generally share the position that in a class-based society, each class is tempted to want more for itself from time to time and that the greatest danger usually comes from those with much rather than those with little. Since Machiavelli's approach is fairly representative, let me begin a discussion of these issues by briefly examining his position regarding a class-based republic.

Even though all of Machiavelli's citizens have substantive stakes in their society, he assumes significant class differences and attempts to shield the stakes of the many against the designs of the few. In his class-divided society, Machiavelli attempts to avert concentrations of wealth and power that enable any citizen to act independently of the state because, he fears, those with great wealth and power have no attachments to the polity. Moreover, they are continually tempted to transform republican politics by employing their vast resources to steer the regime away from the public good to their own good. Finally, with the appearance of private centers of wealth and power, more and more citizens depend less on the republic and more on those with greater power and wealth for their security and well-being. Once-patriotic citizens now come to invest their primary allegiance to the rich and powerful on whom they have become dependent, and their primary allegiance is no longer directed to the republic but to those on whom they rely for their welfare. They are then not apt to be tempted to undermine the prosperity of their masters, even if the designs of the wealthy and powerful undermine the free institutions of the republic and diminish the liberty of its citizens. Armed with this reading of the relationship between wealth and politics, Machiavelli attempts to place ceilings on what any one person can possess, not because of justice issues but because of its effects on republican politics.

Machiavelli also separates the political institutions open to the ordinary property-owning citizens from those reserved for wealthy citizens. In doing so, he offers institutional arrangements which are not only conservative and protective but also populist. The wealthy hold some offices but are barred from others in order to shield ordinary citizens from the manipulation of the few. Without such protections, Machiavelli fears the wealthy will fill all offices which they will then use to serve their own purposes and thereby thwart the republican principle of political equity. The issue communitarians need to take up today is not whether Machiavelli's protective division of power remains desirable—it does not—but whether some kinds of protection are necessary beyond contemporary constitutionalism and proceduralism to assure the stakes, political equality, and liberty of ordinary citizens.

Rousseau moves away from a class-divided society and attempts to narrow the range of economic differences that separate citizens. In doing so, he presents us with one of the strongest political arguments for a one-class society. By his account, every citizen is a property owner and no one is so poor as to sell himself and no one so rich as to be able to buy someone. Rousseau's floors and ceilings provide the framework in which a common civic outlook emerges among citizens. For him, distributions of property enhance or diminish the prospects that citizens share a common background and important experiences. He goes on to claim that extensive economic inequalities lead to political inequalities. When inequalities occur within a narrow range of differences, he expects that citizens will draw from common experiences, concerns, and stakes as they formulate their politics. Rousseau's one-class society is said to banish the politics of resentment and to facilitate a politics of cooperative, shared undertakings.[130]

Whether it is a class-based economy or a one-class economy, strong republicans are attentive to the political consequences of economic distributions on republican politics. For them, the economy is not autonomously located in civil society and separated from the political. They disagree about the best pattern of economic distributions but they acknowledge that any distribution must enable every citizen to meet necessity, overcome insecurity, and see in their property an investment in the republic. Strong republicans go on to agree that the economy should be arranged in such a way that some citizens are not dependent on others for their well-being but should recognize their debt to the republic. Good citizenship for Aristotle, Machiavelli, and Rousseau does not require people to suspend interest in themselves when they participate in politics; these strong republicans expect patriotic citizens to care about themselves and to see that their well-being is linked to republican politics. For strong republicans, patriotism not only is expressed in a readiness to sacrifice for the republic in times of crisis but also is practiced by alert citizens who use republican politics to shield themselves from those who wish to employ public power for their own purposes.

Self and Society, Not Self or Society

As important as tradition, civic virtue, education, and renewal are in strong republicanism, these goods do not stand independently from the reoccurring experiences of citizens. Aristotle, Machiavelli and Rousseau never expect that republican citizenship is compatible with acute poverty and insecurity. For this reason, strong republicans are concerned not only about the moral foundations of society but also about its distributional ones. They attempt, in a variety of ways, to promote arrangements and practices that bring citizens together and also assure each citizen a modicum of security and well-being. For this reason, concrete stakes in the form of private property are a requirement for full republican citizenship and not merely a desirable characteristic or an exclusionary device.

Aristotle, Machiavelli, and Rousseau enjoin political philosophers to recognize that people care very much about themselves and one of the tasks of political philosophy is to explore how personal attachments can take on a civic dimension and how citizens come to understand they have an investment in their republican institutions. These strong republicans also appreciate that a politics that successfully protects the stakes of citizens in a peaceful and prosperous society introduces a profound paradox, making civic participation less compelling and inviting private preoccupations or factional politics. Aristotle, Machiavelli, and Rousseau acknowledge that citizens with stakes can readily become self-absorbed,[131] and they attempt to contextualize stakes politically by demonstrating the civic foundations of private goods. They offer renewal, crisis, respect for law, education, civic virtue, and civic participation as remedies to challenge the deconstructive pull of personal attachments and thereby prolong the life of the good republic.

The social conditions on which Aristotle, Machiavelli, and Rousseau build their argument for private property as stakes have, in many critical senses, become frail and their specific views about what constitutes stakes are no longer compelling.[132] Moreover, the foundational institutions of society are no longer stable and continuous but changing and often disconnected today. Even so, the strong republican case for stakes carries important implications for liberal democracies in advanced capitalist economies. Even though the precise character of stakes has changed in the late modern world, their relationship to citizenship has not: those who have no investment in their society or only weak stakes are not likely to be attached to their regime and have little interest in maintaining it.

The move from partial political inclusion based on concrete stakes to universal political inclusion has procedurally democratized politics but not substantively. Now there is a compelling reason to move quickly to formal citizenship for everyone and ignore substantive qualifications for full citizenship. If we wait for everyone to have the necessary substantive stakes for full citizenship, many members of society will remain citizenless. But in extending formal citizenship to every adult, the substantive requirements of democratic citizenship do not disappear. Indeed, without every citizen carrying concrete stakes, the process of democratization remains incomplete. Strong republicans repeatedly emphasize that citizenship is defective if some continually struggle with necessity.

What constitutes a stake today is a question that invites disputes and no single answer can be the settled one. Two considerations, however, seem helpful in sorting out the issue. For one, stakes would somehow have to include a solid place for rights. Second, the mythic benefits attributed to private property ownership, particularly agrarian property, no longer make sense in a postindustrial world, and we ought not to dwell too long on private property as the relevant stake in contemporary democracy. Property holdings, particularly agrarian property, are valued in strong republicanism because of their purported relationship to liberty, security, and autonomy. On this view, private property provides the foundations for the freedom necessary to construct a moral life, affords a reasonably manageable environment for citizens, precludes dependency, nourishes attachments between the citizen and political society, and provides the leisure necessary for political participation.[133] Agrarian property in particular is also thought to carry natural limits to ambition and acquisition and hence to forestall the problems of corruption. On this view, the common core of shared values, traditions, or civic virtue of strong republicans builds on the concrete attachments of citizens to their society.

The late-modern world brings a much different understanding of property. It no longer connotes independence. When agrarian property is replaced by commerce, finance, and industry, the holdings of ordinary men and women are no longer a surety for escaping necessity, scarcity, and dependency. More and more people depend on wages and salaries in the larger economy, and their property becomes their abode, means of transportation, or personal possessions. Property, as such, does not necessarily bring autonomy.

Nor does modern property carry the sense of limits associated with agricultural property. By the time Jefferson wrote about the importance of agriculture, he knew it was already too late to maintain the old republican values based on the yeoman farmer. Jefferson's fear of a commercial society is compounded in the modern world by its incessant mobilities,[134] instabilities, and dissatisfactions. And as Claus Offe and others have argued, much of this dissatisfaction comes from the structure of modern life, which leaves many vulnerable and uncertain.[135] Finally, the nature of work has changed dramatically with the division of labor, the bureaucratization of the economy, and the growth of the corporation. What then are the stakes of citizens in the late-modern world? Two candidates for stakes in contemporary liberal democracies would appear to be equality of opportunity in an economy of growth and procedural rights.

Equality of opportunity can be seen as replacing private property in liberal democracies and can be understood as providing people with access to the economy and a realistic chance of earning a livelihood for themselves and their family. However, the analogue between equality of opportunity and the expectations that strong republicans attach to private property is tenuous for several reasons. Most obviously, modern liberal democracies claim inclusiveness but the economy operates in ways which ignore or marginalize many individuals who continue to face unrelenting necessity. In addition, some groups are systematically discounted in the economy, and the equality premise that resides in equality of opportunity is diminished. Third, equality of opportunity, as currently practiced, intensifies inequalities, something strong republicans think is inimical to good government.[136] Finally, the motivations embedded in equality of opportunity rest on a dissatisfaction with a person's present position and an abiding desire to improve. However, such dispositions serve to detach citizens from the civic, thus undermining the central purpose of stakes in strong republicanism. My point is not that equality of opportunity is inimical to democratic principles but that it cannot be substituted for substantive stakes.[137]

Procedural rights also appear to qualify for stakes in modern liberal democracies.[138] Procedural rights offer citizens, regardless of background, a chance and a choice to speak, assemble, worship, and participate in society, politics, and the economy, as well as engage in a variety of other activities that do not contravene a harm principle. As critical as procedural rights are, they can not qualify as a substitute for substantive stakes in the strong republican sense. Among other things, substantive stakes are expected to enable individuals to subdue necessity but that is not what procedural rights are expected to accomplish. The goodness and significance of procedural stakes are not sufficient to energize citizens to invest in the well-being of the republic particularly when they are insecure and vulnerable.

A democratic community that does not recognize the importance of providing citizens with stakes is deficient in meeting the strong republican requirement for overcoming necessity as a prelude to full citizenship. Strong republicans remind us that substantive stakes are not rights but requirements for full citizenship. If we take their arguments seriously at the theoretical level but ignore them in practice, we need to acknowledge, it seems to me, that we do not care whether some members of society are not destined to be full citizens.

At the same time it is important to notice that in the strong republican position, citizens are both the recipient of substantive stakes and the carriers of civic obligations. Thus strong republicans search for ways to make politics responsive and open and to make citizens responsible for their own well-being as well as for the republic's. Citizens in the strong republic are property owners and are also expected to contribute to the republic in significant ways. I am not sure precisely what this means today but suspect that it means something very different than what is embedded in procedural rights. A problem in much of the current debate is that too many communitarians stress the responsibilities of stakes without providing them, and too many liberals today emphasize the rights of the vulnerable to goods that often look like stakes but refuse to talk about the duties associated with stakes. In emphasizing rights to cover a wide array of vulnerabilities, procedural liberals forget there are important goods besides rights, such as justice, democracy, or fairness and that the way of meeting such goods means shifting away from the exclusive use of the language of rights to other political languages such as a language of robust citizenship.

Although we need rich commentaries that simultaneously address the vulnerabilities of many citizens as well as their responsibilities, the present debate does not seem destined to take us far. Contemporary rights talk simply has a very difficult way of dealing with responsibility, and communitarian critiques seldom address the requirements for full citizenship. In looking at strong republicanism, we encounter a theory that is sensitive to both the prerequisites for and responsibilities of citizenship and weaves them closely together.

Strong republicans are also helpful in reminding us that the preoccupation of people with their own lives is not unique to a liberal form of politics but occurs in any mode. For Aristotle, Machiavelli, and Rousseau, self-regardingness is both natural and healthy, provided it remains within bounds. Every regime, not only republican ones, must challenge the tendency of ordinary people to become self-involved. Impassioned appeals about being civic-minded or persistent complaints about individualism and materialism do not effectively confront the issue. As strong republicans know, civic ideals and traditions are viable only if routinely practiced and rewarded and that is highly dependent on citizens seeing their own well-being is substantively linked to the well-being of the republic.

Notes

1. The importance of private ownership and the dangers of significant inequalities is hardly limited to strong republican literature. See Plato, *The Laws,* for the argument that every citizen should possess some minimum property and an upper threshold of five times the original allotment should be imposed on all citizens (Book 5, 744d–745a).

2. For extended discussion of multiple needs, see Stephen Salkever, *Finding the Mean* (Princeton: Princeton University Press, 1990), and Michael Ignatieff, *The Needs of Strangers* (New York: Penguin, 1986).

3. In everyday life, for example, people who are seriously ill are preoccupied with their own pressing crisis. They hardly surrender their civic identity during these troubled times, but it is not their primary way of understanding themselves nor are they moved to become civic at such moments. Republican politics faces its crisis when people are so preoccupied with their own private concerns that they leave politics to others.

4. I am not claiming that well-being means people can obtain everything they desire for the asking. I assume, along with strong republicans, that citizens must work for a living and their work provides them with an existence that allows them to overcome necessity, thereby freeing them to attend to many of their other needs.

5. I recognize there are solid reasons to ignore the arguments of strong republicans that property is essential to citizenship. It is a restrictive and exclusionary requirement, opening political participation only to some. I take up these objections later in this chapter, not to defend private property ownership as a requirement for citizenship today but to argue that a strong republic requires that all citizens have substantive investments in their regime and carry concrete stakes in its well-being.

6. Why democracy should protect private property, see Friedrich Hayek, *The Political Order of a Free People* (Chicago: University of Chicago Press, 1979), and Robert Nozick, *Anarchy, State, and Utopia* (New York: Basic Books, 1974). Why democracy should redistribute private property, see Graeme Duncan, ed., *Democracy and the Capitalist State* (New York: Cambridge University Press, 1989), and Frank Cunningham, *Democratic Theory and Socialism* (Cambridge: Cambridge University Press, 1987). Why property should be subordinate to principles of justice, see John Rawls, *A Theory of Justice* (Cambridge: Harvard University Press, 1971). For a critical discussion of growth see David Marquand, *The Unprincipled Society* (London: Fantana, 1987).

7. See Claus Offe, *The Contradictions of the Welfare State* (Cambridge: MIT Press, 1984); Norberto Bobbio, *The Future of Democracy* (London: Polity Press, 1987); and Hayek, *Political Order.*

8. Stakes need not necessarily be restricted to private property; we can talk about other kinds of stakes that complement or replace private property or that might even create a tension with private property.

9. *Sources of the Self* (Cambridge: Harvard University Press, 1989).

10. Robert Bellah et al, *Habits of the Heart: Individualism and Commitment in American Life* (Berkeley: University of California Press, 1985).

11. Consider Michael Sandel's list of "qualities most plausibly regarded as essential to a person's identity—one's character, values, core convictions, and deepest loyalties" (*Liberalism and the Limits of Justice* [New York: Cambridge University Press, 1982], 74). Whether people are secure and able to earn a living escapes the attention of Sandel and most other communitarians when they consider a person's identity.

12. See J. G. A. Pocock, *The Machiavellian Moment* (Princeton: Princeton University Press, 1971). Also see his *Virtue, Commerce, and History* (Cambridge: Cambridge University Press, 1985), chaps. 2 and 3. Quentin Skinner, *The Foundations of Modern Political Thought* (Cambridge: Cambridge University Press, 1978); also see his "On Justice, the Common Good, and the Priority of Liberty" in *Dimensions of Radical Democracy* edited by Charles Mouffe (London: Verso, 1992).

13. *Moment*, 212.

14. *Moment*, 210.

15. *Moment*, 203.

16. Skinner, "On Justice," 217. Skinner's effort to make room for Cicero and the stoics as the founding republicans does not coincide with his own views about property. Reflecting the custom of the day, Cicero's citizens are property owners, but he pays little attention to why property should be important to citizenship, does not emphasize its contributions to the development of civic virtue, and certainly does not take property to be a stake that connects citizens to their republic. As Skinner himself stresses, when Cicero looks to ways to fortify civic duty, he calls for a classical education to provide the basis for civic virtue, particularly the willingness to place the common good before personal goods. In this way, Cicero has more in common with most communitarians today than he does with the strong republicanism of Aristotle, Machiavelli, and Rousseau.

17. Skinner, "On Justice," 220.

18. "On Justice," 221.

19. See Jeffrey Isaac, "Republicanism vs Liberalism? A Reconsideration," *History of Political Theory*, 9 (1988): 351. For a sensitive discussion of the importance of equitably distributed property in a republic, see Frank Michelman who argues that private property underpins "the independence and authenticity of the citizen's contribution to the collective determinations of public life." Michelman calls on contemporary republicans to strive "through public law for the broadest feasible distribution of whatever property in whatever form is considered minimally prerequisite to political competence" ("Law's Republic," *Yale Law Journal*, 97 (1979): 1493–1537.

20. See Salkever, *Finding the Mean*; Judith Swanson, *The Public and the Private in Aristotle's Political Philosophy* (Ithaca, N. Y.: Cornell University Press, 1992); William Booth, "The New Household Economy," *American Political Science Review* 85 (1991): 59–75.

21. *Finding the Mean*, 138.

22. *Finding the Mean*, 153.
23. *Finding the Mean*, 161,
24. Aristotle, *On Rhetoric* (New York: Oxford University Press, 1991), I.5.3.
25. *Rhetoric*, I.5.4.
26. *Politics* (Chicago: University of Chicago Press, 1984), bk. 1, 1253a.
27. Salkever finds that Aristotle's universe is "composed of interdependent parts which are themselves wholes" (*Finding the Mean*, 51).
28. This perspective would have difficulty, for example, in accepting capital-intensive models for the Third World that emphasize a universalistic approach to economic development and pretend local conditions are not important.
29. *Politics*, 1276b. Elsewhere, Aristotle holds that "you cannot make a state out of men who are alike (*Politics*, 1, 1261a).
30. *Politics*, I, 1253a.
31. Arendt makes a forceful argument that Aristotle consigns the household to an inferior position in *The Human Condition* (New York: Doubleday, 1958).
32. *Politics*, 2, 1262a. For a discussion of the importance of the private in Aristotle, see Swanson, *Public and Private*.
33. In *Ethics*, Aristotle argues that "the household is prior to the city and more necessary" in addressing the elementary, daily needs of persons (1162a16-19).
34. *Politics*, IV, 1288b-89a.
35. *Politics*, II, 1261a. According to Aristotle, "What was said to be the greatest good for cities actually destroys them; yet the good of each thing is surely what preserves it. It is evident in another way as well that to seek to unify the city excessively is not good. For a household is more self-sufficient than one person, and a city than a household; and a city tends to come into being at the point when the partnership formed by a multitude is self-sufficient. If, therefore, the more self-sufficient is more choiceworthy, what is less a unity is more choiceworthy than what is more a unity" (*Politics*, II, 1261b).
36. *Politics*, II, 1261b.
37. *Politics*, II, 1262b.
38. *Politics*, II, 1261b.
39. Aristotle holds that those who would take pleasure only in themselves alone should consider "philosophy, for the other [pleasures] require human beings" (*Politics*, II, 1267a).
40. *Politics*, II, 1267a.
41. One of the consequences of money is acute inequality, and Aristotle holds that a city with impoverished citizens "produces factional conflict and crime" (*Politics*, II, 1265b).
42. See *The Politics*, book 1, chapter 8 for his argument for boundaries to the acquisition of property and chapter 9 for a discussion about limits to "wealth and possessions."

43. *Politics*, II, 1261a.
44. William Booth, "The New Household Economy," *American Political Science Review* 85 (1991): 61.
45. *Politics*, I, 1265b.
46. Booth, "Household Economy," 61
47. *Politics*, VI, 1317b.
48. *Politics*, VI, 1218b.
49. Some minimal commerce occurs in this setting but that is not the primary characteristic of Aristotle's agrarian economy.
50. The politics of redistribution generally refers to taking from the rich and giving to the poor. Such a reading is incomplete for Aristotle who finds redistribution also occurs when the rich takes from the poor.
51. Aristotle also finds that extensive poverty contributes to the corruption of democracies (*Politics*, VI, 1320a).
52. For Aristotle's discussion of commerce, see *Politics*, I, chaps. 8–9.
53. *Public and Private*, 110. See Aristotle, *Politics*, V, chaps. 2–3.
54. This view is contrary to one advanced by Swanson who claims that "Where virtue is not the norm, legislators should expect that money-making will attract most men; accordingly if they are concerned to preserve the regime, they should legislate only to discourage, not to prohibit, money-making among citizens" (*Public and Private*, 77). Aristotle wants to challenge the role of money with more than legislation. If people have sufficient property to exercise autonomy and if their education teaches them that the goods they value are dependent on the health of the republic, they are more apt to resist the corruption of money than when either or both of these conditions are absent.
55. *Politics*, V, 1309a.
56. *Politics*, VI, 1317.
57. *After the Revolution* (New Haven: Yale University Press, 1970).
58. *Politics*, 1984, III, 5.
59. Booth, "Household Economy," 63. For Aristotle: "Being at leisure . . . is held itself to involve pleasure, happiness, and living blessedly. This is not available to those who are occupied, but rather to those at leisure" (*Politics*, VIII, 1338a).
60. "Household Economy," 63–64.
61. *Finding the Mean*, 243.
62. Communitarians need to ask whether the tendency of many American families to spend an extraordinary amount of time working is moving away from what Aristotle might have hoped and whether a society that countenances work as its central way of understanding worth is approaching a telos. Also see Salkever, 227–28.
63. Commerce is not natural to Aristotle, but that hardly means he takes it to be evil or something to be avoided at all costs. As a human construction, it carries no natural instructions as to its best uses. It is up to us to determine how it can contribute to our happiness and for that we need to place it in the context of the many other goods we seek.

88   *Chapter 2*

64. Just as there are many reasons for crime, and not just poverty, Aristotle recognizes that there are many reasons why people invade public space with their own private agenda. A common one is that those with great wealth want more, but that does not lead Aristotle to argue against wealth. Rather he wants to guard against it, knowing that no solution to tether the political ambitions of wealthy will be fixed in time.

65. See Pocock, *Moment*; Skinner, *Foundations*; and Bruce Smith, *Politics of Remembrance* (Princeton: Princeton University Press, 1985).

66. Pocock links civic and military virtue and holds

> Military virtu necessitates political virtue because both can be presented in terms of the same end. The republic is the common good; the citizen, directing all his actions toward that good, may be said to dedicate his life to the republic; the patriot warrior dedicates his death, and the two are alike in perfecting human nature by sacrificing particular goods to a universal end (*Moment*, 201).

In Pocock's formulation, the citizen directs "all his action" to the good of the republic and does so unreservedly. Moreover, Pocock's citizens who are patriot warriors are the best citizens, that is, they are always ready to dedicate their death to the republic.

67. Machiavelli's dark, foreboding reading of human nature is lost in Pocock's rendering, which makes *fortuna*, and not human pride, the great menace to the republic. For Machiavelli, politics should work with the assumption "that all men are bad and ever ready to display their vicious nature, whenever they may find occasion for it. If their evil disposition remains concealed for a time, it must be attributed to some unknown reason, and we must assume that it lacked occasion to show itself" (*Discourses* [New York: Random House, 1940], 1.3). For recent criticisms of Pocock's reading of Machiavelli, see Ian Shapiro, "J. G. A. Pocock's Republicanism and Political Theory," *Critical Review* 4 (1990): 433–71, and Vickie Sullivan, "Machiavelli's Momentary 'Machiavellian Moment,'" *Political Theory* 20 (1992): 309–18.

68. *Discourses*, I, 37.

69. *Discourses*, III, 5. In contrasting the many and the few in chapter 9 of *The Prince*, Machiavelli argues that most, but not all, are content with enjoying what they presently possess. "For in every city these two opposite parties are to be found, arising from the desire of the populace to avoid the oppression of the great, and the desire of the great to command and oppress the people. And from these two opposing interests arises in the city one of the three effects: either absolute government, liberty, or license" (*The Prince* [New York: Random House, 1940], Chap. 9).

70. Machiavelli condemns mercenary troops and tells the Prince he needs to rely on a citizen militia. In *The Art of War* (Indianapolis: Library of Liberal Arts Press, 1965), Machiavelli sings the praises of the militia, and in *Discourses*, he repeatedly talks of the central role it plays in the vitality of the republic. Unlike mercenaries, Machiavelli's republican citizens have an

investment in their republic through their normative and substantive attachments. See *Art of War*, 18, 20.

71. *Discourses*, III, 25. Sheldon Wolin observes that Machiavelli holds that "the best political matter was to be found in those who have possessions and want to retain them, not in those who want to acquire more" (*Politics and Vision* [Boston: Little Brown and Company, 1960], 230).

72. Although Machiavellian citizens do not build walls of separation between the public and private as some see in the liberal tradition, his citizens expect the republic will not interfere with their most important attachments: their families and property.

73. *Discourses*, II, 2.

74. Machiavelli tells the Prince that "he must encourage his citizens to follow their callings quietly, whether in commerce, or agriculture, or any other trade that men follow so that this one shall not refrain from improving his possessions through fear that they may be taken from him and that one from starting a trade for fear of taxes, but he should offer rewards to whoever does these things" (*Prince*, 21).

75. Machiavelli argues that "Well ordered states and princes have studied diligently not to drive the nobles to desperation and to satisfy the populace and keep it contented" (*Prince*, 19).

76. *Discourses*, III, 23.

77. According to Machiavelli, corruption is "generally the result of idleness and peace, whilst apprehension and war are productive of union" (*Discourses*, II, 25).

78. *Discourses*, I, 6.

79. For Machiavelli's view of the corrupt regime, see his *History of Florence* (London: Dent, 1965). For extended discussions of corruption in the republican and civic humanist traditions, see Pocock, *Moment*, and Skinner, *Foundations*, vol. 1.

80. Machiavelli argues "The faults of the people spring from the faults of their rulers" and the reason, he explains, is that the latter leave the former no choice. They manipulate laws, and the worst evil "was that the people became impoverished . . . [and] the stronger amongst them endeavored to make good their losses by plundering the weaker" (*Discourses*, III, 29).

81. *Art of War*, 11. In *Art of War*, Machiavelli's hero, Cosimo, defends his grandfather against the charge that he does not live up to the standards of ancient civic virtue. Cosimo responds that he does "not believe there was any man of this time who detested a soft and delicate way of life more than [his grandfather] did or loved more the austere life you have praised. Nevertheless, he found it impossible either for himself or for his sons to practice what he most approved . . . [because of] the corruption of the age in which he lived" (11).

82. See *Discourses*, I, 56.

83. Horatius had saved Rome but then killed his sister, and Machiavelli condemns the Romans not for putting him on trial but for acquitting him. Machiavelli's argument is not one of justice but of politics. If "a citizen who

has rendered some eminent service to the state should add to the reputation and influence which he had thereby acquired the confident audacity of being able to commit any wrong without fear of punishment, he will in a little while become so insolent . . . as to put an end to all power of law" (*Discourses*, I, 24).

84. See *Discourses*, II, 2.
85. *Discourses*, I, 55.
86. *Discourses*, I, 55.
87. Machiavelli holds that if the law is written to favor some at the expense of the rest, the equal application of the law only institutionalizes inequality and thereby undermines the good republic.
88. *Discourses*, I, 55.
89. *Discourses*, I, 37.
90. *Discourses*, III, 25.
91. *Moment*, 204.
92. Pocock tells us that Machiavelli's citizens practice civic virtue to challenge fortuna, that is to forestall corruption. But Machiavelli does not take corruption to be related to chance; he finds that it should be expected to arrive at regular intervals of every ten years. To confront corruption, Machiavelli does not call on the civic-virtuous citizens to respond appropriately but appeals to officials to employ the relevant laws to "strike terror into the hearts of man." The purpose of this terror, he tells us, is to bring republics "back to their original principles." The best republics "must have within themselves some goodness, by means of which they obtain their first growth and reputation, and as in the process of time this goodness becomes corrupted, it will be of necessity to destroy the body unless something intervenes to bring it back to its normal condition" (*Discourses*, III, 1).
93. Carole Pateman, *Participation and Democratic Theory* (Cambridge: Cambridge University Press, 1970); Benjamin Barber, *Strong Democracy* (Berkeley: University of California Press, 1984); and David Held, *Models of Democracy* (Stanford: Stanford University Press, 1987).
94. See C. Fred Alford, *The Self in Social Theory* (New Haven: Yale University Press, 1991); William Connolly, *Political Theory and Modernity* (London: Basil Blackwell, 1988); Roger Masters, *Political Philosophy of Rousseau* (Princeton: Princeton University Press, 1968); Alan Ryan, *Property and Political Theory* (London: Basil Blackwell, 1984); Judith Shklar, *Men and Citizens: A Study of Rousseau's Social Theory* (Cambridge: Cambridge University Press, 1969). The reading I advance is contrary to commentaries that find Rousseau is a precursor of "totalitarian democracy." See J. L. Talmon, *The Rise of Totalitarian Democracy* (London: Secker and Warburg, 1952).
95. *The Social Contract* (London: Dent, 1983), I,i.
96. J. J. Rousseau, *A Discourse on the Origin of Inequality* (London: Dent, 1983).
97. Rousseau's innocent person has no self-conscious interests and therefore cannot be corrupted by them.
98. *Origins of Inequality*, 76, 89, 93; See *Social Contract*, III,15

99. Rousseau opens *The Social Contract* with the claim that he will take "men . . . as they are," by which he means individuals who no longer have the attributes of the noble savage but carry all the complications, vulnerabilities, and opportunities that come with civilization, including a self-conscious regard for themselves (165).

100. Although they reach their conclusions with different arguments, Aristotle and Rousseau both find that profound changes that occurred ages ago repeal natural limits and introduce new contingencies in a world where individuals become self-referential. Aristotle emphasizes money as the primary source of change while Rousseau attaches importance to the invention of tools, leisure, and wealth. Both are concerned about how these changes profoundly complicate the way people think about themselves, what they think they are due, and how they organize their lives or accept the organization of their society.

101. *Origins of Inequality*, 80.

102. *Origins of Inequality*, 80.

103. *Origins of Inequality*, 33.

104. *Origins of Inequality*, 81.

105. MacIntyre speaks extensively of the importance of our roles when we construct a narrative of our lives. I assume that he takes it that our roles provide us with a sense of dignity and purposefulness, but he never addresses the issue of what happens to people whose roles are often demeaning and degrading (*After Virtue* [Notre Dame: Notre Dame University Press, 1981]).

106. *Origins of Inequality*, 86; also see Ryan, *Property*, 49–72.

107. See *Political Economy*, 134, for Rousseau's discussion of the importance of a large middle class and the dangers to republican government from great wealth and extreme poverty.

108. In this way, he attempts to avoid the problem of maintaining the kind of equilibrium between classes that Machiavelli makes a central part of his view of republican government.

109. See *Political Economy*, 131, 139; *Social Contract*, 204, 231; *Origins of Inequality*, Dedication.

100. According to Rousseau, the only valid title to property is labor. "It is impossible to conceive how property can come from anything but manual labor" (*Origins*, 85).

111. *Political Economy*, 131–32. Rousseau finds that if "the fundamental conventions" regarding the widespread ownership of property are "broken, it is impossible to conceive of any right or interest that could retain the people in the social union; unless they were restrained by force" (*Political Economy*, 132).

112. *Political Economy*, 138. Later, Rousseau insists, "It should be remembered that the foundation of the social compact is property; and its first condition, that every one should be maintained in the peaceful possession of what belongs to him" (*Political Economy*, 145).

113. *Political Economy*, 139.

114. *Origins of Inequality*, 86–88.

115. *Social Contract*, II,11; also see *Origins of Inequality*, 144. Earlier in *The Social Contract*, Rousseau argued that "the social state is advantageous to men only when all have something and none too much" (I,9).

116. See *Social Contract*, III,15.

117. Michael Brint, in *Tragedy and Denial* sees Rousseau's citizen losing himself to the public good. "A citizen's personal ambitions would be directed toward the greater priority of the general good. . . . All achievements would be hailed as tributes to the glory of the state as a whole" (*Tragedy and Denial* [Boulder: Westview Press, 1991], 55). Such a reading makes Rousseau's citizen so contrary to his celebration of the citizens of Geneva and so antithetical to his claims for liberty, we must ask what is going on in this fairly typical reading. Without denying the heavy burdens Rousseau imposes on citizens and without ignoring the dangers in his project, particularly to independently standing rights, Rousseau's citizen is not so lost in a welter of civic obligations that an independent identity no longer exists.

118. What follows departs from William Sullivan's view that Rousseau's general will is "abstract" (*Reconstructing Political Philosophy* [Berkeley: University of California Press, 1982], 82).

119. *Social Contract*, II,3.

120. See Rousseau's discussions of monarchy, aristocracy, and democracy as distinct forms of administration and how each can implement the general will (*Social Contract*, III,3-8).

121. See Rousseau's claim that it is necessary to avoid bargaining when citizens seek the general will (*Social Contract*, II,3). This suggests that even when good republican citizens come together to identify the general will, they are under constant temptation to attend to their own concerns first.

122. *Social Contract*, II,10.

123. Rousseau sees great dangers to the republic when "domestic affairs are all-absorbing" (*Social Contract*, III,15).

124. *Social Contract*, III,15. Italics in original.

125. For a reading of Rousseau as a writer who tries to strip away any independent identity of citizens, see Talmon, *Rise of Totalitarian Democracy*. For a review of debate on Rousseau as a totalitarian democrat, see John Chapman, *Rousseau—Totalitarian or Liberal* (New York: Columbia University Press, 1956).

126. *Origins of Inequality*, 92–93; also see *Social Contract*, III,15.

127. *Origins of Inequality*, 89. On the inadequacy of procedural equality, Rousseau holds that "Under bad governments, this equality is only apparent and illusory; it serves only to keep the pauper in his poverty and the rich man in the position he has usurped" (*Social Contract*, I,9).

128. Emile is happiest when he is strong enough to be physically independent of others but not yet old enough to spawn new, unachievable desires. Even Emile is subject to disappointment and unhappiness because he grows older. No longer satisfied with the limited desires he only recently longed for and could achieve, Emile becomes buffeted by a stream of temptations to

desire more than he can realize. What is true of Emile, Rousseau thinks, applies to each of us.

129. *Social Contract*, III,4.

130. For another version of the relationship between politics and a one-class society see Alexis de Tocqueville's discussion of equality of conditions in America (*Democracy in America* [New York: Vintage, 1957]).

131. Disappointed socialists have found that as economic conditions improve, workers become protective and conservative rather than participatory and radical.

132. Arendt's helpful distinction between property and wealth looms even larger today than it did when Aristotle and Rousseau were concerned about these issues (*Human Condition*).

133. See Arendt, *Human Condition*; Pocock, *Moment;* John Reid, *The Concept of Liberty in the Age of the American Revolution* (Chicago: University of Chicago Press, 1988), 141.

134. See Michael Walzer for a discussion of the political implications of mobility in "The Communitarian Critique of Liberalism," *Political Theory*, 18 (1990): 6–23.

135. *Contradictions of the Welfare State*.

136. See John Schaar, "Equality of Opportunity and Beyond," in *Equality, NOMOS*, vol. 9, edited by R. Pennock and John Chapman (New York: Atherton, 1967), and Fred Hirsch, *The Social Limits to Growth* (Cambridge: Harvard University Press, 1976).

137. Equality of opportunity also undercuts the republican requirement for leisure and stability.

138. Charles Beitz, *Political Equality* (Princeton: Princeton University Press, 1989).

Chapter Three

Noisy Republicans: Mythologizing the Founding and Justifying Conflict

The preceding chapter discussed the paradox of why stakes are essential to good republican citizenship and how they can undermine and ultimately destroy republican politics. In this chapter, I consider why Machiavelli and Rousseau think that the inevitable decay can be delayed and how each generation has it in its hands to rescue republican politics.

As I indicated in chapter 2, the greatest domestic threat to republican liberty comes from two different but related phenomena. In the first place, the peace and security that citizens covet divert their attention from the civic to the private, and the stakes that once served to attach citizens to their republic are reconstituted into strictly personal concerns. At such a time, citizens retreat from civic space into their own private enclaves. When this happens, strong republicans expect a few who are personally ambitious will seek to fill the political vacuum and use public power to further their own interests. The second threat concerns ambitious citizens who wait for no vacuum but seek public power for their own private ends. In either case, the issue for strong republicans is whether citizens will resist the incursions of the ambitious, which threaten both the foundational principles of the republic and their own liberty, or whether lethargic citizens will find their private pleasures and attachments more attractive. However important the foundings and traditions of a republic are to strong republicans, they know that the civic commitments and sacrifices of any generation cannot bind future generations who will either maintain republican vigilance or become preoccupied with their own private lives, allowing republican politics to deteriorate into factions and liberty to decay.

Differences, Disagreements, and Agreements

Both friends and critics of modern liberal democracy have been impressed with the highly diverse character of its citizens and their very different backgrounds, identities, and demands. For many, recognition of these differences is welcome evidence that liberal democracies are addressing questions of rights and equity in regimes that have historically tended to favor some and ignore or penalize others. Critics, however, find that contemporary liberals are so closely attached to their claims they lose sight of what they share as citizens, leave public goods unattended, intensify group interests, and breed political conflict. The issue here is not that conflict signals something pathological; after all, democratic regimes are expected to manage conflict in nonviolent ways whereby citizens remain citizens in good standing whether they are winners or losers.

Some find that today public space is fractured by competing interest groups who threaten the vitality of the democratic regime. In very different ways, this is the argument of Machiavelli and Rousseau about factions. If, in their accounts, political conflict occurs between warring factions, winners use their power to make laws that no longer attend to the good of the whole but that serve their own private interests, usually at the expense of the rest. However, Machiavelli and Rousseau invite discord under specific circumstances.[1] How are we to distinguish conflicts that are dangerous to the republic from those that are necessary to its survival?

In advancing a strong case for both maintaining tradition and enhancing "shared self-understandings," many communitarians seem suspicious of conflict and fail to see its role in their own agenda.[2] Most decline to ask whether today's citizens are treated in ways that tie them to the good community or whether they are neglected and asked to fend for themselves.[3] In seeing contemporary politics bereft of any conception of a common good, communitarians such as Sandel, MacIntyre, and Bellah do not take the next step and ask what individuals substantively require to become good citizens and, if those requirements are lacking, whether individuals should then make noise.

The text of much communitarian writing uncovers a fractured people who should and can return to a harmonious community through a uniform civic education and common political language that minimizes difference and diminishes conflict. With many communitarian positions, we find compelling arguments about the danger posed by the Balkanization of society. In raising these specters of dissonance and discord, many communitarians come perilously close to assuming an exclusionary position regarding those who do not readily accommodate to their view of the coherent, unified community.[4] In the process, they leave many deep problems unattended with their appeals to harmony, and we come perilously close to Brazilianization of society.[5]

Many communitarians find liberal democracies are noisy places and see liberals clustering in interest groups to compete over scarce resources, apparently unconcerned about how their success affects the rest of society and unguided by a shared tradition. In contrast to the cacophony of interest-group liberalism, many communitarians offer us a coherent republic where the disagreements that invariably accompany democratic politics are settled by rational discourse employing a shared moral vocabulary. In the communitarian account, we find deliberative citizens advance their own positions as well as learn from their fellow citizens as they search for what is good for the community at large.[6] In distinguishing themselves from liberals, communitarians seek harmony and resist hearing a dissonance of political voices, each detached from any common theme. But, as I shall argue, not all political noise has the same effect, and some noise is necessary for the strong republic.

From the communitarian gloss, we would assume that the textual materials of their tradition that emphasize a robust community would reflect harmony and agreement, indeed would definitionally require harmony and agreement. Accordingly, we should expect republicans historically to stress not only the importance of tradition, civic virtue, and participation, but also political concord and unity. And they do—but not at any price. They also anticipate, even welcome, conflict when foundational principles and practices are threatened or are becoming corrupt. When this occurs, Machiavelli and Rousseau expect patriotic citizens to resist corruption and, if necessary, to resort to conflict to maintain the good republic.

Where do patriotic citizens obtain the material to determine when conflict is necessary? For Machiavelli and Rousseau, the principles embedded in the founding house the highest ideals of a people, providing citizens with a sense of their common identity and an understanding about their civil liberties and their civic responsibilities. From this perspective, the founding represents not so much an accurate historical account of a people but a moral and political account of what is both good and distinctive about a people. The important narratives of the founding are not the stuff of everyday politics but concern the heroic, the patriotic, and even the transcendent. In the myth of the founding, personal considerations are less important than civic obligations; utility and instrumentalism fade before collective goals; and differences among the founders become politically and morally irrelevant. Machiavelli and Rousseau know that politics cannot be sustained by any mythological view of human conduct and that any realistic view of popular government must take account of contingencies, differences, and inequalities that describe any society. For them, a realistic understanding of the republic works with an idealized view of the founding to remind citizens of what unites them and to provide a standard for judging politics beyond instrumental advantage. But they do not take the founding as a replacement for the experiences of citizens or as an autonomous force that corrects the dangers posed to the republic by ambitious citizens or shifting locations of power.

Concerns about their own well-being are never far away from ordinary people, and the founding offers a way to interpret the routine and to remind citizens of the ideals that bind them. The founding myth attempts both to crystalize the distinctive identity of a people and to provide them with a legitimate basis for a government to secure their liberty and harness chance. In the strong republican gloss, such standards, however, are not embedded in the origins of every regime; some are "unlucky," and their origins are marred by division, suspicion, and subordination.[7] These regimes lack the moral and civic materials that are necessary not only for good citizenship but also for judging policy and conflict.[8] If the founding principles are defective, citizens will repeatedly fight among themselves about issues that were initially unresolved and their conflicts will revolve around factional interests, thereby hastening corruption.[9] For both Machiavelli and Rousseau, the politics of a free people can never escape pride, ambition, and complacency, and the most effective response to decay seldom comes with appeals to once-patriotic citizens to return to the principles of the founding. Machiavelli and Rousseau do not simply rely on renewing tradition, appealing for sacrifice, or promoting civic education. And although their constitutional arrangements speak to the issue of ambition, strong republicans do not hold that institutional and legal remedies, any more than a robust tradition, are sufficient by themselves to correct all of the distorting effects of ambition.[10] They are always ready to employ politics.

Foundations, Ambition, and Equilibrium: The Case of Machiavelli

What makes Machiavelli's republicanism particularly provocative is his effort to link civic virtue to the nature and purposes of power. Power, for Machiavelli, is unavoidable and is both a resource and a danger. Whether we like it or not, he tells us, social relations are informed by power, and the issue is not whether power is employed but the purposes that power serves. Individually or collectively, we can use power to protect what is important to us or to gain more for ourselves. Because others can be counted on to do the same, conflict is inevitable.[11]

Machiavelli's republic is designed to tame domestic power and channel it in ways that transform ambitious individuals into virtuous citizens. Relying heavily on tradition and civic practices to define and arrange social relationships, he hopes to subvert some of the causes of ambition and conflict. For him, the foundational principles of the republic identify common standards of good and evil and serve as the standards for honor and shame. At the same time, Machiavelli appreciates that a common religion or tradition cannot invariably trip ambition, and he accordingly introduces a variety of institutional arrangements to address the inherent vulnerabilities of his normative framework. Some of his republican institutions are designed to generate similar experiences for all citizens, some are expected to assure the liberty of citizens and the stakes they have in their republic, and some are expected to provide a stable equilibrium of power among different and potentially hostile groups. Machiavelli's good republic requires an equilibrium of wealth, power, and property that will remain satisfying to future generations, even though his equilibrium reflects significant inequalities within society. Critical to Machiavelli's republican politics are both the attachments of good citizens to their tradition and their satisfaction with the distributional arrangements the founding legitimizes. Good citizens, then, are content with their own situation and do not covet the places of others. He expects citizens to use these materials and dispositions to recognize when the traditional equilibrium is disturbed by ambitious individuals or factions and act to restore the earlier balance.[12]

Holding that neither tradition nor virtue can eradicate the causes of every serious conflict in the republic, Machiavelli wants to assure that political confrontations, however hostile, are not irreconcilable and that the parties to a controversy return to their earlier civic undertakings. For this to happen, winners must be satisfied with returning to the approximate equilibrium which described the distribution of power and privilege before the crisis. Should winners define victory by destroying, humiliating, or impoverishing losers, a new equilibrium is created, one distanced from the founding and unable to convince losers they should once again become loyal citizens.[13] If the bonds that once joined citizens are rent, it is no longer possible to talk about the purpose of politics serving the common good. Politics becomes corrupt and is understood as winning advantages for one's own faction.

The Foundational Principles of the Republic

The moral foundations of Machiavelli's republic rest on both the religious beliefs of a people and their foundational principles of justice and fairness. In his view, religion ought to avoid the kind of transcendence he criticizes in certain aspects of Christianity, and his quasi-pagan alternative reflects his effort to place the natural concern people have about themselves within a larger moral order.[14] However, he wants religion to do more than provide a thin accommodation with the contingent and transitory. Admitting that no religion can, by itself, continually convince citizens to forget their temporal concerns, he finds religion is at its best when it provides believers with an identity so compelling it moves people at critical times to suspend their preoccupations with temporal matters. As they think about themselves in the religious terms proffered by Machiavelli, they are not continually asked to deny their secular attachments such as family or private property or repudiate all of their personal aspirations; rather they are expected to contextualize their contingencies within a moral framework.

Machiavelli never asks about religion, "Is it true?" For him, the important issues are functional: does religion add to the vitality of citizenship or does religion subvert civic life?[15] Machiavelli's central questions about religion are political and sociological, not theological,[16] reflecting his view that the self-referencing inclinations of individuals will lead to corruption and conflict unless individuals are reconstituted into citizens. Religion is essential to his efforts at civic reconstruction because, left to their own devices, people become fixed on temporal advantages.

> So powerful is the sway that ambition exercises over the human heart that they never relinquish it, no matter how high they have risen. The reason is that nature has so constituted men that, though all things are objects of desire, not all things are attainable; so that desires always

exceed the power of attainment, with the result that men are ill content with what they possess and their present state brings them little satisfaction.[17]

However, Machiavelli insists, people need not be left to nature and their own devices, and he assigns to both religion and politics the task of restraining the dark side of human nature. Indeed, he finds it difficult to think about a robust civic sphere without a firm religious grounding. When he turns to Rome, his exemplary republic, he celebrates not Romulus, the legendary founder of the city, but Numa, the founder of Roman religion. Numa is presented as working with a "very savage people." Wishing "to reduce them to civil obedience by the arts of peace, [he] had recourse to religion as the most necessary and assured support of any civil society."[18]

According to Machiavelli, Numa provides Rome with shared beliefs and obligations, and his religion instills fear of the gods whose standards and strictures are deeply internalized by the citizens. It does even more; in uniting the Romans around common standards, Numa's religion covers "the wicked with shame."[19] According to Machiavelli, religion provides citizens with the material to judge themselves and their fellow citizens and enables them to tame their personal desires and criticize ambition in others. Without religion, or more specifically, without the kind Numa offers, interests would have a freer hand in Rome, which would then be a place where people constantly get in one another's way. For these reasons, Machiavelli can conclude

> that the religion introduced by Numa into Rome was one of the chief causes of the prosperity of that city; for this religion gave rise to good laws, and good laws bring good fortune, and from good fortune results happy success in all enterprises. And as the observance of divine institutions is the cause of great republics, so the disregard of them produces their ruin, unless it be sustained by the fear of the prince, which may *temporarily* supply the want of religion.[20]

Both Machiavelli's prince and religion originally rely on fear, but the prince can only use fear effectively to threaten those who think they might be detected. The gods, however, constantly intrude into our private activities and thoughts, and become constant monitors of our behavior. In becoming an essential part of our understanding of right and wrong, Machiavelli's religion is an important source of moral identity as well as guilt. And we accept its claims to truth and goodness, whether or not we benefit instrumentally when we obey divine injunctions. We do not wonder whether we are better off telling the truth or performing our duties. Indeed, we accept such standards as good, appropriate, and applicable to us without using some rational or instrumental test. When moral principles become a habit, they trip the ambition that Machiavelli thinks so natural to the human condition.[21] However, Machiavelli never credits religion with the ability to eradicate all concerns about the self. In tandem with civic virtue and republican institutions, Machiavelli believes religion can tame ambition.

For Machiavelli, religion is distinct from politics and the secular founding but inseparably related to them. When they become detached from one another, he fears people increasingly turn to instrumental reason to understand themselves and society. In this sense, religion is one of the necessary pillars sustaining the good republic, which also requires a network of social and political standards and institutions that complement and reinforce one another.[22]

Machiavellian Justice

Machiavelli turns to the founding to capture the best moments of a people and teach them about their best selves. The civic ideals of the founding celebrate shared sacrifices, common institutions, and civic spirit that rise above instrumental rationality, utilitarian considerations, and personal gain. As such, the founding symbolically links the citizens' well-being with the integrity of the republic. For Machiavelli, the founding shows citizens how much their good depends on their republic and how it, in turn, depends on their patriotism.

In his account of the founding, Machiavelli joins justice with fairness, but not in the Rawlsian sense, which depends on both the rationality and the risk-aversion of the representative man behind the veil of ignorance. Machiavelli's republican justice as fairness reflects the traditions, duties, practices, and aspirations of the members of a community over time as protected and supported in the community's principles, institutions, and practices. People are assumed to accept settled social relations and distinctions as basically fair so long as their liberty, security, and political presence are assured; and he expects citizens to resist the efforts of others to destabilize and reorganize these arrangements. This emerges in Machiavelli's account of the early foundings of communities which, he believes, are initially formed for reasons of self-preservation but which leave the realm of necessity to embody justice.

As the human race increased, the necessity for uniting themselves for defence made itself felt; the better to attain this object, they chose the strongest and most courageous from amongst themselves and placed him at their head, promising to obey him. Thence they began to know the good and the honest, and to distinguish them from the bad and the vicious; for seeing a man injure his benefactor aroused at once two sentiments in every heart, hatred against the ingrate and love for the benefactor. They blamed the first, and on the contrary honored those the more who showed themselves grateful, for each felt that he in turn might be subject to a like wrong; and to prevent similar evils, they set to work to make laws, and to institute punishments for those who contravened them. Such was the origin of justice. This caused them, when they had afterwards to choose a prince, neither to look to the strongest nor bravest, but to the wisest and most just.[23]

Machiavelli's original polity rests on the voluntary agreement of its members who choose their leader and accept rules that they take to be necessary for their protection and for the good of their community at large. They quickly understand they cannot individually defend themselves against the attacks of marauders and realize their fate is inseparably linked to the community's. The members also know their duties and are ready to punish those who ignore their civic responsibilities. For Machiavelli, the transparent need for wisdom and justice prompts the first generation to choose its leaders prudently. However, time clouds experience, and what was once important fades and loses its strength to convince people to abide by their foundational principles.[24]

In Machiavelli's account, the fragility and unreliability of civic memory to sustain the original principles of wisdom and justice explain the instability of pure types of governments and why they pass through cycles: from monarchy to tyranny to aristocracy to oligarchy to popular government to a corrupt regime and to a return to monarchy. The lesson he draws from his historical construction of the origins and decay of aristocracies applies to all pure regimes: unless disciplined, civic loyalties decay into personal ambition. Immediately after brave and virtuous aristocrats overthrow the tyrannical regime, they prefer "public interests to their own and . . . administer and protect with greatest care both public and private affairs."[25] But time inevitably dims the original impetus for justice and public-regardingness among later generations of aristocrats who become preoccupied with themselves, not the common good. Their corruption, in turn, unleashes a public reaction that ends their rule.

The very problematic nature of politics leads Machiavelli to observe that "all kinds of government are defective; those three which we have qualified as good because they are too short-lived and the three bad ones because of their inherent viciousness."[26] To overcome the threat of decay he calls for political arrangements that combine the various forms of government so that each part "will watch and keep [the] other reciprocally in check."[27] In this way, Machiavelli's political settlement requires a dispersal of power among classes which share understandings of the good but are nevertheless also tied to their own distinct interests.[28] The issue for Machiavelli, then, is how to bring power into a viable equilibrium that protects the principles embodied in the founding.

Tumult in Rome and Florence

In Machiavelli's politics, no community can long escape conflict, and the issue is how it faces such an eventuality. One way is to emphasize its unity, hoping that such appeals will quiet ambition. But, Machiavelli argues, "those who hope that republics can be unified" merely by making such moral appeals, "are greatly mistaken in this belief."[29] Republican politics are vulnerable because ordinary people think that their common institutions and traditions assure their perpetual liberty and security without the need for their continued political service. Deluded that their institutions no longer require their active presence, citizens are tempted to concentrate on their personal interests. However, Machiavelli fears that political withdrawal leads to "tranquillity, and tranquillity [brings] laziness, and laziness chaos, and chaos ruin."[30]

Political lethargy is hardly the mark of Machiavelli's Roman republic or his own Florence. He sees republican Rome not only as a community of patriots and disciplined citizens, but also as a politically tumultuous society where the plebs are often pitted against the nobles. It is only natural to him that the two sides should periodically come into conflict because their fundamental class differences cannot be entirely bridged by their many agreements, including religious and civic ones. Although every Roman partakes of the same tradition, there is always the possibility that some interpret fairness appropriate to their own circumstances that others find breaks foundational principles.

Machiavelli repeatedly acknowledges that intense internal strife has destroyed many republics,[31] but he holds that internal conflicts in republican Rome had an opposite effect and were "the primary cause of Rome's retaining her freedom."[32] In Rome, civil strife "instead of harming, rather benefitted the republic. And from this we draw the conclusion that, where the mass of the people is sound, disturbances and tumults do no serious harm; but where corruption has penetrated the people, the best laws are of no avail."[33]

According to Machiavelli, the most pronounced source of conflict in republics is the desire of the nobility to dominate while most citizens "merely desire not to be dominated." Regardless of which class disturbs the traditional equilibrium and establishes standards of equity and justice, it should expect the other side to protect itself. If the aggrieved side wins and is animated by a desire to restore the founding principles and the earlier equilibrium, conflict is not only beneficial but also necessary to the maintenance of the good republic.[34] Positive conflict, in Machiavelli's account, does not create new winners and losers but aims to preserve the republic and to make good law. "[G]ood laws in their turn spring from those very agitations which have been so inconsiderately condemned by many. . . . These agitations . . . have given rise to laws that were to the advantage of public liberty." For Machiavelli, the proud achievement of Roman republicanism is that it affords "the people the opportunity of giving vent, so to say, to their ambitions"[35] without destroying the basis of future cooperation and interdependence necessary for its maintenance. Patriotic citizens demonstrate their civic virtues not only in time of war but also when they defend their political liberty and the foundational principles of the republic against domestic threats.

This positive view of conflict needs to be contrasted with his account of conflict in Florence. Machiavelli's Florence is corrupt: a city where "religion and the fear of God seem to be alike extinct," where "bad men are received with the approbation due to virtue, and good ones are regarded only in the light of fools," where "the young are idle, the old lascivious," where "hatred, animosities, quarrels, and factions" abound, and where "bad men" are full of "ambition and avarice and necessity compels the good to pursue the same course."[36] Its politics is so deplorable because even the virtuous person finds "it impossible either for himself or for his sons to practice what he most approved."[37] To be civically-regarding in a corrupt society means that one's own security and well-being are hostage to those who use power for their own personal purposes.

When a sense of fairness and restraint disappears and corruption becomes the norm, the resolution of conflict is no longer marked by a return to an equilibrium of power and fairness. Ignoring the foundational principles of their republic, the contestants destroy the republic itself because winning factions know no limits in the settlements they impose on losers and have no sense that they share something essential with their political opponents.[38] In Florence, as Machiavelli understands it, the

> laws, statutes, and civil ordinances are not, nor have they ever been, established for the benefit of men in a state of freedom but according to the wish of the faction that has been uppermost at the time. Hence, it follows that when one party is expelled or faction extinguished, another immediately arises; for in a city that is governed by parties rather than by laws, as soon as one becomes dominant and unopposed, it must of necessity soon divide against itself.[39]

To avoid such a calamity, Machiavelli wants citizens to be guided by their religion, tradition and civic norms when they take account of themselves. When they see corruption, his patriotic citizens reach to their foundational standards to judge and to act, not to avenge themselves but to protect the republic. The readiness of citizens to protect the republic is what Skinner has in mind when he observes that Machiavelli not only wants political involvement revolving around service and sacrifice but also requires the intense political involvements associated with tumult as "a manifestation of the highest civic *virtu*."[40] From his perspective, Machiavelli's successful republic rests on the continued attention of citizens to politics and even their occasional noise. Machiavelli would readily agree with Skinner that in the good republic, traditions and religion embody principles and standards which move citizens beyond their material interests, instrumental rationality, and personal ambitions. Unlike Skinner, Machiavelli does not expect citizens to be unconcerned about their own well-being whenever the republic is threatened internally. As important as tradition and renewal are to Machiavelli, he knows they are not always sufficient to unite citizens around the welfare of the republic and convince them to put its vitality before their own well-being. Machiavelli never expects foundational principles to make self-referenced interests vanish. He wants the personal attachments of citizens to be civic investments that prompt citizens to see that attacks on republican institutions and the current equilibrium are attacks on their own well-being.

Machiavellian citizens move through their republic with both personal and civic attachments and, when they judge public affairs, they draw on both their individual experiences and stakes as well as their shared foundational principles. For Machiavelli, republican noise or turmoil can come only from citizens who read their prior experiences as just and fair. Coupling the ideals of the founding with their own experiences and stakes, they know when efforts to alter political and distributional arrangements threaten the established equilibrium that protects their liberty and republican institutions. At such times, Machiavellian citizens respond quickly, publicly, and noisily. This form of conflict is required by Machiavelli to return the republic to its founding principles and to the rule of settled law. Passivity and apathy can do as much to subvert the traditions and institutions of the good republic as can individual ambition and pride.

As important as political participation is to Machiavelli's republican politics, he never transforms civic activity into a telos around which all else is organized. Machiavelli could never accept Pocock's claim that "by the institutionalization of civic virtue, the republic or polis maintains its own stability in time and develops the human material composing it toward that political life *which is the end of man*."[41] Machiavelli's understanding of life is too complicated to lend itself to such a formula. A perfectionism commentary[42] that makes republican politics "the end of man" ignores that Machiavelli has a dark view of human nature; that his confidence in institutions is generous but always guarded; that his fears about pride, ambition, decay, and corruption are continuous; and that his reading that ordinary citizens want to attend to their own lives is a sign of their humanity and not their weakness.

Machiavelli's republicanism is more circumscribed and more generous than recent revisionist commentaries would make it. He thinks people cannot become political perfectionists but he believes that they can, with attention and work, combine a commitment to the republic with a healthy concern about themselves and the good republic provides the normative, political, and substantive materials to do both.

Passivity, Agitation, and the Longevity of Rousseau's Republic

In some of the commentaries on the participatory Rousseau, we are introduced to socially extended, active citizens who labor for the good of the republic, neglecting and even sacrificing themselves in the process. That Rousseau wants citizens to extend themselves for civic purposes is clear enough. Ignored in discussions about the developmental and civic purposes of Rousseauian participation are the protective dimensions he attaches to politics. In this section, I take up Rousseau's argument about the relationship between liberty and the protective, sometimes disorderly, participation of citizens in the good republic.

Machiavelli and Rousseau hold that individual interests are not fixed but situational, with different settings stimulating different aspirations. Rousseau particularly emphasizes the social origins of desires and political expectations and goes on to argue that the intersection of convention and institutional practices can produce the alienated person and corrupt society or the patriotic citizen and strong republic. As is the case with many other strong republicans, Rousseau looks to social institutions to help quarantine corrupting interests while fostering a self which is restrained and civic. In this regard, he observes:

> If it is good to know how to deal with men as they are, it is much better to make them what there is need that they should be. The most absolute authority is that which penetrates into a man's inmost being, and concerns itself no less with his will than with his actions. It is certain that all peoples become in the long run what the government makes them.[43]

"What government makes them" is not merely or even primarily a matter of the state mobilizing traditions or other formal expressions of a prior good but rather involves blending the moral standards, political arrangements, and social institutions that Rousseau's citizens hold in common. Rousseau's elaborate constructions in *The Social Contract* and *The Government of Poland* are designed to create conditions that lead to the general will, foster cooperation, and forestall decay.[44] His institutions are credited with challenging the attractions of corruption and withdrawal not merely by appealing to the common good but also by showing property-owning citizens they have a stake in resisting ambitious citizens who seek public power for private benefits. Rousseau also seeks to prohibit certain forms of economic activities and acquisitions that promise citizens that they are best off when they attend to their own private concerns and jettison their civic responsibilities. People who think and act as if their well-being depends on their independent exertions send signals to other citizens who observe that their own civic service is neglected but individualistic behavior is rewarded. At such times, Rousseau sees citizens withdrawing from public undertakings and everyone becoming a civic free rider.[45] Like Machiavelli, he fears that the demonstration effects of personal ambition threaten to destroy liberty for everyone.[46]

The Founding

The principles that animate Rousseau's community are based on neither force nor reason. Overt force is antithetical to Rousseau's idea of community, which must receive the voluntary assent of its members. For him, "force is a physical power, and I fail to see what moral effect it can have."[47] But reason is of no help when it stands by itself, for then it is employed strategically by citizens to disclose how best to attend to their own personal interests and is unable to produce any general agreement. Without shared understandings, talk is particularistic and not general. To be able to speak and act with others in ways that contribute to the general will, Rousseau's citizens are expected to share grounded principles. To achieve this end, Rousseau assigns the founding-legislator the task "of transforming each individual" into a citizen.[48] The comprehensive moral framework provided by the founding-legislator is expected to move people from instrumental and utilitarian modes of reasoning and provide them with a new form of knowledge to understand themselves and their society.[49] In laying down founding principles, the founding-legislator establishes a code that people are expected to make a central part of their own personalities. To achieve this transformation, the great founders, according to Rousseau, must "have recourse to divine intervention and credit the gods with their own wisdom," inspiring citizens to "obey freely."[50] Why anyone should be inspired to "obey freely" is clearly a complex matter, and the investment of the self in the community is critically important. In Rousseau's account, part of this investment is concrete and practical, such as a person's family and property. When their stakes are insecure or endangered, he asks, how can we expect citizens to love their country "if their country be nothing more to them than to strangers and afford them nothing but what it can refuse nobody? It would be still worse, if they did not enjoy even the privilege of social security and if their lives, liberties, and property lay at the mercy of persons in power."[51]

The other part of the citizens' identity is psychological and moral. His good citizens value the republic as a good in itself and internalize deep attachments to it. The importance of this moral association is pressed by Rousseau who holds that the "most important" of all laws

> is not graven on tables of marble or brass but on the hearts of the citizens. This forms the real constitution of the State, takes on every day new powers, when other laws decay or die out, restores them or takes their place, keeps people in the ways in which it was meant to go, and insensibly replaces authority by the force of habit. I am speaking of morality, of custom, above all of the force of public opinion.[52]

These shared meanings are expected to be continually reinforced through the incentives and penalties generated by social institutions.

Just as Machiavelli before him, Rousseau sees "public opinion" or civic morality as critical but fragile, subject to flux and deterioration unless strongly reinforced by the experiences of citizens who share common civic investments. The standards provided by the founding-legislator are not so potent that they can consistently defeat the daily experiences of citizens if those experiences teach some their well-being has no relationship to the republic and if their experiences are so disparate that it is no longer possible to talk about what is common or to agree about the meaning of foundational principles.[53]

Rousseau does not specify the contents of foundational principles because no formula can cover all situations and take account of all the historical, geographic, economic, social, and religious characteristics that describe a particular people. But he makes it clear that whatever its specific features, its basic legislation "precisely consists [of] the greatest good of all" and has as its "main objects, [the] liberty and equality" of every citizen.[54] To Rousseau, equality has both political and economic dimensions. Under the former, every citizen is assigned political liberty and the responsibility to participate in civic undertakings, particularly in the expression of the general will. Economically, Rousseau's good republic allows "neither rich men nor beggars. These two estates which are naturally inseparable, are equally fatal to the common good; from the one come the friends of tyranny; and from the other tyrants. It is always between them that public liberty is put up to auction; the one buys, and the other sells."[55]

Rousseau is concerned about the distributional patterns of civil society because he knows civic dispositions are tied to the ability of citizens to meet their multiple needs.[56] He thinks this requires the absence of great inequality among citizens, leading him to argue that "one of the most important functions of government [is] to prevent extreme inequality of fortunes." Rousseau hardly calls for the expropriation of the great wealth or generous subsidies to the poor but seeks to regulate the economy so as to preclude the accumulation of wealth in the first place.[57] Rousseau claims that

> the encouragement of the arts that minister to luxury and of purely superfluous arts at the expense of useful and laborious crafts; the sacrifice of agriculture to commerce; . . . and, in short, venality pushed to such an extreme that even public esteem is reckoned at a cash value, and virtue rated at a market price; these are the most obvious causes of opulence and of poverty . . . [and] of the corruption of the people."[58]

Here and elsewhere, Rousseau makes it clear that a one-class society is critical for the vitality of the republic. When that relationship is undermined by acute economic inequality, the liberty and political equality of citizens are threatened and, if not corrected, will disappear. He also assumes that his good citizens care about their families, properties, and civil liberties and that they see the relationship between the political and personal and protect republican institutions and practices when they are threatened. The shared self-understandings of his citizens come not just from their traditions but also from their daily experiences, which tend to be similar in his one-class society and reinforce the founding principles.

Shame, Honor, and Political Motivation

In addition to various institutional arrangements designed to promote civic virtue and a general good, Machiavelli and Rousseau also rely on honor to structure meaning and choice. Honor requires an audience who shares public standards for judging conduct and is ready to acknowledge and reward what is honorable and condemn what is blameworthy. To assure and maintain agreements about the meanings of honor and its converse shame require more than a common moral vocabulary. Even in a Rousseauian society with its penchant for agreement and equality, civic honor rests on the concrete experiences that citizens share with one another and are strong enough to annul, for political purposes, the various particularities that distinguish citizens.

Rousseau is concerned with what citizens routinely honor. More than medals, proclamations, or other trophies, such a recognition depends on what is, in fact, rewarded, neglected, or penalized from day to day. The problem with rewarding civic virtue only with tokens is that most citizens recognize the token for what it is, a substitute for wealth, status, power, or office which others are winning for themselves through self-regarding action. Honor depends not on what a society professes to prize but what it teaches it values through its routine conduct. When institutional incentives signal that civic virtue brings only thin tokens of honor, the foundational principles of the republic are marginalized by delivering private gains and the corrupt society emerges.[59]

Political Conflict

Rousseau shares with Machiavelli the expectation that some people, even in the good republic, seek to advance their own interests at the expense of their civic obligations and thereby undermine the institutions that secure their liberty and equality. Sooner or later, ambition infects enough people who see political power as a prize for the winner, and one of the rewards they covet is the institutionalization of their spoils. The issues for Rousseau are whether other citizens see that this is occurring and whether they care.

With Machiavelli, Rousseau deplores factions, those groups that attempt to translate their particularistic wills into public policy. In Rousseau's account, "when particular interests begin to make themselves felt and the smaller societies to exercise an influence over the larger, the common interest changes and finds opponents, . . . [and] contradictory views and debates arise."[60] He would reverse this slippage with vigilant citizens who continue to prize their liberty and devote their energies to preserving the free institutions of the republic. However, "When the citizens are greedy, cowardly, and pusillanimous, and love ease more than liberty, they do not long hold out against the redoubled efforts of the government," which has fallen sway to victorious partial interests.[61] At such times, political language becomes debased and no longer conveys shared meanings. In the corrupt society, "the meanest interest brazenly lays hold of the sacred name of 'public good,' the general will becomes mute, . . . and iniquitous decrees directed solely to private interest get passed under the name of laws."[62]

The defense of liberty requires action, and the action Rousseau has in mind is political conflict. According to him, "A little disturbance gives the soul elasticity; what makes the race truly prosperous is not so much peace as liberty" and what protects liberty is political agitation.[63] Political activity means breaking through lethargy and pulling away from private satisfactions. Rousseau recognizes the attraction of the quiet and personal life and how it can divert our attention from what should be central to us—our autonomy—and exaggerates the secondary. When Rousseau claims "Where right and liberty are everything, disadvantages could for nothing," he is focusing on political apathy and personal profit, not about the need for citizens to sacrifice themselves.[64]

Like Machiavelli, Rousseau recognizes the damage that factions can visit on the republic, and, with Machiavelli, he distinguishes between conflicts that serve to protect and even invigorate the foundational principles of liberty from those that seek to advance private interests.[65] If a republic has not slid too deeply into corruption, Rousseau believes noisy republicans can intervene to restore the original normative and institutional contexts for thinking about oneself and one's relation to the community. As they did for Machiavelli, Rousseau's founding principles provide the basis for judging disagreements and furnishing citizens with standards of fairness and justice, which they are expected to employ to renew the republic and secure their own liberty. For this to happen, Rousseau expects the standards of the founding will be continually renewed in the daily experiences of citizens and that these experiences teach citizens that the things they care about most deeply depend on their active civic attention and participation.

Another Republican Paradox

The issue is not whether a republic experiences political conflict, even deep conflict, but why there is conflict. What becomes important in noisy republics is the preservation of foundational principles that are invested with moral meaning. Although they readily criticize the many modes of conflict that undermine the principles of the republic, Machiavelli and Rousseau each seek to promote conflict to restore the republic's equilibrium.

Each finds the republican founding provides a community with its moral purposes and moves its members away from pure instrumentalism. For Machiavelli, the founding celebrates the liberty and security of citizens; for Rousseau, it commemorates their equality and liberty. Each fears that these principles are lost when citizens become preoccupied with their own personal lives and gratify their personal desires. In this reading of conflict in the good republic, some conflicts are meritorious and even necessary. For Machiavelli and Rousseau, politics *is* disputation. Their good republic is hardly a place where citizens have only obligations to serve the state or a public space where like-minded citizens bind themselves in participatory cooperation. To be sure, they emphasize obligation and participation in their conceptions of the good republic, but they expect much more. They recognize that different people, no matter how much they partake in a common tradition and moral vocabulary and no matter how much they share a common political fate, will often have different understandings of the good. The issue for Machiavelli and Rousseau is that politics, it turns out, has little to do with civility or polite disagreements about marginal issues. They fear silence as much as unbridled ambition. But the irony attached to peace and prosperity is not only that self-involved citizens become lethargic and corrupt, but also that they become hostile toward noisy politics because it distracts them from enjoying their private concerns and bids them to leave their insularities. The paradox that Machiavelli and Rousseau detect in political agreement is that it can dampen the noisy conflict that is necessary to resist ambition and decay.

Machiavelli and Rousseau share an important position in their appreciation of the persistence and unavoidability of politics and the need to address political conflict in a straightforward way, rather than trying to constrain politics or mute disputes. What is arresting in the present debate between many liberals and communitarians is the tendency of each to seek to constrain politics, the former by appeals to a neutral proceduralism and the latter by celebrating traditional values as a way of achieving harmony and avoiding conflict. In their own very different ways, many communitarians and procedural liberals depoliticize democratic politics and prefer to discover broad answers that cover everyone rather than promote contestation. For Machiavelli and Rousseau, no stable republic can persist without allegiance to broad moral principles, but such civic principles cannot, by themselves, sustain the strong republic. For that, politics is central.

Notes

1. I have not included Aristotle as a noisy republican because to do so would force him into an uncomfortable fit. True, Aristotle offers us an open, fluid mode of politics (see Stephen Salkever, *Finding the Mean* [Princeton: Princeton University Press, 1990], 144–45; 262–64) and he favors a constitutional solution which balances different kinds of power. However, Aristotle does not develop an explicit argument for noisy republican politics, and I think this is not a matter of his having different concerns than later republicans or we do. Rather, Aristotle places greater efficacy on education to promote virtue, on the importance of constitutional arrangements to secure a stable society, and on the sagacity and prudence of the statesman much more than Machiavelli and Rousseau. Even though he overstates the case, Josiah Ober captures Aristotle's emphasis in his observation that "the social system on which [Aristotle's] regime was based was designed to be inflexible and was to be maintained by the laws" ("Aristotle's Political Sociology: Class, Status and Order in the *Politics*," in *Essays on the Foundation of Aristotelian Political Science*, edited by Carnes Lord and David O'Connor [Berkeley: University of California Press, 1991], 28). Moreover, Aristotle repeatedly shows how democracy can deteriorate and is suspicious that noisy, popular dissent can correct the defects of democracy because, he fears, it is highly susceptible to the manipulation of demagogues (see Barry Strauss, "On Aristotle's Critique of Athenian Democracy," in *Essays on the Foundations of Aristotelian Political Science*, edited by Carnes Lord and David O'Connor [Berkeley: University of California Press, 1991]).

Salkever also makes the point that although Aristotle wants citizens to be political, he also wants to protect them "against the charm of civic republicanism" because he fears "those who are single-mindedly committed to the political easily make the kind of mistakes proper to slavemasters and lovers of war—in their treatment of foreigners if not of fellow citizens" (*Finding the Mean*, 148).

None of this is to deny Judith Swanson's argument that Aristotle promotes "public-spiritedness" to protect what is important (*Public and Private* [Ithaca: Cornell University Press, 1992], 138). But this "public-spiritedness" does not take the form of republican noise.

2. Although Benjamin Barber expects and invites noisy politics on occasion, most other communitarians largely ignore any beneficial effects that conflict might contribute to democratic politics (*Strong Democracy* [Berkeley: University of California Press, 1984]). Will Kymlicka finds that communitarians are generally silent about diversity and conflict (*Liberalism, Community and Culture* [Oxford: Oxford University Press, 1989], 86).

3. Kymlika faults communitarians for failing to take account of manginalized groups (*Liberalism*, 87).

4. For criticisms along this line, see Will Kymlicka, *Contemporary Political Philosophy* (Oxford: Oxford University Press, 1990), 224–30, and Amy Gutmann, "Communitarian Critics of Liberalism," *Philosophy and Public Affairs* 14 (1985): 318–22.

5. This term signals very deep and persistent inequalities in a society that purports to respect liberty and democracy.

6. For Michael Sandel, liberalism leaves individuals without "shared self-understandings" (*Liberalism and the Limits of Justice* [New York: Cambridge University Press, 1982], 173). Today, "we cannot justify political arrangements without reference to common purposes" (Michael Sandel, "The Procedural Republic and the Unencumbered Self," *Political Theory* 12 [1984]: 5). With the absence of common purposes, community falls into disarray, and political language becomes corrupted. For Sandel, we require "a common vocabulary of discourse and a background of implicit practices and understandings within which the opacity of the participants is reduced if never finally dissolved" (*Liberalism*, 172–73). This is the very opposite of what he sees liberalism offering with its emphasis on the separateness and distinctiveness of individuals. Without "constitutive attachments," we find a "person wholly without character, without moral depth" (*Liberalism*, 179) and are left with the people who are "unsituated" in their own society.

7. See Aristotle (*Politics* [Chicago: University of Chicago Press, 1984], V, 1301a-91b) for a discussion of the "initial and fundamental" errors that create unbridgeable factions and subsequent political "disaster." Also see Alexis de Tocqueville's lament about the unhappy origins of French democracy (*Democracy in America* [New York: Vantage, 1957]).

8. There is a vast literature on the positive function of social conflict. For an early, influential work, see Georg Simel, *Conflict and the Web of Group-Affiliations* (Glencoe: Free Press, 1951). For more recent treatments, see Lewis Coser, *The Functions of Social Conflict* (New York: Free Press, 1956), and

Ralf Dahrendorf, *Class and Class Conflict in Industrial Society* (Stanford: Stanford University Press, 1957).

9. See chapter 7 where I discuss Lincoln's view that a flawed origin, namely slavery in the American founding, requires a later generation to re-found the republic.

10. Consider the elaborate ways Rousseau develops institutions in the last half of *The Social Contract* (London: Dent, 1983) and Machiavelli's treatment of the subject in the latter part of book 1 of *The Discourses* (New York: Random House, 1940).

11. See Sheldon Wolin who argues that Machiavelli presents us a world filled with ambition and conflict and offers us an "economy of violence" to meet it (*Politics and Vision* [Boston: Little Brown and Company, 1960], 195-238).

12. When this fails, Machiavelli argues in his account of the causes of the fall of republican Rome, citizens are no longer content with their present situation and eagerly support politicians who manipulate them with promises of more benefits.

13. These may be options Machiavelli recommends to victorious states as they attempt to manage their external affairs, but they are not tenable for him when he talks of settling domestic conflicts among republican citizens.

14. Although Machiavelli joins religion and politics, he neither offers a theocratic approach nor constructs a civil religion. As developed by Robert Bellah, civil religion invests politics with a meaning that transcends the factions and interests of any given period. Focusing on American civil religion, Bellah finds "the Declaration of Independence and the Constitution were the sacred scriptures and Washington the divinely appointed Moses who led his people out of the hands of tyranny" ("Civil Religion in America," *Daedalus* 90 [1967]: 9). Machiavelli, for one, would reject this formulation. His view of religion is important to his politics not because it inspires admiration for the regime but because it instills fear. He wants people to believe in the omniscience of the divine who detects our every thought, including those that are conspiratorial and make us experience guilt and fear divine retribution. This no state can do. For Machiavelli, religion should be an inseparable component of everyone's civic identity. See also *The Prince* (New York: Random House, 1940), chap. 26.

15. J. Samuel Preus argues that "Machiavelli came to have enormous respect for the psychological power of religious belief . . . No analysis of political reality could afford to neglect religion" from Machiavelli's perspective ("Machiavelli's Functional Analysis of Religion: Context and Object," *Journal of the History of Ideas*, 40 [1979]: 173).

16. Isaiah Berlin finds that Machiavelli carries no serious belief in God into his writings ("The Originality of Machiavelli," *Against the Current: Essays in the History of Ideas* [New York: Viking, 1980]).

17. *Discourses*, I,37.

18. *The Discourses*, I,11.

19. Sociogical accounts of religion usually emphasize the importance of guilt and the fear of future, eternal punishments as monitors of current conduct. Guilt is internal, depending on deeply internalized moral standards to regulate behavior. Shame, however, has a social basis and relies on what external observers think of conduct. For someone who cares about reputation, the prospect of social condemnation acts as a check to proscribed actions. Machiavelli's Romans are always alert to the importance of acting honorably as patriotic citizens and the shame attached to ambition, envy, and cowardliness. The materials for honor and shame come from Machiavelli's civic principles while the principles for guilt come from religion.

20. *Discourses*, I,11; italics added.

21. See Machiavelli's discussion of how religion is used "to preserve order in their city, and to carry out their enterprises and suppress disturbances" in *Discourses*, I,13.

22. See Hannah Arendt, *Human Condition* (New York: Doubleday, 1958) on the coupling of religion, tradition, and political authority in republican Rome.

23. *Discourses*, I,2.

24. See Bruce Smith, *Politics of Remembrance* (Princeton: Princeton University Press, 1985).

25. *Discourses*, I,2.

26. *Discourses*, I,2.

27. *Discourses*, I,2. The different classes need to watch one another because Pocock's civic virtue is, for Machiavelli at least, insufficient to protect the republic.

28. Although Machiavelli appears to reflect a modern view of the dispersal of power, as reflected in Madison's aphorism that ambition must be made to counteract ambition, Machiavelli's solution is indebted to the classical position of Aristotle and Polybius who argue that class differences are intractable and power needs to be institutionally dispersed in ways that no particular class dominates.

29. *Discourses*, VII,1.

30. *Discourses*, VII,5. Machiavelli complains that "after an effective and well-organized militia has produced victories, and these victories have ensured tranquility, the strength of such brave minds cannot be corrupted with a more honorable laziness than that of literature" that is, philosophy. He goes on to argue that "nations have come to ruin because of this" honorable laziness (*History of Florence* [London: Dent, 1975], vol. 1).

31. *Discourses*, I,40.

32. *Discourses*, I,3.

33. *Discourses*, I,17.

34. *Discourses*, III,8. This assumes a fairly static conception of fairness and should be compared with Lincoln's views, discussed in chap 7, that require losers to adjust to a new equilibrium.

35. *Discourses*, I,4.

36. *History*, 114. Gisela Bock shows that Machiavelli believed the revolt of the Ciompi, the Florentine woolworkers, in 1378 is best explained by

"historical development and change." In arguing that Machiavelli both favored and rejected "tumult," Bock fails to notice that Machiavelli only endorses conflicts that served to return the republic to its foundational principles and he continually rejects conflicts that sought the gains of a particular class, faction, family, or party at the expense of the whole ("Civil Discord in Machiavelli's *Isorie Florentine*," in *Machiavelli and Republicanism*, edited by Gisela Bock [Cambridge: Cambridge University Press, 1990]).

37. *Art of War*, 11–12.

38. Machiavelli credits Piero deMedici, a friend of republican institutions, with the following lament. "I could never have believed that the time would come when the actions of my friends would cause me to turn in love to my enemies, and regret that my victory had not been a defeat, because I never expected to find such a boundless measure of greed in men, who after they had been revenged upon their enemies were not content to live in peace and security. But now I fear I am greatly deceived and that I know little of the natural ambition of men, and less of yours . . . . You have taken the possession of your neighbours, you have sold justice, have disregarded the laws, have oppressed peaceful citizens, and encouraged the insolent . . . . [I]f you continue to follow in these paths, . . . I will make you repent of having made such an evil use of that victory." (*History*, 7, 298–99) See also *History*, III,1.

39. *History*, III, 1.

40. *Moment*, 181.

41. *Moment*, 183; emphasis added.

42. On Pocock's attribution of perfectionism to Machiavelli, see *Moment*, 167, 201.

43. *Political Economy* (London: Dent, 1983), 127).

44. *Social Contract* and *The Government of Poland* (Indianapolis: Library of Liberal Arts, 1972).

45. See William Connolly for a discussion of Rousseauian politics as an effort to challenge the free rider problem (*Political Theory and Modernity* [London: Basil Blackwell, 1988], 54–57).

46. Rousseau claims that people should be "forced to be free." If they pursue their own interests, they are said to begin a process that obliterates the moral, institutional, and distributional foundations of the republic.

47. *Social Contract*, I,3. Rousseau goes on to argue that "if force creates right, the effect changes with the cause: every force that is greater than the first succeeds to its right" (*Social Contract*, I,3).

48. *Social Contract*, II,7. For a comparison between Machiavelli's founder and Rousseau's legislator, see Roger Masters, *Political Philosophy of Rousseau* (Princeton: Princeton University Press, 1968), 364–68.

49. "The legislator therefore, being unable to appeal to either force or reason, must have recourse to an authority of a different order, capable of constraining without violence and persuading without convincing" (*Social Contract*, II,7).

50. At this point, Rousseau approvingly cites Machiavelli's observation that "there has never been . . . an extraordinary legislator who has not had

recourse to God." Like Machiavelli, Rousseau takes a sociological rather than theological approach to religion (*Social Contract*, II,7).

51. *Political Economy*, 131.

52. *Social Contract*, II,12.

53. Rousseau's expectation that private and public life are complementary requires a regime in which "there is no need to lay on any man burdens too heavy for a man to bear" (*Social Contract*, II,10).

54. *Social Contract*, I,11. For Rousseau's discussion of taxation, see *Political Economy*, 146, where he holds that those "who possess only the common necessaries of life should pay nothing at all."

55. *Social Contract*, II,11.

56. See Rousseau's discussion of Romans and work in *Social Contract*, IV,4.

57. In *Political Economy*, Rousseau argues, "It is one of the most important functions of government to prevent extreme inequality of fortunes; not by taking away wealth from its possessors but by depriving all men of means of accumulating it; not by building hospitals for the poor but by securing the citizen from becoming poor" (*Political Economy*, 134). In *The Social Contract*, he admits that "a thorough-going equality" is impossible (*Social Contract*, III,5).

58. *Political Economy*, 134.

59. Machiavelli and Rousseau remind us that honor counts only in a particular kind of society. If a society continually rewards greed or consumerism, appeals to surmount a narrow individualism will have little effect. Those communitarians who want to restore honor to society need to ask what they want to reward institutionally in society.

60. *Social Contract*, VI,1.

61. *Social Contract*, III,14.

62. *Social Contract*, IV,1.

63. *Social Contract*, III,9, note 1.

64. *Social Contract*, III,15.

65. *Social Contract*, II,3, where Rousseau favorably cites Machiavelli's distinction between factional strife and beneficial political conflict.

Chapter Four

Anxious Liberals I: The Moral Individualism of John Locke

John Locke, Adam Smith, and John Stuart Mill hold that ordinary people are due rights both to act on their personal concerns as well as to develop morally. Our concerns are often good: family, friends, religion, jobs, homes, property, and citizenship are valuable to us, not because we are weak but because it is through such attachments we develop our identity, connectedness, and character. But some of our concerns may be dangerous to us or to others, and Locke, Smith, and Mill credit us with the ability to distinguish good from evil and lead principled lives. Recognizing that we live in a world full of moral pitfalls, they appreciate that we often inflate the significance of what is important to us and risk succumbing to our own pride. Their uneasiness about the possibilities that rights-carriers will construct a narrow understanding of the self make Locke, Smith, and Mill anxious liberals. In this way, they address some of the same issues as do strong republicans.

Anxious liberals see the possibility that as free people we will make a narrow understanding of our interests the touchstone of our identity and the basis of our happiness. In their own way, anxious liberals recognize that in promoting freedom they give agents a tacit permission to exaggerate one or another of their attachments. It is in this context that Locke, Smith, and Mill examine how concern about one's self intersects with moral standards and how ordinary people can flourish in a world that is vulnerable to corruption.[1]

Liberal Choice and Responsibilities

In the many exchanges that have surrounded his work, John Rawls has shifted some positions but never abandoned his primary argument about the need to treat everyone fairly according to the procedures embodied in just institutions.[2] For Rawls, the accidents of contingency ought not to determine what a person is due. We all have an equal claim to "all social primary goods—liberty and opportunity, income and wealth, and the bases of self-respect—[which] are to be distributed equally unless an unequal distribution of any of or all of these goods is to the advantage of the least favored."[3] The problem, as Rawls sees it, is

> the existing distribution . . . is the accumulative effect of prior distributions of . . . natural talents and abilities—as these have been developed or left unrealized, and their use favored or disfavored over time by social circumstances and such chance contingencies as accident and good fortune. Intuitively, the most obvious injustice of the system of natural liberty is that it permits distributive shares to be improperly influenced by these factors so arbitrary from a moral point of view.[4]

Rawls attempts to defeat chance with his theory of just institutions and fair procedures. To do this, he places an abstracted, contingent free person in the original position. There, his "representative man" uses reason to move beyond accident and chance to construct a just society. Rawls has acknowledged his debt to Kant in thinking through this solution. In the debate that has followed, critics have made most liberals into Kantians who know only abstracted, not encumbered, persons and who have only one source of knowledge, reason, rather than additional sources, such as found in their tradition.

Rawls finds that prior conceptions of the good favor some at the cost of others and circumvent standards of neutrality or fairness and that conceptions of the good ought to be private matters and not determine how the advantages and disadvantages in society are distributed.[5] Critics see these moves as examples of liberal tolerance opening the way to an empty relativism and claim that liberals are afraid or unable to make choices about a moral life.

In arguing that contingency is critical but arbitrary, Rawls appears to free individuals of responsibility for their action. He claims that it is "clear that the effort a person is willing to make is influenced by his natural abilities and skills and the alternatives open to him."[6] This appears to mean that the character a person develops is problematic:

your good character is as accidental as my bad character. Because our backgrounds are the product of (good and bad) luck, so is our character. Galston is horrified at such a conclusion, and finds that "Rawlsian moral freedom liberates us from all antecedent principles—all duties and obligations, all intrinsic values other than freedom itself."[7]

Rawls and other procedural liberals are, in many ways, more confident in ordinary persons than anxious liberals are. Rawls is not troubled about the ways individuals exercise their freedom so long as they abide by the rules of justice. Anxious liberals take a very different position and worry that individuals often deceive themselves about what is best and that their society invariably houses seductive temptations that appeal to their vulnerabilities. The response of anxious liberals is not to make people choose the good but to look to several ways of fortifying individuals: through their moral education as children; through their intimate social lives with family and friends; through encouraging traditional practices of the good; and through persistent warnings about the seductions that surround people.[8]

In another way, Rawls is less confident about ordinary people than anxious liberals. Along with many other procedural liberals, he finds that because the contingent characteristics that describe any life are undeserved and serve to advantage some and handicap others, it is a cruel hoax to talk about responsibility. Anxious liberals such as Locke, Smith, and Mill are mindful that contingencies, such as poverty or illiteracy, make a profound difference in both the kinds of choices that await individuals and the resources people bring with them when they make choices. But they do not conclude that because the burdens of responsibility are heavier for some than for others, it is necessary either to withhold rights until the burdens can be equalized or to support the position that individuals can carry rights without a corresponding responsibility.

Abstracted vs. Busy Liberals

A major problem in liberalism, as critics understand it, is its heavy reliance on the abstracted self, particularly as presented by Kant and extended by Rawls. They are said to introduce us to a person without a history, tradition, morality, social relationships, talents, or aspirations. The only property attached to the Kantian-Rawlsian abstracted person is reason, which enables the contingent-free thinker to distinguish the just from unjust and the ethical from unethical. In relying on a Kantian conception of the person, many contemporary liberals leave behind another part of their tradition, one indebted to John Locke,[9] Adam Smith, and J. S. Mill who offer us persons whose lives are crowded with contingencies that agents are expected to address. Even when anxious liberals work with abstract principles, they then return to a busy world where agents employ both reason as well as traditional and cultural standards to understand themselves and the good.

Whether there is a distinct state of nature in early liberalism as we find in John Locke,[10] a prehistoric time of innocence as Adam Smith argues, or a primeval period of conflict as J. S. Mill holds, the effect remains the same in much liberal theory. What is uncovered by Locke, Smith, and Mill in their excursions into the state of nature or back to prehistory is a self that is essentially equal to every other self and that has evaluative powers, such as Locke's rational faculties, Smith's moral sentiments, or Mill's developmental capacities. With these views of the self, no person has any natural dominion over another, and the contingent properties of persons do not qualify some individuals to become rights-carriers and disqualify others.

The anxious liberal construction of free and equal persons, particularly Locke's efforts in the early state of nature or Smith's prehistorical account, provides us with a simple person in a simple environment, not an abstracted person. The Lockean rendition of the simple self or Smithian view of the historically innocent self is usually accompanied with an account of peace, harmony, goodwill, and rationality in an uncomplicated society which retains a rough economic equality and is unmarked by institutionalized subordination or political inequalities. Unlike Hobbes's view that perfect freedom and perfect equality are inherently unstable because the desires of individuals inevitably conflict, the members of Locke's early state of nature and Smith's innocent society of hunters and gatherers avoid conflict and retain their freedom and equality so long as matters remain "naturally" simple.[11] With the appearance of money or fixed property (which depends on who is telling the story), contingency matters in new and profound ways, and people begin to get in each other's way. In the Lockean and Smithian accounts, before the secular fall and the loss of innocence, our needs are natural (such as feeding and clothing ourselves), simple (in the sense that we can readily meet them), and limited (because we want only what we can consume before it spoils). After the secular fall, artificial desires envelop us, reason becomes complicated (and in the process, not always reliable), and society begins to carry corrupting influences. Anxious liberals use simple settings to assign equality and freedom to simple persons but they quickly move to a more complicated, crowded world where reason is often problematic and the pursuit of personal desires often preoccupies rights-holders.

In spite of all the changes that distinguish simple from complex settings, anxious liberals believe that new moral possibilities await men and women after the secular fall and that ordinary people can lead moral lives. The rights attributed to persons in Locke's simple state of nature or Smith's innocent beginnings turn out to be necessary to their theories of moral autonomy and development. Because contingency counts for so much in civil society and complicates arguments about who deserves what,[12] the strategy of moving to a simple setting with simple persons attempts to avoid the complications introduced by inequality. The Lockean move to abstraction, however, is only partial. Unlike Kant's or Rawls's pure reasoners who detach themselves from their surroundings, Locke's persons in the state of nature apply their rational capacities to their contingent situations. They feed and cloth themselves to satisfy their elementary needs, and Locke uses these simple needs and examples of direct labor to show that everyone can behave rationally and morally in this simple environment. Moreover, the individuals he discovers in early civil society have families, property, and shared expectations about rights and fairness before government is formed.

According to Locke, after the invention of money people invented or "adopted" desires or interests with a view to gaining pleasure or happiness. In this account, interests are particularistic in contrast to rights, which are said to be general. Whether it is Locke, Smith or Mill, each argues that a free society opens choices for men and women and, in turn, creates the possibilities both for human flourishing and moral failure. People are free to become better; but their rights open the possibility to become worse as well. From this perspective, the members of a liberal society can become morally autonomous or they can succumb to the temptations housed in organized society. To explore the status of interests and the moral life in early liberalism, I examine three important contributors to anxious liberalism: Locke is the subject of this chapter and Mill of the following chapter, and I then turn to Smith to engage him in a debate with libertarians and interest-group liberals.

Liberal Imperfections: Autonomy and the Good Life

What is the best life and who can achieve it? Premodern answers often assume that moral inequality is a natural fact to be taken into account in answering both questions. In rejecting earlier perfectionist views and taking moral equality as a fact, anxious liberals hardly move away from the question of the good life. For them the issue is how everyone, including ordinary people, can advance morally in a world increasingly described by new needs and desires. For anxious liberals, the vexing problem of particularities intensifies with the expansion of rights and opportunities for economic advancement. People are now free either to develop morally and socially or to pursue some of the very things that can defeat their own happiness and interfere with the happiness of others.

The anxious liberal view of autonomy holds that people want and deserve to control their own lives in significant ways and that they have the moral capacities (because of their reason or their moral sentiments) and materials (such as provided by tradition, religion, or philosophy) to make moral choices. This being so, people are said to be responsible—in whole or in large measure—for their choices and the character they fashion for themselves. In the theories I shall be discussing, choice is never unbounded and the writers under review could easily agree with Harry Frankfurt's observation that what "has no boundaries has no shape."[13]

Autonomy for anxious liberals requires freedom, and if they disagree among themselves about what precisely constitutes freedom, each associates it with the ability to make important choices honestly. For some it signals new religious choices with the growth of Protestantism; for others, it comes with the decline of arbitrary power in government; and for still others, it is marked by the demise of feudalism and the opening of new commercial opportunities. Writers such as Locke and Smith believe these kinds of changes give a new and robust meaning to autonomy in providing men and women not only with choices unavailable before but also with the responsibility for their own lives. People are free not only to worship God as they please, but also to transgress God's word; not only to enjoy basic rights, but also to abuse those rights; not only to choose to live principled lives, but also to subvert their own integrity.

The idea of personal responsibility is central to the anxious liberal theory of autonomy which holds that when people voluntarily choose a certain path, they cannot shift responsibility for their choices to others. We "own" our decisions, which give us a moral identity. Responsibility is not restricted to wise or prudent persons but to everyone; and through the pattern of our choices and the way we assume responsibility for them, we give ourselves a moral identity. In this sense, liberal autonomy is not reserved to those who make the correct or "perfect" choices but applies to everyone. Moreover, liberal theories of autonomy are largely insensitive to the backgrounds of agents. This means that disadvantages do not count in the assignment of either rights or responsibility for anxious liberals.

The discussion of anxious liberals that follows builds on recent scholarly research that seriously questions the claim that early liberals justify a narrow instrumentalism and offer us a morally empty self.[14] Recent discussions show that Locke, Smith, and Mill insistently deny that material or other conventional pleasures can ever provide an adequate way of defining what should be important in the life of a person.[15] In examining why Locke, Smith, and Mill think it is possible for individuals to develop morally, even if imperfectly, I question criticisms that hold that liberalism celebrates the particularities of individuals or at least is bogged down in them, ignores standards of the good, and detaches persons from their community. I go on to argue that anxious liberals find that freedom is simultaneously necessary for a principled life and a heavy burden.

Radical Individualism and the Problem of Subjectivity

Ordinary people often inflate the importance of many of their attributes, linking what is valuable to them with the good and calling obstacles bad. This intersection of moral evaluation and contingency is nowhere more elaborately developed than in Hobbes who broaches the problem of subjectivity clearly: people call good what pleases them and evil what displeases them, and they accept their constructions as true. In many ways, this argument about the subjective basis of what constitutes the good is not unique to Hobbes. Socrates, for example, raises this issue to defeat the subjective and contingent in favor of a universal standard. But Hobbes argues that all that we have is the contingent, and he places subjective reasoning at the center of his political philosophy in several important senses. First of all, he holds that all conceptions of good and evil are reducible to a personal calculation and that there is no inherent or shared human understanding of the good that can command a consensus. Within the context of his epistemology and psychology, Hobbes gives us a state of nature where there are no conventional and institutional restraints on individual desires. There, an almost perfect equality reigns: no one can institutionally control others, but everyone has the capacity to harm others. Moreover, everyone in Hobbes's state of nature believes she is best suited to identify the good for herself. For Hobbes, this means there is no moral subordination of one to another in his state of nature as each pursues her own subjective understanding of the good.

People invariably get in one another's way in the condition of perfect freedom and equality that characterizes Hobbes's state of nature. Some desire to dominate others, and some want others to honor them. Most people, however, simply want to be left alone and resist the attempts of others to dominate. These incommensurable psychological predispositions eventually collide, thereby creating Hobbes's state of war. To escape the chaos flowing from a radical individualism that knows no limits, Hobbes holds that people are driven into the Leviathan, which is expected to protect them through binding rules and punishments if its laws are breached. In this sense, the Commonwealth creates boundaries to tether unmediated subjective behavior. For Hobbes, government is created to direct individualism in ways that avoid the state of war and promote a stable milieu for people to pursue their "safe" preferences.[16] Hobbes offers us "that great Leviathan, or rather (to speak more reverently) . . . that *Mortall God*." Like the Old Testament God, the Leviathan is presented as an angry and jealous god who brooks no false gods or competing standards of justice to its own.[17]

As much as liberals depart company with Hobbes over the unlimited power of the Leviathan, they remain in his debt in two important ways. However much they modify his argument, liberals from Locke to Rawls accept Hobbes's claim about the equality of persons and never return to earlier arguments about natural inequalities. Moreover, liberals agree with Hobbes that the state is created not to make people good but to provide them with a manageable environment in which they develop. By taming Hobbes's Leviathan, anxious liberals do not overcome the problem of subjectivism and radical individualism and attempt to address them within the framework of a free society.

Making Freedom an Opportunity and a Burden: John Locke's Anxious Liberalism

The Locke we have come to know is someone who claims rights for everyone, requires government to rest on consent, insists on a limited government that protects private space (including private property), expects government to act infrequently and neutrally, and justifies rebellion when government breaks its trust. Locke is also regarded as one of the towering figures of the Enlightenment for his celebration of reason. But ever since he wrote, Locke has been the subject of controversy and the disputes have not abated.[18] Many of these debates have focused on whether it is possible to be as detached and neutral as Locke claims; whether there are real essences and fixed truths waiting to be discovered as he thought; whether his distinction between the public and private is helpful or valid; and whether his justifications of rights and consent are too loose, too restrictive, or simply wrong.[19] Moreover, controversy has recently emerged about Locke's influence on Anglo-American thought and whether rival traditions overshadow Lockean liberalism in America.[20] Yet Locke remains significant today for several reasons, one of the most important being that many critics find that his theories and claims about rights, obligation, tolerance, and consent mirror their own construction of liberalism in important ways.

The persistent presence of Locke in liberal discourse has animated much of the continuing criticism of his work. In mounting their objections, his critics are, for the most part I think, seldom interested in Locke's positions for the sake of correcting historical texts or joining late–seventeenth-century debates about epistemology, religion, or politics. Rather, in challenging or defending Locke's theories, assumptions, outlooks, and language, critics address one or another part of contemporary liberal thinking, and, by implication, demonstrate what they take to be defective or worthwhile about liberalism.[21]

In this section, I take up Locke's view of reason and interests and their place in his theories of moral autonomy. I mean to show that some of the received interpretations about Locke are inadequate in understanding him or his version of liberalism. In mapping out this position, I turn to Locke's discussion about the way ordinary people think, the obstacles they encounter in thinking clearly, and how they acquire their moral knowledge. In emphasizing Locke's position concerning the rationality of ordinary people, I depart from the usual treatments of Lockean rationality, which address the innovative, sophisticated, and complex theories he presents in *Human Understanding*. There and elsewhere, he offers an elegant analysis of how we begin life without prior moral knowledge, how we use our sense impressions and a hedonistic calculus to determine what is good and bad, how we acquire simple ideas and combine them into complex ones, and how we can move beyond the nominal meaning or essence of a thing to its real meaning or essence.[22]

Not surprisingly, many current controversies about Locke center on these and related issues, raising questions for epistemology, logical consistency, psychology, moral philosophy, the sociology of knowledge and the philosophy of science. In concentrating on his views of ordinary people, I bypass many of these arguments to consider why ordinary people can lead a moral life even though these are the very people Locke expects are least likely to think in the detached, self-reflective ways he recommends in *Human Understanding* or to benefit from his ideal education.

The Power and Frailty of Reason

Locke privileges reason in several critical ways. First and foremost, he believes that every person has an elementary capacity to reason and to make basic choices to protect his or her life, liberty, and estate. For Locke reason is an essential component of freedom, arguing that "so far as this Power reaches, of acting or not acting, but the determination of his own Thought . . . so far is a Man free."[23] Reason enables us to "suspend the execution of and satisfaction of any of [our] desires" and to "examine, view, and judge" the morality of our choices. "This," Locke concludes, "seems to me the source of all liberty."[24] For Locke, this means our choices ought not be the product of our instincts, impulses, desires, or public opinion. We become our own masters, on his account, when we call up our grounded standards to guide us in our choices.

To show how people acquire their moral standards, Locke relies on a hedonistic psychology. Confusions between his descriptive and moral hedonism have been a major source of controversy since Locke wrote *Human Understanding*.[25] In that book, he claims that nature, "has put into man a desire of happiness and an aversion to misery: these indeed are innate practical principles which (as practical principles ought) do continue constantly to operate and influence all our actions without ceasing."[26] Because people define happiness in ways that make sense to themselves, "Good and evil . . . are nothing but pleasure or pain, or that which occasions or procures pleasure or pain to us."[27] Although it appears that the desire both to seek pleasure and avoid pain moves people, it is pain that Locke places as the foundation of choice. In his substantial additions to the second and subsequent editions of *Essay*, Locke rejects the idea that pleasure carries equivalent power with pain in determining choice, and he makes uneasiness and pain trump ease and pleasure.

> All pain of the body of what sort so ever, and disquiet of the mind, is *uneasiness*: And with this is always join'd Desire, equal to the pain or *uneasiness* felt; and is scarce distinguishable from it. For *desire* being nothing but an *uneasiness* in the want of an absent good, in reference to any pain felt, ease is that absent good.[28]

The anxious Locke sees little relief in this busy life.[29] After we fulfill one desire, another appears and we are uneasy until it is satisfied. Rest eludes us with each new intrusion as we commit ourselves again to quieting our new uneasinesses. Along the way, we often form assessments about what will make us happy without reflecting on our choices or their consequences. Our judgments often prove to be unreliable, sometimes because we are confused about time. According to Locke, choice is complicated by the future tense; when we consider what constitutes our present pleasures or pains, we never make a mistake. If I am hungry, I satisfy my uneasiness by eating. In this example, the causal relationship between my efforts and my satisfaction of immediate pleasures is simple and direct. But what I currently take to be pleasant or painful sometimes undermines my prospects for achieving a greater pleasure or avoiding a greater pain in the future. According to Locke, people must be convinced that there is some good reason to suspend their immediate pleasures in favor of an absent pleasure and to recognize that not every action is "concluded within itself" but draws "consequences after it." Because any given moment is superseded by new ones, Locke wants rational individuals to take into account the effects of their present choices on their future welfare. For him,

> Actions carry not all the Happiness and Misery, . . . but are the precedent Causes of Good and Evil, which they draw after them, and bring upon us, when they themselves are passed, and cease to be; our desires look beyond our present enjoyments, and carry the Mind out to the absent *good*, according to the necessity which we think there is of it to the making or increase of our Happiness.[30]

Locke wants us to stand back from our desires and use our reason to think about the consequences of our choices. However, he finds people are deeply committed to their own constructions of what is good even if they are mistaken. Locke holds that for such people "it is not in the power of Reason to help us, and relieve us from the Effects of" our misunderstanding.[31] Tied to our own private understanding of what is good for us, we often fail to be self-reflective and self-critical.[32] As Locke surveys the world around him, he sees a pervasive failure to reason properly: "There is scarce a Man so free from" this vulnerability which is expressed not merely at moments of passion, but most especially "in the steady calm course" of a person's life. In his account, this inability to reason clearly is "a weakness to which all Men are so liable; . . . a Taint which so universally infects Mankind."[33] Because "all men are liable to Errors, and most Men are in many points, by Passion or Interest, under Temptation to it," Locke fears that if we choose without grounded standards, we will lead our lives in a "fleeting state of Action and Blindness."[34] Whatever else defines Locke's conception of the human condition, this weakness in human rationality leaves Lockean agents fragile and vulnerable—but Locke does not mean to leave matters here.

Text and Context: Before and After the Secular Fall

How do we reconcile the view of Lockean reason as faulty in most people much of the time with Locke's positive celebration of reason in the *Second Treatise* wherein ordinary people in the state of nature use their reason to recognize that they and others carry rights? Actually, Locke offers us two distinct contexts for thinking, each with its own properties. One context occurs in the early state of nature, before the invention of money, where Locke hypothesizes the needs of agents are simple and limited, their desires are natural and not acquired, and inequalities and background differences are narrow and inconsequential.[35] In Locke's early state of nature, agents move only in the present, never concerning themselves about any future consequences stemming from their current behavior because, he believes, there is no incentive to desire anything that will spoil in a few days.[36] The other context appears after these idyllic conditions deteriorate with the proliferation of acquired desires, the appearance of complex cause-effect relations, growing inequalities, and increasing conflict.

In Locke's early state of nature, what I think is due to me I also acknowledge is due to others; as I claim the fruits of my labor as my own, Locke expects me to understand that the product of the labor of others is theirs, and not mine for the taking. In Locke's account, I can meet my needs at this time without harming others and, therefore, I reason others have no need to harm me. I come to these conclusions by a simple rational process that Locke believes is available to everyone.[37] If people are incapable of these simple moral judgments, then whatever moves a person, regardless of its consequences on others, becomes permissible to that person. To avoid this kind of Hobbesian condition, Locke insists that the elementary rational capacities of persons in the early state of nature enable individuals to understand both the boundaries of their rights as well as their reciprocal obligations not to harm one another. These assumptions enable Locke to assign rights to everyone and make them responsible for their actions.[38] Choice and responsibility, in Locke's reading, give persons their moral character.

In an important sense, everyone in Locke's premonitary society is an ordinary thinker, requiring no special training or education to sort through complexity, explore causality, penetrate time, or weigh probabilities because the world is simple, cause-effect is direct, time is always in the present, and the consequences of a person's actions are clear and unproblematic. Once money appears, we encounter the second context. We meet a new set of agents encumbered with a proliferation of diverse contingencies and acquired desires. The invention of money irreversibly overwhelms the adequacy of simple rationality and static time found in Locke's early state of nature. Locke's text about the agent changes because the agent's context changes. At this point, agents reconstitute themselves.[39]

But to what? To see how reason becomes more complicated and the role of contingency takes on a pressing importance, it is helpful to explore Locke's account of the consequences of the secular fall. After the invention of money, Locke no longer ties people to a subsistence economy where they take from nature only what they can immediately consume, but now locates them in an economy where the exchange of goods and services for money enables them to work beyond what it takes to satisfy their simple, natural needs for physical survival. People now have an incentive to appropriate much more from nature than they had before and to save the "overplus." With money, they move beyond their natural needs and acquire or "adopt" new, artificial needs that they take to be essential to their well-being. Locke also sees money introducing growing inequalities which, he expects, lead to conflict.[40] By the time we reach the eighth chapter of *The Second Treatise,* we have left the "*Golden Age*" with its goodwill and harmony and find ourselves in the midst of strife as people seek a government to provide a manageable environment and to secure our rights.[41] After the fall, artificial desires multiply, uneasiness intensifies, the future counts, inequalities abound, and reason is not always simple or accessible.

Why reason should become so problematic takes us back to Locke's treatment of time: he thinks it is appropriate for people to concentrate exclusively on the present only in the early state of nature because the consequences of an action there immediately follow the action and can, therefore, be judged to be rational or not.[42] However, linear causality is seldom so simple or direct in civil society where behavior often carries complex consequences into the future.[43] People now frequently misunderstand the future significance of their present conduct and, in Locke's account, make decisions that undermine their chance for happiness because they employ a hedonistic calculus of pleasure and pain that is stuck in the present. What Locke thinks is rationally available, universal, and reliable in the early state of nature becomes vulnerable after the secular fall, and what was an almost automatic consultation with the laws of reason diminishes in the highly complicated world that evolves after the introduction of money.

Acquiring Moral Knowledge

Even though he rejects the idea that the sophisticated reason he proposes in *Human Understanding* can apply to people who do not have the time for a rigorous education, Locke believes we retain our rational capacities in civil society. As he sees it, elementary reason tells us both before and after the secular fall that murder or theft is wrong. For example, Locke argues that the rationally derived principle of self-preservation shows us that we, not others, have a right to our life and that we do not have a right to the lives, liberties, or estates of others.[44] Moreover, he believes our society reflects many of these basic moral principles in its conventions and laws which individuals generally accept as true.[45]

His position here is critical to his defense of equality and moral autonomy. If people cannot be depended upon to know elementary moral standards, they cannot be expected to recognize the valid rights-claims of others and cannot be held responsible for their actions.[46] Locke wants to deny both positions. An essential part of his argument about equal rights rests on his view that each of us knows that no one has a warrant to deny other persons their basic rights. What is involved here, from a Lockean perspective, is *simple* reciprocity.[47]

However, Locke holds that this kind of elementary moral reasoning is not always sufficient to guide conduct after the secular fall and he looks at two very different ways people can acquire reliable moral knowledge: one is to have the right kind of parents[48] and the other is to be a Christian.[49] To have the "right" kind of parents means that a child has the opportunity to receive a solid Lockean education and to engage in complex rationality while the "wrong" kind of parents are unable or unwilling to provide a rationally grounded preparation for adulthood and leave the child open to a crude hedonism or public opinion to form ideas about good and bad. Because a solid Lockean education is time-consuming, parents must devote a large part of their day to educating their children or pay full-time tutors. This, Locke thinks, means that most children will be ineligible for a rigorous education.

Locke overrides parental deficiencies by introducing Christianity.

To live outside a Christian culture means to Locke that agents lack a consistent, coherent, and especially compelling standard and are not consistently able to detect their moral mistakes. In his account of history before Christ, Locke discovers a time that is bereft of comprehensive and compelling moral principles. He sees popular norms resting on superstitions or false opinions, often inviting the pursuit of immediate, sensual pleasures, or, at best, providing only a partial grasp of moral conduct. Prior to Christ's arrival, people "made so little use of their reason. . . . Sense and lust blinded their minds in some, and a careless inadvertency in others." People were morally rudderless, and even their best efforts at reason could not provide them with a steady moral direction. "In this state of darkness and ignorance of the true God, vice and superstition held the world. Nor could any help be had or hoped from reason; which could not be heard, and was judged to have nothing to do in the case."[50]

Allowing that some ancient philosophers had made solid moral discoveries, Locke insists they did not carry the entire corpus of moral wisdom and, just as critical to Locke, they could not muster convincing arguments to compel ordinary people to pursue a moral life.[51] This is important to Locke who holds that ordinary people, whether in Christian or non-Christian societies, cannot achieve a comprehensive moral view on their own. To think otherwise would mean we could turn "all day-laborers and tradesmen, the spinsters and dairy-maids into perfect mathematicians, as to have them perfect in ethics." Locke would have the day-laborers and milk-maids of the world hear plain commands which, he believes, is "the sure and only course to bring them to obedience and practice. The greatest part cannot know, and therefore they must believe."[52] This argument corresponds to his observation in *The Essay* that people who employ their time in daily labor "require *some Foundation or Principles to rest their Thought on* and they *take them upon trust.*"[53] For Locke, the Christian faith is the most reliable and deserving form of trust.

According to Locke, Jesus comes into the world because he is needed.[54] With the teachings of Jesus, Locke holds that we are not only given an account of all we need to know to lead a moral life but also that Christ provides convincing incentives to act morally, something the ancient philosophers could not supply. Locke's Jesus gives us inducements to overcome temptations with the threat of eternal damnation and to lead a moral life with the promise of eternal salvation.[55] In this sense, Locke's natural law of physical self preservation that is so important in *The Second Treatise* is extended to eternal self-preservation, which is said to override our immediate desires. For him,

Christianity challenges the preoccupation of ordinary people with their too ready accommodations to their immediate contingencies by introducing considerations that transport them out of the present and make them think about eternal self-preservation.

Locke's Christianity occupies a central place in his theory of the acquisition of moral knowledge and moral incentives for ordinary people; it also has important political implications. As John Dunn shows, Locke wants to harness pride and to deny envy a standing in civil society, not because Locke believes all contemporary privileges and disabilities are justified but because he fears pride and envy carry profoundly disruptive effects for both the individual and society.[56] Locke wants each person to attend to his or her own calling and derive satisfaction from it. Moreover, Locke's Jesus teaches self-denial, which acts as a gatekeeper to present gratifications. With these moves, Locke expects a stable moral identity and settled political and social expectations from ordinary people.

Locke's agents are embedded in an imperfect world, with their desires following them constantly and robbing them of their peace and tranquillity.[57] Moreover, they are said to be surrounded by temptations that make their lives turbulent. In this busy world, Locke wants to invest agents with the requisite materials to judge what is appropriate and what is not. In both the *Essay Concerning Human Understanding* and *The Reasonableness of Christianity*, we meet countless examples of people who are weak and confused and who mistake apparent goods for the real good. Locke's secular rationality and his Christian culture are not presented as perfectionist strategies if this means people are now expected to transcend their contingencies in search of the good. For Locke, the issue is not only how people come to know moral standards but also whether they will use these standards to develop morally or will be stuck on their immediate desires.

Locke's communitarian critics may not like his use of Christianity as a substitute for a telos because it lacks a civic concreteness, but they need to acknowledge that Locke's liberalism relies heavily on a comprehensive moral doctrine.[58] He confronts the tendency of agents to be self-centered with an education that teaches agents to be self-reflective as well as with a Christian culture to provide deeply internalized standards for judging. Character enters Lockean liberalism in a different guise than it does in republicanism, but it enters nevertheless. Agents are at their Lockean best when they step back from their own concerns to wonder about the moral meaning they are giving to themselves. To the extent that Locke's ideas are transported into democratic vistas today, he needs to be seen as skeptical of interests rather than exonerating them.

Locke's Liberalism and Ours

We often use Lockean language to talk about what is valuable or wrong about liberal democratic society, but we also know that our conception of rights and their coverage is more expansive than Locke's, our understanding of consent and the franchise is broader, our assignment of tasks to the state covers more, and our ideas regarding fixed moral principles discovered by reason are less certain. But something is often lost in correcting or expanding Locke, and I want to consider several themes that deserve more attention than procedural liberals give to them today, namely the continued vulnerability of persons to moral failure in a free society and the necessity for both grounded standards and self-reflection to develop fully.

Before considering procedural liberalism, it is helpful to consider the communitarian claim that liberals are morally empty and lonely. Although the first charge cannot be sustained against Locke, the heavy moral responsibilities assessed on liberal agents by Locke leave them more lonely than is often supposed. They are expected to exercise their moral autonomy without regard to any considerations of background, except for the religion or education provided by their parents. Not only does Locke disregard differences among the rich and poor, the favored and the despised, the learned and the illiterate, his agents exercise their rights and make moral choices in a society that is morally unreliable. Whether they obtain their principles of choice and conduct from a rigorous Lockean education or from Christianity, Locke wants them to reflect on who they are becoming as moral beings, and contingency is irrelevant in this quest.[59] The Lockean personality who emerges is not a "possessive individualist"[60] but a moral individualist. Locke's moral individualist does not construct a personal morality but is made responsible for the kind of person she becomes. She may employ her reason to discover the fixed truths embedded in the laws of nature (because of her education) or she may call up the grounded standards she learned as a Christian. Whatever the source of her moral knowledge, however, she and she alone is responsible for leading a moral life. For Locke, background conditions should not be considered when we assign rights or moral responsibility. Each belongs to everyone.

Today, many procedural liberals not only spurn Locke's claim that individuals are responsible for their own character, procedural liberals also reject his arguments for moral individualism. Although Locke's reading of responsibility may be overdrawn, it is a mistake to assume that one is either wholly responsible for individual choices or not responsible at all. Procedural liberals need to ask whether we want to talk about free persons who are not responsible for their choices, and if we do, what that would mean. If agents can deny personal responsibility when they harm themselves or others, can these same agents conclude they have no responsibility for their actions that are helpful, positive or beneficent? To leave agents without any responsibility is not the most satisfying way to respond to a theory of personal responsibility that ignores important contingent backgrounds. For all of their disagreements with Locke's theory of responsibility, procedural liberals still need to return to his concern about fostering a moral character which equips agents with the materials to challenge a narrow or conformist construction of the self.

The institutional practices and normative standards on which Locke relies have historically been challenged by many liberals who find that what harmonizes for some, even a majority, does not for them. Locke's views of the naturalness of the patriarchal family, for example, are often seen as contrary to his claims for universal autonomy. This is a dispute not so much with Lockean liberalism as with the restrictive, patriarchal culture on which he is so reliant.[61] Locke works with existing distributions of authority, power, and privilege sponsored by the dominant institutional practices of his particular society and legitimized by its reigning culture. When some find that the promise of liberalism and the performance of society are contradictory, the pattern has not been to jettison liberalism with its claims to rights and celebration of autonomy but to summon liberal principles to confront a nonliberal culture and nonliberal practices.

Procedural liberals need to do more than acknowledge that Locke's comprehensive moral standards do not fit comfortably in the late modern world. As I have already argued, Locke deserves attention from liberals today because of his continuing preoccupation with the moral character of liberal agents and the dangers inherent in an unreflective, loosely restrained pursuit of interests. Contemporary liberals carry the continuing challenge of asking how and where agents obtain the principles to judge themselves and the many competing interests that they carry into politics today. The specific association Locke draws between rights and moral standards may not be convincing today but the relationship between autonomy and grounded principles remains compelling. Liberals, whether anxious or procedural, want agents to be in charge of their lives. However, procedural liberals forget what Locke emphasizes: moral standards ought not be left to chance but must be cultivated and nourished.

Anxious liberals want agents to have standards to judge both themselves and the world around them. Accordingly, they insist the moral socialization of children is an essential component of the life of free persons. The anxious liberals I discuss continually sound a warning that without a moral grounding, individuals are apt to be adrift and squander their rights. Like all good liberals, they want children to learn to be tolerant but they also expect them to be educated in the particular morality chosen by their parents. Galston has challenged his fellow liberals to move away from a uniform defense of the priority of rights over the good in order to assure that liberals do not ravage the practices and standards they need, such as a coherent moral environment for children. Unlike most contemporary liberals but in many ways similar to anxious liberals, Galston wants to be sure liberals do not disturb or undermine the many goods required by the autonomous person. Particularly troubling in contemporary liberalism is the silence about one of the most vulnerable groups in society: the young and how they are prepared for adulthood.

What is embedded in Locke's liberalism is a commitment not only to rights but also to a moral life. The latter part of his project has often been ignored by procedural liberals in their own project to extend our conceptions and applications of freedom, but a principled life remains as important today as it did in Locke's time. However much we differ with Locke in our understandings of what constitutes a moral life, any view of morality has to do with more than showing equal respect and regard to others. A moral life also has a substantive content that proceduralism can not furnish, and for this reason, liberals today need to ask whether they are promoting or hindering nonjudicial sites that can provide the materials for a moral life. Any conception of autonomy requires not only freedom but also a standard for making choices that leads to a morally flourishing life. The dignity that procedural liberals prize can be thwarted by external impediments, but, as Locke argues, dignity can be subverted by the person, and this is most apt to occur when agents have no moral compass.

The argument I am advancing also holds that the view of liberal politics as one that is relatively safe for private interests is contrary to Locke's project. He wants to make politics a place that is relatively safe *from* private interests. The critique of Locke as the new Adam of self-interested, individualistic liberalism whose original sins have come to corrupt each succeeding generation of liberals does not help us understand either Locke or ourselves.

Notes

1. The narrative I unfold about early liberalism here is a partial one. I will not be dwelling on those critical chapters of liberalism that detail the expansion of rights to cover more people in more ways largely because that part of the story has been told often. What should be noticed in the struggle to extend rights is that liberalism provides important requirements for full autonomy to those who have been institutionally denied equal rights, as then practiced, in liberal society. In other words, the language of liberalism yields some of the most compelling materials for the expansion of rights to new claimants who come asking not first and foremost for justice or economic fair shares but for rights. And the rights they demand are those generally available to some large segment of the population, such as the propertied, males, and whites. The universal vocabulary of rights becomes a resource for those who want to be rights-carriers, but are not yet recognized as such.

2. Critics such as Michael Sandel (*Liberalism and the Limits of Justice*: [New York: Cambridge University Press, 1982]) and Charles Taylor (*Sources of the Self* [Cambridge: Harvard University Press, 1989]) have characterized Rawls's just solutions as procedural. Taylor sees proceduralism resting on the premise that each person has "his or her conception of the good or worthwhile life" and social institutions—governmental, legal, economic, familial, and the like—ought not to fear some individual preferences over others. To favor some conception of the good as more worthwhile than others would breach "the principle of equality of nondiscrimination" (*Sources*, 164).

3. John Rawls, *Theory of Justice* (Cambridge: Harvard University Press, 1971), 303.

4. *Theory of Justice*, 72.

5. For parallel arguments concerning neutral or fair standards, see Bruce Ackerman, *Social Justice and the Liberal State* (New Haven: Yale University Press, 1980); Ronald Dworkin, *Taking Rights Seriously* (Cambridge: Harvard University Press, 1978); and Robert Nozick, *Anarchy, State, and Utopia* (New York: Basic Books, 1974) who assume that there are rational standards that we should apply to cover social relations. For a liberal claim that politics cannot always be neutral, see William Galston, *Justice and the Human Good* (Chicago: University of Chicago Press, 1980).

6. *Theory of Justice*, 312. For a further discussion of undeserved inequalities, see James Fishkin, *Justice, Equality of Opportunity, and the Family* (New Haven: Yale University Press, 1983).

7. "Moral Personality and Liberal Theory," *Political Theory* 10 (1982): 516.

8. Locke and Smith want to see a robust Christianity while Mill looks for a variety of traditional practices to provide a source of groundings for persons. For anxious liberals, the issue is which standards and practices should be dismantled and which retained. This reading is contrary to the conventional view that liberalism, growing out of the Enlightenment, attempted to shatter tradition and other nonrational beliefs. For example, Margaret Moore holds that "[L]iberalism initially conceived of itself as opposed to tradition, as wiping away the centuries of obedience to irrational superstition and deferential subordination to traditional authority by applying the power of reason to social and ethical questions" (*Foundations of Liberalism* [Oxford: Clarendon Press, 1993] 125). However, the process of dismantling is highly selective.

9. Locke is often seen as offering us an abstracted self in the state of nature, but, as I argue below, Locke introduces us to a simple person, not an abstracted one.

10. Many liberals reject a state of nature; Hume attacks Locke for this move, and many contemporary liberals, such as Dworkin, proceed without Rawls's abstracted person behind the veil of ignorance. For critiques of the abstracted individual, see Ian Shapiro on Locke in *The Evolution of Rights in Liberal Theory* (Cambridge: Cambridge University Press, 1986), and Michael Sandel on Kant in *Liberalism*.

11. Compare with Aristotle's society of farmers before the invention of money.

12. Smith asks whether the wise, the virtuous, the wealthy, the experienced, or the strong should rule. And if it is the wise or virtuous, how do we tell who qualifies, particularly when almost all think they are wise and virtuous?

13. Harry Frankfurt, *The Importance of What We Care About* (New York: Cambridge University Press, 1988), ix.

14. Reprentative scholarship includes John Dunn, *The Political Thought of John Locke* (Cambridge: Cambridge University Press, 1969); Alan Ryan, *J. S. Mill* (London: Routledge and Kegan Paul, 1974); D. D. Raphael, *Adam Smith* (Oxford: Oxford University Press, 1985); John Colman, *John Locke's Moral Philosophy* (Edinburgh: Edinburgh University Press, 1983).

15. Nathan Tarcov, *Locke's Education for Liberty* (Chicago: University of Chicago Press, 1984), John Robson, *The Improvement of Mankind* (Toronto: Toronto University Press, 1968); Bernard Semmel, *John Stuart Mill and the Pursuit of Virtue* (New Haven: Yale University Press, 1984).

16. See Deborah Baumgold, *Hobbes' Political Theory* (New York: Cambridge University Press, 1988); Richard Flathman, *Thomas Hobbes: Skepticism, Individuality, and Chastened Politics* (Newbury Park, CA: Sage, 1993); and Stephen Holmes, *Passions and Constraint* (Chicago: University of Chicago Press, 1995), 69–99.

17. Thomas Hobbes, *Leviathan* (Harmondsworth, U.K.: Penguin, 1972), bk 2, chap. 17).

18. In the century after his death, Shaftsberry, Rousseau, and Hume were, in very different ways, important critics of Locke's basic arguments. For a

discussion of seventeenth-century criticisms of Locke, see Richard Ashcraft, *Revolutionary Politics and Locke's Two Treatises* (Princeton: Princeton University Press, 1986). Also see Locke's own numerous responses to criticisms of his work. For example, in the seventh volume of *The Works of John Locke* (London: Tegg, 1823), the first third contains his essay "The Reasonableness of Christianity," and the remainder consists of Locke's "Vindications" of that work.

Extensive bibliographical materials on the current debates about Locke can be found in Ruth Grant, *John Locke's Liberalism* (Chicago: University of Chicago Press, 1987) and Edward Harpham, ed., *John Locke's Two Treatises of Government* (Lawrence: University Press of Kansas, 1992).

19. These positions have been taken, respectively, by Willmore Kendall, *John Locke and the Doctrine of Majority Rule* (Urbana: University of Illinois Press, 1941); John Rawls, *Justice*; and Carole Pateman, *Participation and Democratic Theory* (Cambridge: Cambridge University Press, 1970).

20. Bernard Bailyn, *Ideological Origins of the American Revolution* (Cambridge: Harvard University Press, 1967); Gordon Wood, *Creation of the American Revolution* (New York: Norton, 1969); and J. G. A. Pocock, *The Machiavellian Moment* (Princeton: Princeton University Press, 1975).

21. John Pocock and others have argued that the received Locke is not the real Locke, that the purported influence of Locke has been greatly exaggerated, and that alternative discourses competed with the Lockean paradigm at the very time it was said to be robust in the United Kingdom and United States. See Pocock, *Moment*; also see his "Civic Humanism and Its Role in Anglo-American Thought," in *Politics, Language, and Time* (New York: Atheneum, 1971). Pocock's arguments notwithstanding, the fact remains that Americans speak a Lockean language when they talk about rights or when they debate the proper boundaries between the state and civil society. Locke may not be right or even helpful, but we use Lockean language to think about basic rights and negative liberty (See Mary Glendon, *Rights Talk: The Impoverishment of Political Discourse* [New York: Free Press, 1991]).

22. There are several extended discussions of this theme; for a philosophically grounded analysis, see R. S. Woolhouse, *Locke* (Minneapolis: University of Minnesota Press, 1983) and John Yolton, *Locke and the Compass of Human Understanding* (Cambridge: Cambridge University Press, 1983). For a discussion of the political implications of Locke's ideal rationality, see Grant, *Locke's Liberalism;* Colman, *Locke's Moral Philosophy;* and Thomas Spragens, *The Irony of Liberal Reason* (Chicago: University of Chicago Press, 1981).

23. John Locke, *An Essay Concerning Human Understanding* (Oxford: Oxford University Press, 1979), 2.21.21.

24. *Essay*, 2.21.47.

25. For criticisms of Locke's hedonism, see Roberto Unger, *Knowledge and Politics* (New York: Free Press, 1975); Frederick Vaughan, *The Tradition of Political Hedonism From Hobbes to Mill* (New York: Fordham University Press, 1982), and Benjamin Barber, *Strong Democracy* (Berkeley: University

of California Press, 1984). However, recent research amply demonstrates that Locke separates his psychological hedonism from his view of grounded reason. See Spragens, *Irony*; Grant, *Locke's Liberalism*; Tarcov *Education* (105, 210); Dunn, *Political Thought* (195–97), and Pamela Krauss, "Locke's Negative Hedonism," *Locke Newsletter* 15 (1984): 43–63, who emphasize that Locke assumes that people can transcend a narrow view of pleasure and pain through a Christian culture, a moral education, and grounded standards (see John Locke, *Some Thoughts Concerning Education* in *The Educational Writings of John Locke*, edited by James Axell [Cambridge: Cambridge University Press, 1968], par. 33; Cf. 56, 61; 116–17). With these resources, Locke claims that people have the materials required to move beyond their contingent interests and pleasures and construct a moral existence for themselves that brings them happiness.

26. *Essay*, 1.3.3.
27. *Essay*, 2.28.5.
28. *Essay*, 2.21.31; also see 2.20.2; 2.21.44).
29. For a discussion of Locke's psychology, see Uday Singh Mehta, *The Anxiety of Freedom* (Ithaca, N. Y.: Cornell University Press, 1992).
30. *Essay*, 2.21.59.
31. *Essay*, 2.21.13.
32. *Essay*, 2.21.3. Locke reminds the readers of *The Essay* that the person who detects the "least flaw" in another person, "if it is at all different from his own, every one is quick-sighted enough to espie in another, and will by the Authority of Reason forwardly condemn, though he be guilty of much greater Unreasonableness in his own Tenets and Conduct, which he never perceives, and will hardly, if at all, be convinced of" (*Essay*, 2.33.1).
33. *Essay*, 2.21.3.
34. *Essay*, 4.20.17 and 4.16.4.
35. For two different readings of Locke's treatment of the invention of money, see C. B. Macpherson's argument that Locke holds that "accumulation is morally and expediently rational *per se*, and then found that the only thing that prevented it being rational in man's original condition was the absence of money and markets" (*Possessive Individualism*, 235; also see 203–11). Richard Ashcraft finds that Locke sees the invention of money "to be compatible with the advancement of the common good of mankind" (*Revolutionary Politics and Locke's Two Treatises of Government*, 274). In what follows, I do not argue that Locke detects no positive good flowing from the invention of money; rather I concentrate on its mixed moral effects on society and the individual.
36. John Locke, *Two Treatises of Government*, Peter Laslett, ed. (Oxford: Oxford University Press, 1988), 5.36; hereafter referred to as *Second Treatise*.
37. *Second Treatise*, 2.6.
38. *Second Treatise*, 2.6–7). For Locke, ordinary reasoners are distinguished from "lunatics" and "madmen" who lack the capacity to reason or children who have not yet developed their reason (*Second Treatise*, 6.60).

39. *Second Treatise*, 5.50; 8.108.
40. *Second Treatise*, 2.48–50.
41. *Second Treatise*, 8.110–11). Locke discusses the need for government earlier but does not explain why rational people should want to enter government until he makes his case about the secular fall later. The failure to consider the consequences of the fall has lead several scholars to find that Locke alienates his natural self with the contract (See Mehta, *Anxiety of Freedom*). But the natural self has already been alienated by the consequences of the secular fall and the ensuing state of war it introduces.
42. *Second Treatise*, 2.28–31.
43. See *Essay*, 2.21.60.
44. But Locke believes that some elementary laws of nature can be subverted in a corrupt society. For example, he holds that everyone naturally knows they need to work to survive. See Neal Wood, *John Locke and Agrarian Capitalism* (Berkeley: University of California Press, 1984), 120, and Tarcov, *Education*. However, in *Education*, Locke makes it clear that it is necessary to teach people to work beyond mere survival. And in his proposals for reforming the poor laws, he wants to eliminate inducements that reduce what he takes are rational incentives for not working, namely private charity for beggars.
45. *Second Treatise*, 6.59.
46. *Second Treatise*, 6.60.
47. Locke works with an assumption that no longer commands agreement. He believes there are fixed rights that are internally harmonious with one another and the rights of others. Today, there is little agreement about the fixity of natural rights or a harmony of rights.
48. See, Locke, *Education*; Tarcov, *Education*.
49. *Reasonableness*, 138–41.
50. *Reasonableness*, 135.
51. *Reasonableness*, 138–42. Locke thinks non-Christians respect some basic moral rules, such as prohibitions on murder and theft, because of the strength of public opinion and civil law.
52. *Reasonableness*, 146.
53. *Essay*, 1.3.24; italics in original.
54. *Reasonableness*, 135.
55. *Reasonableness*, 150.
56. *Political Thought*, 248.
57. *Essay*, 2.21.31.
58. However, see Alasdair MacIntyre's treatment of Augustine and Aquinas in *Whose Justice? Which Rationality?* (Notre Dame, Ind.: Notre Dame University Press, 1988).
59. Except, as I argued above, for the contingencies of having certain kinds of parents or being a Christian.
60. Macpherson, *Possessive Individualism*.
61. Rogers Smith holds that liberalism is not only about rights (for some) but also about hierarchy and inequality ("Beyond Tocqueville, Myrdal, and

Hartz: The Multiple Traditions in America," *American Political Science Review* 87 [1993]; 549–66). An alternative way of reading the hierarchies and inequalities that characterize outlooks and practices in a liberal society is to see them embodied in a nonliberal culture.

Chapter Five

Anxious Liberals II: J. S. Mill on Overcoming the Natural Self

John Stuart Mill reflects many of the same concerns that make Locke an anxious liberal. Mill seeks to enlarge the domain of liberty and works with the assumption that ordinary men and women can construct a plan of life for themselves that is personally fulfilling and morally grounded. At the same time, Mill finds his age emphasizing a narrow, materialistic conception of the successful self, thereby undermining the moral development of persons. To counter this new, sweeping challenge to autonomy, Mill seeks to expose the new conformity to commercial norms as well as point to alternative ways of conceptualizing the good that takes account of both the individuality and social constructedness of human beings. In this chapter I follow Mill's arguments about the need for both liberty and grounded moral principles.

J. S. Mill offers one of the most robust claims for autonomy in the liberal literature. For him, everyone not only deserves to be autonomous but also requires autonomy to develop fully as a human being. Although Mill's own view of what it means to be developed is highly contested, the basic features of his argument for autonomy occupy a central place in liberalism. This is reflected in the familiarity given to such Millian views as the importance of free speech, the necessity to broaden political liberty (notably the franchise), the need to extend political participation throughout society, and his arguments for the autonomous agent who carries "a sense of dignity."[1] For Mill, each of us needs to construct a moral life for ourselves, by which he means we need to reflect on the kind of person we want to become and what we are doing to achieve our plan of life. For the ordinary person, "his own mode of laying out his existence is the best, not because it is the best in itself, but because it is his own mode."[2] This is so, according to Mill, because our plan must make sense to us, reflecting our own aspirations, sentiments, ideals, and feelings. For him, we are "progressive beings," capable of revising and improving our plans as we move beyond our current expectations for ourselves and expand socially and develop morally.

Mill wants individuals to cultivate their moral, social, and intellectual properties, and for this he finds several conditions are required.[3] Most obviously, he wants people to be formally free from a despotic state, and he sees the decline of arbitrary government and the steady growth of democratic institutions as necessary steps. He also insists that people must have real choices if they are to author their own plan of life. Because we are not sheep following one shepherd, to use Mill's metaphor, a single standard or even a narrow range of alternatives thwarts our development.[4] The human faculties of perception, judgment, discriminative

> feeling, mental activity, and even moral preference, are exercised only in making a choice. He who does anything because it is the custom makes no choice. He gains no practice either in discerning or in desiring what is best. The mental and moral, like the muscular powers, are improved only by being used.[5]

Millian choice can be undermined in two ways. One can be prevented from exercising a choice by an external source, and Mill finds that any extrinsic restraint "partakes, either in a great or small degree, of the degradation of slavery."[6] Historically, this is embodied in the arbitrary state and monopoly church, and Mill believes these impediments have largely—but not completely—been overcome in the West, which now faces a new, pressing challenge. The great danger to autonomy he detects in his own generation is a growing conformity that revolves around standards of economic success. Finding that alternative standards of identity are crowded out in commercial society, Mill fears people are suspending their independent judgment. They unwittingly allow themselves to be driven by the criterion of economic achievement to define who they are and to identify their success and failure as human beings, as if almost nothing else matters.

Mill's Account of the Beginnings of Human History

Unlike the Lockean rendition of the original peaceful agent in the early state of nature, Mill sees the natural self as instinctive, aggressive, cruel, and antisocial, which the morally constructed self must overcome. The progressive path that Mill invites us to take moves us away from the natural self to a self who carries moral standards, is socially extended and self-disciplined, and is guided by its developed conscience.

Mill follows Locke in looking at the earliest stage of history as simple, but Mill finds no peace or self-directed harmony. Rather, he sees a self-involved, passionate being who has no sense of reason or morality and is moved by unmediated and immediate pleasure. Where nature rules supreme, Mill sees the "savage," that aggressive primordial individual who is always ready to make war. Mill's purpose in looking at people in this prehistoric period is not to lay the grounds for rights as Locke does but to show how the raw ego can be transformed to a new personality that ultimately requires autonomy to develop. Even though Mill is more optimistic than Locke about the possibility of influencing environmental factors to favor moral development, he is closer to Hobbes's bleak pessimism in his original reading of human nature. In Mill's view, nature lacks structure, reason, and discipline and produces only chaos and cruelty. Offering no moral guidance, nature

> impales men, breaks them as if on the wheel, casts them to be devoured by wild beasts, burns them to death, crushes them with stones like the first christian martyr, starves them with hunger, freezes them with cold, poisons them by the quick or slow venom of her exhalations, and has hundreds of other hideous deaths in reserve, such as the ingenious cruelty of a Nabis or a Domitian never surpassed. All this Nature does with the most supercilious disregard both of mercy and of justice, emptying her shafts upon the best and noblest indifferently with the meanest and the worst.[7]

Mill's "savage" sees no real distinction between good and evil in raw nature where "the most criminal actions are to a being like man, not more unnatural than most of the virtues."[8] When people leave their natural self-centeredness, they learn to sacrifice "a present desire to a distant object for a general purpose which is indispensable for making the actions of the individual accord with his own notions of his individual good." In Mill's account, civilization "assuredly requires in most persons a greater conquest over a greater number of natural inclinations to become eminently virtuous than transcendently vicious." Finding that nature is a description of "things as they would be, apart from human intervention," Mill argues that to claim otherwise is "irrational, because all human action, whatever, consists in altering, and all useful action in improving, the spontaneous course of nature."[9] And to insist that nature carries standards of right and wrong is "immoral because the course of natural phenomena being replete with everything which when committed by human beings is most worthy of abhorrence any one who endeavored in his actions to imitate the natural course of things would be universally seen and acknowledged to be the wickedest of men."[10]

Mill sees the exodus from nature to organized society leading to gradual but profound changes, particularly the appearance of internalized moral standards that lead to self-discipline and the extended social self.[11] He holds we develop in our society in the sense that it teaches us moral principles and instructs us socially and psychologically. We learn to take account of others as well as to restrain a narrow egoism. It is in society where we learn what Mill calls the higher pleasures.[12] Even though individuals develop socially and morally once they leave raw nature, self-interest and self-deception continue to follow people, even in Mill's "civilized" society. For this reason, he wants people to realize that "the character which improves human life is that which struggles with natural power and tendencies, not that which gives way to them."[13]

Developing the Millian Conscience

Mill aims to show that people have the ability to learn how to overcome their natural instincts and understand that their immediate desires may not be best for them. Equipped with his associational psychology, Mill charts the development of the mature conscience.[14] In his account, people have the capacity to expand their understandings of what brings them pleasure and pain. If we learn to feel guilty about acts that are "selfish" or "barbaric," to use Mill's language, we no longer look at such acts as sources of pure pleasure and move on to a higher standard of conduct. Those who have a weak conscience and follow their sensual desires only show Mill that the associations he wants in place have not yet matured. "It is not because men's desires are strong that they act ill; it is because their consciences are weak."[15]

> The internal sanction of duty, whatever our standard of duty may be, is one and the same—a feeling in our own mind; a pain, more or less intense, attendant on violation of duty, which in properly-cultivated moral natures rises, in the more serious cases, into shrinking from it as an impossibility. This feeling . . . is the essence of Conscience—the simple fact is that the conscience is encrusted over with collateral associations, derived from sympathy, from love, and still more from

fear; from all the forms of religious feeling; from the recollections of childhood and of all our past life; from self-esteem, desire of the esteem of others, and occasionally even self abasement.[16]

Whatever else Mill's conscience is, it is not tranquil. He expects people to develop standards and feel guilty when they ignore those standards. Mill would have us develop an "internal sanction of duty," which "is the essence of conscience."[17] Today, he laments, we see "the ease with which, in the generality of minds, conscience can be silenced or stifled."[18] He particularly wants his contemporaries to develop internalized standards that are ready to challenge the widespread assumption that happiness and "money-getting and money-having" are inseparable. If unexamined associations become our second nature, then, he argues, we have escaped the worst features of nature but fail to develop fully and lack control over our own lives.

In Mill's account, the new standards of commercialism have channeled individuals into a narrow conception of life that pivots around production and consumption. He sees modern men and women always seeking more and never taking the time to enjoy where they are or who they have become.[19] And he detects an emptiness in the spirit of the age, "which has been described as 'destitute of faith, but terrified at skepticism'—in which people feel sure, not so much that their opinions are true, as that they should not know what to do without them."[20]

Mill sees commercialism filling the void created when modern skepticism denies the vitality of standards of good and evil. However, he insists that commercial norms appeal to what is egoistic rather than social, possessive rather than just, and materialistic rather than moral. It is not only the content of commercialism that Mill deplores but also its pervasiveness. For him, men and women no longer think for themselves but rather are guided by extrinsic forces that overwhelm the self. Production and consumption have become so consuming, people have little time for shared activities in their communities; when they do gain time for themselves, Mill sees them turning to their solitary hobbies.[21] However, Mill also believes this is a time that can bring opportunities for social and moral development and human flourishing.

The Wiles of Commercial Society

Mill complains that commercial society is regressive; its greatest promise is to satisfy sensual gratifications, particularly material ones.

He sees commercialism making economic success the primary standard of the good and in this sense is merely a sophisticated variation of the earlier understandings of sensual pleasure that he discovers in nature. That people satisfy their sensual appetites in more elaborate, sophisticated ways than earlier generations does not make them less sensual. Food, clothing and shelter speak to our biological needs and satisfy our lower pleasures, not our higher ones.[22] Mill recognizes that none of us can escape our biological needs nor should we deny ourselves pleasures in meeting them. The issue is whether we get stuck on necessity and are unable or unwilling to move beyond the elaborate ways we satisfy them in commercial society.

Mill finds the spreading conformity of commercial norms robs agents of choice and liberty itself. As mass standards insinuate themselves into the human psyche and become a person's second nature,[23] they wear down self-reflective, independent judgments as well as the distinctive properties of each person.[24] In his account, "he who lets the world, or his own portion of it choose his plan of life for him, has no need of any other faculty than ape-like imitation. He who chooses his plan for himself, employs all his faculties."[25] According to Mill, the members of commercial society "exercise choice only among things commonly done . . . until by dint of not following their own nature, they have no natures to follow."[26] With Mill's reading, modern freedom is full of irony. No longer bounded by powerful external restraints, people are now in danger of being molded by a powerful public opinion. They may have given up beliefs in the power of witches to harm them but have uncritically accepted beliefs in the power of money to make them happy.

Challenging the idea that "money-getting and money-having" should be the hallmarks of individual success, Mill does not want people to deny the importance of economic well-being but rather to place it in perspective. One problem with exaggerating the importance of money and other external goods is that, like a favorable reputation, they can become ends in themselves. They can move us toward the things that provide us with one of the means to happiness but they cannot, by themselves, be satisfying. Mill fears that "the love of money is not only one of the strongest moving forces of human life, but money is, in many cases, desired in and for itself; From being a means to happiness, it has come to be itself a principle ingredient of the individual's conception of happiness."[27]

Like Aristotle earlier, Mill holds that a free people can misunderstand the nature of freedom, thinking that it means doing whatever a person wants to do. For this reason, Mill wants to develop an "equipoise" between internalized moral standards and freedom. Formal freedom has delivered us from the intrusive, arbitrary state, but this does not mean we will accept the invitation of freedom to take charge of our own lives. Unless we find internal ways to develop our moral character, he fears, we will be created by the commercial norms of our society rather than by ourselves.

J. S. Mill and the Renewal of Tradition

In looking at the status of tradition or culture in liberal society, we encounter two very different theories. One emphasizes an autonomous, distinctive liberal culture which both promotes and requires individualism, tolerance, and rights. The other argues that liberalism has no viable culture of its own but lives off of the capital of an autonomous culture in order to promote the moral life. Some of those who see a distinctive liberal culture emphasize its positive dimensions and focus on toleration and respect for rights.[28] In responding to its individualistic themes, however, others see a liberal culture housing relativism, possessiveness, and hedonism and thereby spawning moral infertility and social irresponsibility.[29] What both of these positions share is the belief that there is a particular liberal culture that generates its own standards and practices, for better or for worse.

Taking a much different approach, writers such as Joseph Schumpeter, Fred Hirsch, and Daniel Bell argue that early liberals did not have to confront a possessive, instrumental individualism because liberalism developed within an extant culture that grounded identities, moderated desires, and directed action.[30] From this perspective, a theory that is heavily reliant on individualism does not have the internal, independent capacity to generate coherent moral practices or moderation but can nevertheless use materials from an autonomous culture or tradition to achieve these ends. However, those who emphasize an autonomous culture find that Western societies have been subject to significant secular changes and the institutions and practices that once fortified traditional culture have grown weak or disappeared. With these changes, the members of liberal society fill the gap created by a decaying tradition with individualistic and materialistic understandings of themselves. For these writers, the current flabbiness of moral standards in liberal society is not best traced to liberalism but to secular change.

Mill works with both arguments. He sees once-robust traditions now grown tired and unable to animate but also believes some of the past is positive and should be recovered and renewed. He also finds that some elements of earlier traditions were restrictive, exonerated inequality and subordination, and have no place in a liberal society. He goes on to argue for a sturdy liberal component for contemporary culture, one characterized by a generous tolerance, a regard for diversity, and a commitment to autonomy. Neither traditions nor liberal principles are substitutes for one another in a Millian conception of culture; they require each other.

Millian Civilizations

There are, Mill tells us, two ways of thinking about the meaning of civilization. On the one hand, we can consider a country civilized if it promotes "the best characteristics of Man and Society; farther advanced in the road to perfection: happier, nobler, wiser" than non-civilized countries. On the other hand, a country can be called civilized if its wealth and power distinguish it from "the savages or barbarians." In this sense, we can "speak of the vices or the miseries of civilization" and question "whether civilization is on the whole a good or an evil." Mill insists that "civilization in this sense does not provide for" the highest good, and there is a tendency for this type of civilization "to impede the highest good." In spite of significant material and technological improvement, Mill does not find the present age "as either equally advanced or equally progressive in many of the other kinds of improvement. In some it appears to us stationary, in some even retrograde."[31] As Mill surveys his society, he finds much that is welcome and salutary, although his writing often emphasizes what he considers to be its darker side. Positively, he sees this as a time of freedom, a necessary ingredient for the progressive journey Mill wants men and women to travel.[32] To facilitate this journey, he wants grounded, practiced standards available to act as countervailing forces that will check the conformist tendencies of the age. According to Mill, "all that we are in danger of losing we may preserve, all that we have lost we may regain . . . only by establishing counter-tendencies, which may combine with those tendencies and modify them."[33]

Revolutionaries and Reactionaries

Although Mill believes the French Revolution performed a valuable service in eliminating innumerable obstacles to freedom, he holds that it "was not ripe for doing effectually any other work than that of destruction." For him, the revolutionaries made a mistake when "they did not acknowledge the historical value of much which had ceased to be useful, nor saw that institutions and creeds, now effete, had rendered essential services to civilization and still filled a place in the human mind, and in the arrangements of society, which could not without great peril, be left vacant."[34]

Mill finds the response of Coleridge and other writers "of the reactionary school" provides an important tonic to the blind destruction of tradition.[35] They remind us of the importance of anchored, moral principles and practices and show that individuals cannot construct their own standards of excellence in a cultural vacuum. However, Mill argues, the Tories push their case too far. They misunderstand the present and the past and are insensitive to the relation between moral excellence and practice. Their mistake about the past comes in their assumption that ancient standards can be codified and ritualized for the modern world. What once made such standards important and vital was that they were animating principles that men and women coherently applied in their daily lives. Because empty rituals do not convince individuals to move beyond a narrow conception of the self, each age requires its own understanding and application of moral principles.[36]

Mill also complains that Tories ignore what he calls new moral facts, and the paramount one is liberty. In his scathing letter to Carlyle who had defended slavery in America, Mill argues that such past practices are vicious and that we know enough today to realize that some earlier ways of categorizing people into superior and inferior races is simply unwarranted. But to discard the morally noxious does not mean an entire tradition need be jettisoned. Indeed, in the modern world, Mill wants to modify traditions in keeping with his principle of "moral facts," which recognize the capacities of each person to develop fully and freely.

The Participatory Mill

If modern society is becoming morally vacant, if consumption is the standard of success for ordinary men and women, and if nature provides no reliable guide for conduct, what does Mill recommend? In *On Liberty*, where the benefits of free speech are celebrated, he offers an important part of the answer. Free speech provides more than a forum to advance ideas, it also invites people to listen to others and to learn from them. Mill wants speech to challenge the new orthodoxy of commercialism, but even here, he denies that discourse can uncover a standard of perfectibility that applies to everyone. For Mill, each person is unique, carrying his or her own sentiments, aspirations, attachments, and past experiences, and the person's character is reflective of these properties. After they speak, listen, and reflect, Mill expects agents to return to the real world where they pursue their plan of life with others.

For Mill, it is simply unimaginable to believe that people are exercising free choice if they merely have a chance to talk about familiar ideas of the good. They require credible alternatives to practice their conception of the good, and Mill turns to local venues to provide concrete settings where people extend themselves socially. Mill fears that because people use more and more of their time in making and spending money, there is less time available to participate in the many local traditions which are dying from lack of attention.[37] He is particularly alarmed about what he takes to be the incessant mobility of the modern age, complaining that even farmers are willing to pull up the roots planted by their forbearers in order to improve themselves economically. With continued mobility, once-stable local traditions are abandoned and practices that had taken generations to establish are neglected. In this highly mobile, commercial society, traditional values are discounted and the norms of efficiency assert themselves. This can be seen in the case of the honest shopkeeper who knows and is known by the people who come into his shop. According to Mill, he produces goods of quality and charges his customers an honest price. This changes when people buy from whoever has the lowest price. Mill imagines not only that the quality of goods and services diminishes but that conditions that promote honesty deteriorate. We buy, not from those we know well and who treated us fairly before, but from strangers who can shave a penny or two from the price. In the process, we destabilize local communities in our search for the best price, caring little about our long-standing familiarity with some other members of our society.

In Mill's participatory structures, citizens who share similar self-understandings of the good come together with purpose and frequency.[38] What happens in these local participatory settings varies, but their primary object is not merely or especially to enhance the material comforts of the participants. Rather, Mill's diverse, participatory sites offer a standard of excellence to the members. What is valued in one particular venue is often ignored or even unwelcome elsewhere, but the variety of local options enables men and women to remain with the standards they learned as children or travel from the place of their childhood to new settings that make moral sense to them as adults. If left here, Mill's local communities could be clusters of parochial intolerance where established traditions confine the members rather than liberate them. But Mill expects something different; local venues now exist in an environment of freedom and their members are not as apt to be confined as earlier generations had been. In such a changed milieu, people are more apt to apply standards of liberty to the practices of their own local community.

When Mill turns to cooperation and participation to encourage the extended social self and moral growth, he concentrates on local venues over a national one. We should see what, besides its manageable scale, leads to this recommendation. Unlike national constituencies, local settings tend to be homogeneous, with the participants sharing many similar outlooks and interests, such as a better education for their children in their local schools, the security of their neighborhoods, or safe conditions in their workplace. Or they join with others for aesthetic, religious, or intellectual purposes. They freely associate to pursue a limited number of goals, and their disagreements are apt to be about the strategies and tactics most appropriate to achieve their common interests rather than about what their common interests really are. They settle their differences with speech, not with coercion or intimidation, and their speech reveals a mutual respect among equals who depend on one another to pursue their common undertakings.[39] For Mill, these shared projects may be limited, even narrow, but they provide the settings and incentives for extending the self, assuming responsibilities, sharing commitments, and developing morally in modern commercial society.[40]

But there are some things that do not happen in these participatory groups, or at least Mill never exaggerates the transformative potentials of local participation on men and women for national politics. Nowhere does he claim that a network of intense participatory venues will convert men and women into citizens who will continually desert their own interests to achieve some common national good, although he does believe that ordinary people can learn to think in a more expansive way about a common good than they do presently. Even so, Mill holds that the overlapping interests that draw particular men and women together in local projects as parents, neighbors, or coworkers do not stop being interests when they enter national politics. Even if they learn to respect the opinions of those outside their participatory group and even if they have an enlarged view of politics, Mill believes that ordinary people do not continually escape their interests. Thus, his scheme for national government limits the power of voters;

his voters and their representatives are said to be most competent in articulating their interests, learning from debate, and exercising oversight over government,[41] but Millian voters do not elect a legislature that can initiate legislation.[42]

At issue is who teaches us and what we learn. Mill holds that we are constantly learning from those around us; we learn what is called good and evil, what is rewarded, ignored, and condemned, and what constitutes success and failure. If we are increasingly taught by a single teacher, we get stuck on the uniform message and today that means that we learn that economic success is what really counts. Mill wants the vernacular of comfort and security of commercial society to give way to a broader form of discourse and expects the diversity found in a liberal culture to undermine the form of bland speech that characterizes modern politics. He expects participatory men and women in their local settings to gain the materials to judge national politics better and attend to national political debate more attentively. If nothing else, they know that the promises of the good despot are not satisfying and that being left out of political life is a cost, not a benefit.[43]

Mill thinks that we need liberty not only when we are fully flourishing, but also to become flourishing. Only by possessing and using freedom in concert with other free men and women do we leave a narrow conception of ourselves and develop our consciences, our cognitive abilities, our reflective capacities, and our ability to extend our social selves. The task Mill pursues is not how to introduce new overarching standards that will convince men and women to forget their surroundings. Rather, he works at the margin, inviting small steps and securing local venues for the development and protection of independent opinion in a world grown more homogenous and more self-satisfied with its own self-referenced standards. Hence, his celebration of local participation comes not from its redemptive capacities for national politics but from its limited but important social and moral possibilities for individuals in their local exertions. Mill resists the major assaults of his day on democracy, but when he assesses contemporary democratic politics in liberal society, his theories continue to carry much of the weight of Locke's anxious liberalism, which seeks to enhance the prospects for developing a moral life and exercising independent judgment.

Mill attempts to address many of the very things that trouble communitarians when he assails the relativism, skepticism, and materialism of contemporary society as well as when he challenges its narrow individualism, apathy, and insularity. But Mill's answer is not a comprehensive moral code for everyone. Rather, he wants a diversity of communities which not only invites participation but which nourish and extend the moral life. In a world that remains skeptical and relativistic, where a narrow individualism neglects social cooperation, and where traditional standards are challenged by efficiency and consumption, Mill argues that the need for local participatory communities are all the more pressing if men and women are to find sites that accord with their own aspirations for themselves and enable them to implement their plan of life.

Is Mill a Genuine Liberal?

Some commentators on Mill emphasize what they take to be antiliberal features in his work and make him into a republican masquerading as a liberal. In the revisionist reading, Mill either is incoherent and self-destructive in his aim to promote both freedom and self-discipline or he is a secret, but sterile, republican.[44] Part of the confusion in some recent readings of Mill stems from a faulty understanding about what constitutes anxious liberalism. As an anxious liberal, Mill distinguishes the idea that people should be free to do whatever they want from the idea that people should exercise self-discipline or self-restraint as they make morally grounded choices. If Mill is read as a nineteenth-century anxious liberal, he remains a liberal and not a confused republican in disguise. An anxious liberal reading of Mill allows him consistency when he assigns the state a positive role for fostering the conditions for moral improvement but refuses to call on it to make people good.

Mill's commitment to a culture that respects rights and tolerates difference can be seen in his tolerance of the Mormons, even though he is opposed to their views on marriage. So long as a woman freely elects to join the Mormons and is free to leave them if she chooses to do so, Mill believes state efforts to require Mormons to conform to the dominant marriage standard is wrong. Even more to the point, Mill refuses to protect people when they should know right from wrong but act on their impulses or passions rather than on a moral standard. When debating a proposal to require prostitutes in seaports to register in order to stop the spread of venereal disease among sailors, the Victorian Mill insists that such a law is deleterious to liberty and that sailors have the elementary moral capacity to decide their own conduct. For Mill, there is no warrant to require the state to invade the privacy of women for the sake of the protection of sailors. He reaches this conclusion knowing full well that some sailors might infect their wives who become innocent victims of the disease. Whether or not Mill's reasoning is sound on this matter, it distinguishes him from nonliberals who seek to promote the well-being of the entire community at the expense of the rights of some.

A parallel line of discussion about Mill's "secret republicanism" comes in his severe view of parents who have children without being able or willing to provide for them.[45] Mill never imposes an overt moral competency test on the right of adults to have children because that would be a gross invasion of privacy. However, he does call for an economic test: parents should be able to support their children. For Mill, the right to become a parent imposes a duty to provide for the elementary physical well-being and education of the child. None of us controls who our parents will be and, as children, we are dependent on our parents in the most fundamental ways. For Mill, this means that parents must have a livelihood to provide for the elementary survival of the family unit.[46] If such means are not available, Mill argues, and an adult has children, the state can intervene and force the father to work, that is, force the father to fulfill the responsibilities as a parent.[47] The other part of Mill's views on parental responsibility concerns withholding marriage licenses from people who wish to marry but have no visible means of supporting a family.

The feature of Mill's suggestion I want to emphasize here is that he believes such a move will be effective because most parents want to avoid the shame of having children born out of wedlock.[48] When distinctions such as legitimacy and illegitimacy are no longer compelling, that is, when the culture changes, such Millian proposals become quaint and beside the point. What does not become problematic, however, is the need for children to have physical security and a moral grounding, matters that deeply concern Mill.

The most serious charge that Mill is not a consistent liberal but a communitarian comes from revisionists who claim his general arguments on good government require state intervention to promote the moral character of citizens. Mill writes that the "first element of good government . . . being the virtue and intelligence of the [citizens], . . . the most important point of excellence which any government can possess is to promote the virtue and intelligence of the people themselves."[49]

How does he call on government to "promote the virtue" of citizens? Nowhere in his policy positions does he ask the state to "make" citizens virtuous. Indeed, central to his argument in *Representative Government* is that people guard against the "good despot," the state that defines and delivers the good.[50] Mill, like many other liberals of his generation, has an ambivalent view of the state. He sees every state carrying a strong coercive dimension and tending to do more harm than good. A state does the most harm when it attempts to instill a single pattern of the good in its subjects, and it is at its best when it promotes the conditions that take citizens further on their progressive path. One way it contributes to the latter goal is to provide elementary security and protection for citizens and improve the conditions in which people live. The state also promotes conditions for development when it removes obstacles to choice and diversity and expands the range of citizen participation in their own governance. In the end, Mill's policy proposals are designed to assure greater choice. All other things being equal, he holds that educated people have better choices to control over their lives than the ignorant or illiterate, the economically secure face more satisfying choices than the impoverished, and participatory structures extend the choices of their members more than institutions that shelter individuals from social engagements. The Millian state challenges the growing homogeneity of commercial society not by a frontal assault but by fostering the conditions where men and women can freely practice their plan of life. In this sense, Mill is neither a procedural liberal nor a communitarian but someone who is concerned about promoting the conditions that enhance the moral development of agents.

At this point it is helpful to return to arguments that Mill is not a genuine liberal because many of his concerns are central to communitarians. Stewart Justman builds such a case with the following citation of Mill: "The most immoral periods in a nation's history are always ... periods ... when ... each person 'does what is right in his own eyes.'" Justman goes on to observe that it "would take a skillful pleader to 'reconcile' such views with the argument of *On Liberty*."[51] Not at all. Mill never argues in *On Liberty* that liberty means doing whatever a person wants to do. His work presents an argument about the benefits of moral autonomy that can flourish after people become unstuck from the identities they take from commercial norms. Mill's moral utilitarianism aims to defeat the possibility that people will do whatever moves them, never stopping to reflect on who they are. He does not want to force people to think and act in a particular way, however worthy he may find that way for himself. To acknowledge that a free people can abuse their freedom does not lead to the conclusion, at least for Mill, that the way to address the problem is to subvert our commitment to freedom for everyone. One can fault Mill on many grounds here: he is too optimistic that people will leave their old habits or pleasures; his view of self-restraint is either too expansive or too narrow; or he depends too heavily on speech, participation, or renewal[52] and not enough on government to affect change. But none of these objections have to do with Mill's anxieties about the way people often misunderstand their freedom or the dangers that come from a government that seeks to make people good.

Mill's anxious liberalism depends on a willingness to confront many of the same practices and values that critics of modernity in general and liberalism in particular challenge. In undermining traditional ways of thinking and acting, modern society leaves men and women without a firm, animating, credible grounding. There is the recurring view in Mill that people want meaning for themselves and, in the void created by modernity and modernization, they turn to commercial society to provide the answer. The pressing danger Mill detects in this default strategy is that it invites relativism and even nihilism. Mill is not consistently optimistic about the outcome. The forces of commercialism are not merely strong and attractive, but also depleting the last enclaves of moral alternatives and starving individualism. The new conformity is especially dangerous because it does not have the honesty to let people know that they are being deprived of their individual liberty or that they are being seduced by the good despot. They lose their independent judgment at the very time they believe that all is well or continually improving. For all of Mill's deep apprehensions about the tendency of his contemporaries to squander their legacy of freedom, he retains a cautious optimism that stems from his confidence that a free society has the resources to protect and enhance both individual autonomy and local communities. There is nothing in his anxious liberalism that requires a person to choose one but not the other. For Mill, we need both.

The Status of Culture in Mill

Mill sees that if the mistakes people make are excused or become codified in the norms of efficiency of their society, the moral personality he wants to promote is endangered. He wants to encourage people to use materials lodged in their tradition to criticize contemporary social norms and their own behavior. This is a persistent theme for anxious liberals who see that some of the standards and practices lodged in their society are morally unreliable. These norms are what strong republicans often consider to be forms of corruption that exaggerate wealth and power and forget moderation.

To move without a cultural context is to move as if there were no past worth considering or valuing, a position Mill sees as dangerously symptomatic of his age.[53] People today "are not accustomed to look for guidance either to the wisdom of ancestors, or to eminent contemporary wisdom" but rely on commercial norms. Mill finds, "It is impossible . . . that mankind in general should form all their opinions for themselves: an authority from which they most derive them may be rejected in theory, but it always exists in fact." Rather than seeking moral guidance from tradition, religion, or philosophy, modern men and women find their standards "in the opinions of one another."[54] Mill wants us to call on our cultural legacy to put the norms of commercial society into perspective.

The claim that anxious liberals rely on a tradition seems, at first blush, to be a communitarian solution and contrary to the common view that liberalism and tradition are incompatible. Liberals such as Locke and Mill use materials from their tradition to gain self-understanding and to critique the standards of efficiency sponsored by the norms of their society. In their reading, traditions provide materials for reflection and choice. To think that someone can independently author standards that give meaning and purpose to life is to assume that people have a superhuman capacity (Aristotle's gods) or that the passions should govern (Aristotle's brutes), something that anxious liberals readily reject.

Tradition is fragile, and it does not serve as a compelling guide for self-understanding simply because it transmits the teachings of the ancients to later generations. A tradition remains vital only if it is practiced and if contemporary institutions foster rather than ignore or penalize its standards. The practices and institutions I have in mind are not only political but also social: the family, networks of friends and associates, the local community in which men and women live, the relations that describe their work, the way resources are distributed, the kinds of activities they share in their leisure, the stakes they have in their society, the lessons their children are taught, and the kinds of success that are honored in their society. To remain viable, cultural standards cannot be placed on a shelf to be revered but left unpracticed. To emphasize the importance of standards does not reduce the important contributions of anxious liberals to the concept and language of rights but rather recognizes that anxious liberals appreciate that rights are not self-actualized in ways that inevitably lead to the improvement and happiness of the right holder. For them, the good life requires coherent, practiced standards as well.

Anxious liberals reach for grounded cultures to provide men and women with firm standards of the good as well as rely on values inherent in liberalism. The liberal components of culture include commitments to equal rights and tolerance, and these properties establish the framework for autonomy but not its substance. Whether standards of excellence reside in religion as they do for Locke or have a more secular basis as Mill thinks, they are fragile and require time and attention. If emerging social practices divert men and women from standards of excellence, we should expect such principles to become secondary in the life of the community and lose their vitalizing force.

Anxious Liberals: Do We Need Them?

One of the unintended ironies in the writings of anxious liberals lies in the ways their theories have been used to support a politics of interests and moral relativism, something that is clearly antithetical to their intention. They mount a strong, self-conscious attack on a mode of life defined and driven by interests. Their critique of mass standards, their concern about the status of virtue, and their warnings about the ascendancy of interests are at the core of their liberal project. They are attentive both to the justification of rights and the purposes for which rights are employed. For anxious liberals, autonomy requires *both* freedom and moral standards. But in our own time, the moral standards that anxious liberals require have faltered, and self-referencing ones have claimed their place.

Why search for answers to some of our difficulties in the writings of anxious liberals? For better or for worse, liberalism has resided in a world of rapid and intense change, and what makes sense in a stable environment is not readily transportable to a changing one. Change introduces new issues, contingencies, opportunities, and dangers that may be discordant with traditional practices. The importance of anxious liberalism comes not in any specific proposal but in their ironic reading of liberty, which leads them both to defend it and to warn about it. As good liberals are prone to do, they fear the stifling effects that an arbitrary state or a dogmatized reading of traditions can cast over people. But they also fear that conventional celebrations of success can dampen the quest for a moral life, substitute instrumental reasoning for critical reflection, and introduce a narrow politics of interests. As contemporary communitarians avoid the issues of stakes and conflict that are central to strong republicans, too many procedural liberals today ignore central arguments in their own tradition about the importance of moral standards in the life of free men and women.

Notes

1. John Stuart Mill, *Utilitarianism* in *Collected Works* (Toronto: University of Toronto Press, 1969), vol. 10, 212.
2. John Stuart Mill, *On Liberty* in *Collected Works* (Toronto: University of Toronto Press, 1977), vol. 18, 270.
3. See John Robson, *The Improvement of Mankind* (Toronto: University of Toronto Press, 1968); Alan Ryan, *J. S. Mill* (London: Routledge and Kegan Paul, 1974); Bernard Semmel, *Pursuit of Virtue* (New Haven: Yale University Press, 1984); and Carole Pateman, *Participation and Democratic Theory* (Cambridge: Cambridge University Press, 1970).
4. "To give any fair play to the nature of each, it is essential that different persons should be allowed to lead different lives" (John Stuart Mill, *Principles of Political Economy* in *Collected Works* [Toronto: University of Toronto Press, 1965], vol. 3, 998).
5. *Liberty*, vol. 18, 262.
6. *Political Economy*, vol. 3, 938.
7. John Stuart Mill, *Nature* in *Collected Works* (Toronto: University of Toronto Press, 1969), vol. 10, 385; also see 381.
8. According to Mill, nature provides us with a description of unmediated hedonistic conduct. "Conformity to nature, has no connection whatever with right or wrong" (*Nature*, vol 10, 400). He goes on to argue that "there is hardly a bad action ever perpetuated which is not perfectly natural, and the motives to which are not perfectly natural feelings" (*Nature*, vol. 10, 401).
9. *Nature*, vol. 10, 401.
10. *Nature*, vol. 10, 402.
11. See *Liberty*, vol. 18, 219–20.
12. There is considerable controversy as to what Mill means by the higher pleasures. Some observers claim that Mill reflects and legitimizes a cultural elitism. While there is some merit in this assessment, it ignores Mill's larger argument. The things that give pleasure to children ought not remain the things that give pleasure to people who are growing into adulthood or are adults. And Mill would go on to argue that those pleasures associated with the senses ought not become the defining pleasures for any person. The acquired tastes of the gourmand are not pleasures that are superior to the simple tastes of a peasant; neither is higher in a Millian sense. Moreover, not every difference in pleasure requires a judgment as to which is higher. That I like Picasso and you like Rembrandt is not a fit subject for judging who is engaging in higher pleasures. That one of us prefers the morning comics as the only relevant form of visual art that interests us, however, is a subject for assessing Mill's conception of lower and higher pleasures.
13. John Stuart Mill, *Considerations on Representative Government* (Toronto: University of Toronto Press, 1977), vol. 19, 407).
14. Mill summarizes his "Laws of Association" as follows: "Of these laws, the first is that similar ideas tend to excite one another. The second is,

that when two impressions have been frequently experienced (or even thought of) either simultaneously or in immediate succession, then whenever one of these impressions, or the idea of it, recurs, it tends to excite the idea of the other. The third law is then greater intensity in either or both of the impressions is equivalent, in rendering them excitable by one another, to a greater frequency of conjunction" (vol. 10, VI, iv, 3; 852).

For a further discussion of associational psychology, see Howard Warren, *A History of Associational Psychology* (New York: Scribners, 1921), 96–103. For a discussion of the political implications of Mill's psychology, see Wendy Donner, *The Liberal Self* (Ithaca, N. Y.: Cornell University Press, 1991), 9–26; 66–75.

15. *Liberty*, vol. 18, 263.
16. *Utilitarianism*, vol. 10, 228.
17. *Utilitarianism*, vol. 10, 228.
18. *Utilitarianism*, vol. 10, 230.
19. John Stuart Mill, "de Tocqueville on Democracy in America [II]" in *Collected Works* (Toronto: University of Toronto Press, 1977), vol. 18, 193; see also, *Political Economy*, vol. 3, 754).
20. *Liberty*, vol. 18, 233; see also 240. Mill fears that modern skepticism and defensiveness coupled with the narrow understanding that wealth brings happiness keep people from listening to and learning from others. What is needed in the modern era, according to Mill, is robust speech which prompts men and women to exercise reflective, independent judgment when they make choices (*Liberty*, vol. 18, 262–63). But Mill holds that those judgments have grown weak in commercial society (*Utilitarianism*, vol. 10, 265–67).
21. *Liberty*, vol 18, 272. According to Mill, "Men lose their high aspirations . . . because they have not time or opportunity for indulging them; and they addict themselves to inferior pleasures, not because they deliberately prefer them, but because they are either the only ones to which they have access, or the only ones which they are any longer capable of enjoying" (*Utilitarianism*, vol. 10, 213).
22. *Utilitarianism*, vol. 10, chap. 2.
23. *Liberty*, vol. 18, 260–75.
24. See Ryan, *J. S. Mill,* and Eldon Eisenach, *Two Worlds of Liberalism* (Chicago: University of Chicago Press, 1981).
25. *Liberty*, vol. 18, 262. For an elaboration of Mill's fears concerning conformity, see *Civilization*, vol. 18, 121–22.
26. *Liberty*, vol. 18, 265.
27. *Utilitarianism*, vol. 10, 236.
28. See William Galston, *Justice and the Human Good* (Chicago: University of Chicago, 1980); John Rawls, "Justice as Fairness: Political not Metaphysical," *Philosophy and Public Affairs* 14 (1985): 223–57; and Robert Lane, *Political Ideologies* (New York: Free Press, 1962), 401–12.
29. See C. B. Macpherson, *The Political Theory of Possessive Individualism* (Oxford: Oxford University Press, 1962); Leo Strauss, *Natural Right and History* (Chicago: University of Chicago Press, 1953); and

Alasdair MacIntyre, *After Virtue* (Notre Dame: Notre Dame University Press, 1981).

30. Joseph Schumpeter, *Capitalism, Socialism, Democracy* (New York: Harper & Brothers, 1942); Fred Hirsch, *Social Limits to Growth* (Cambridge: Harvard University Press, 1976); and Daniel Bell, *The Cultural Contradictions of Capitalism* (New York: Basic Books, 1976).

31. *Civilization*, vol. 18, 119.

32. On the bright and dark sides of the present age, Mill writes, "There is a great increase of humanity, a decline of bigotry, as well as of arrogance and the conceit of case, among our conspicuous classes; but there is, to say the least, no increase of shining ability, and a very marked decrease of vigour and energy. With all of the advantages of this age," it has brought "little that is distinguished, either morally or intellectually, to the surface" (*Civilization*, vol. 18, 125–26).

33. *Civilization*, vol. 18, 136.

34. John Stuart Mill, *Coleridge* in *Collected Works*, vol. 10 (Toronto: University of Toronto Press, 1969), 138.

35. *Coleridge*, vol. 10, 138.

36. According to Mill, many Tories fail to distinguish the important from the superfluous in their traditions. He sees the Tories of his day striving not to protect the former but defending the latter. He finds a "truer spirit of conservation as to everything good in the principles . . . of our old institutions, lives in many who are determined enemies of those institutions in their present state, than in most of whose who call themselves conservatives" (*Civilization*, vol. 18, 129).

37. See *Liberty*, vol. 18, 272.

38. His credentials as a participatory theorist have been widely certified by theorists and activists who seek to expand democracy both within the polity as well as to the larger society. Pateman and Barber, for example, incorporate Millian arguments in their cases for extensive democratization. Millian participation is said to enlarge the social self, expand tolerance and respect for other members of the group, educate agents about the importance of cooperation, reduce hierarchy and subordination, foster equality, and enhance the participants' sense of their own personal dignity and their contribution to their group.

39. Mill writes, "Associations . . . by the very process of their success, are a course of education in those moral and active qualities by which alone success can be either deserved or attained. As associations multiplied, they would tend more and more to absorb all work-people, except those who have too little understanding, or too little virtue, to be capable of learning to act on any other system than that of narrow selfishness" (*Political Economy*, vol. 3, 793). Also see his laudatory comments in his *Autobiography* on civic participation "in the smaller commonwealths of antiquity" (vol. 1, 241). For an extended discussion of participatory Athens, see his review of Grote's *History of Greece* (vol. 11).

40. See Pateman, *Participation and Democratic Theory*, and Dennis

Thompson, *Representative Government* (Princeton: Princeton University Press, 1976).

41. Mill holds that the advantages of representative government are that it "most widely diffuses the exercise of public functions . . . by excluding fewest from the suffrage," and opens "to all classes of private citizens, so far as is consistent with other equally important objects, . . . participation in the details of judicial and administrative business, as by jury trial, admission to municipal offices, and above all by the utmost possible publicity and liberty of discussion" (*Representative Government*, vol. 19, 436). Jury duty and participation in municipal administration are local undertakings while voting and political discourse are appropriate for both local and national politics. See *On Liberty* for Mill's discussion of "varied experiments" in voluntary associations (vol. 18, 306).

42. Although she would not agree with Mill's restrictions on the legislature, Jane Mansbridge, *Beyond Adversary Democracy* (Chicago: University of Chicago Press, 1983), shares his caution and realism about the limits of participatory democracy. Also see Robert Dahl, *Dilemmas of Pluralist Democracy* (New Haven: Yale University Press, 1982) and *Democracy and Its Critics* (New Haven: Yale University Press, 1989). Dahl emphasizes workplace democracy but does not link it to national politics.

43. See Alfonso Damico, "The Democratic Consequences of Liberalism," in *Liberals on Liberalism* edited by Alfonso Damico (Totowa, N. J.: Rowman and Littlefield, 1988), 167–84.

44. Gertrude Himmelfarb sees two Mills (*On Liberty and Liberalism* [New York: Knopf, 1974], xix), a committed liberal who is "confident and unequivocal" in his support of liberty and a writer who is "questioning and ambivalent" about tradition; John Gray (*Liberalisms* [London: Routledge, 1989]) finds Mill is a multiple liberal who is confused; and when Stewart Justman (*The Hidden Text of Mill's Liberty* [Savage: Rowman and Littlefield, 1991]) looks at Mill, he sees a secret, muddled republican.

45. Some revisionists delight in showing that Mill argues that people who are on the dole should not have the franchise because they have lost their "self-dependency." It seems somewhat ingenuous to attribute a late–twentieth-century view of welfare policy to the cannon of all liberalism, regardless of time and place. Like almost everyone else in his generation, Mill is tied to the view that self-dependency rested, *in part*, on individual work.

46. See *Liberty*, vol. 18, 300, 302.

47. *Liberty*, vol. 18, 295.

48. Mill's use of shame to change attitudes also appears to be a republican solution because it requires strong community standards (which is said to be contrary to liberalism) to work. For Mill, it is natural and appropriate that people should both be offended by certain kinds of acts and want to avoid the derision of their fellows. Believing that people of his generation avoid criticizing each other because such moves are personally unsettling and have replaced politeness and civility for judgment, Mill holds there is a pressing task to reintroduce shame. Although shame has a central place in strong re-

publicanism, a liberal such as Mill wants individuals to develop both a sense of guilt, as Locke also wants, to act as an internal monitor, and a sense of shame to act as an external impetus to move people away from a life dedicated to satisfying the lower pleasures.

49. *Liberty*, vol. 18, 390.

50. *Utilitarianism*, vol. 10, part 3, 399–412.

51. *Hidden Text*, 114.

52. Mill holds that "it is natural and inevitable that in every age a certain portion of our recorded and traditional knowledge, not being continually suggested by the pursuits and inquiries with which mankind are at the time engrossed, should fall asleep, as it were, and fade from memory" and he wants to renew such "traditional knowledge" (*Logic* in *Collected Works* [Toronto: University of Toronto Press, 1974], vol. 8, 681–88).

53. Mill spent much of his working life as an administrator with the East India Company where he held mixed views on Indian civilization. Reflecting the dominant view in England at the time, he thought the British could introduce improvement and progress. However, as Lynn Zastoupil shows, Mill departs from his superiors on several occasions, arguing that Indians should retain most of their own practices because they make sense to Indians even though British officials in India find them inadequate or offensive ("J. S. Mill and India." *Victorian Studies* 32 [1988]: 31–54).

54. *De Tocqueville on Democracy in America* [2], vol. 18, 178–79.

Chapter Six

Interest-Group Liberals and Libertarians: The Critique of Adam Smith

Smith readily qualifies as an anxious liberal. Along with Locke and Mill, he prizes freedom and worries about it, finding its emancipatory qualities rest on fragile foundations that are subject to decay. For Smith, there is nothing about freedom that assures its wise and prudential use. On the contrary, he sees free societies crowded with temptations that, if pursued, invite the unhappiness of free men and women. With other anxious liberals, he promotes freedom as well as the moral development of agents and sounds both a celebration and a warning about liberty. Preoccupied with the deceptions he sees following men and women, whether in a free society or a despotic one, Smith seeks to make space for the expression of the moral sentiments. Moreover, he argues that although the rise of commerce introduces freedom, it provides no guarantee of a happy, moral life.

In addition to his anxious liberalism, Smith offers highly influential theories of economic markets and the emancipatory properties he assigns to them. For this reason, he is an important source for those who find liberal democratic politics explained best by political markets as well as for those who seek to reign in the modern state and protect negative liberty. In this chapter, I work with Smith's anxious liberalism and his theories of economic markets to enlist him in a debate with libertarians and interest-group liberals who rely on fragments of his work to understand democratic politics today.

Interest-Group Liberals

Interest-group liberalism presents itself as both an empirical and normative theory of modern liberal democracy.[1] It employs Smithian metaphors to conclude that citizens, groups and leaders are self-interested political maximizers who are instrumentally rational.[2] Interest-group liberals, ranging from pluralists to economists to rational-choice theorists, work with the argument that democratic politics has largely become secularized and demythologized.[3] Interest-group liberals go on to argue that the basic materials of democratic politics are not persons but organized groups. Bentley, for example, finds that the "individual stated for himself . . . is a fiction." To look at an individual is "of trifling importance in interpreting society." It is the group that "is essential, first, last, and all the time."[4] The political competition interest-group liberals detect in democratic politics follows from their reading of a society that is relatively open, nonhierarchical, and competitive.[5]

Sometimes interest-group liberals focus on the aspirations of political leaders competing for votes[6] and sometimes the model features organized groups competing about public policy.[7] In market models of democratic politics, interest groups compete for advantages for their members, and citizens judge their leaders not by some standard of the general good but by whether their interests are satisfied. The process of bargaining and mutual accommodation in political markets is said to lead to an equilibrium of power and benefits until successfully challenged by a new coalition of interest groups, which reconstitute the equilibrium to reflect its power and interests.[8] In this literature, economic maximizers and interest-bearing voters become analytically indistinguishable from each other.[9] In these accounts, Smith seems a worthy parent of both.[10]

Transporting an economic market analysis to democratic politics is appealing in many ways. Both share common vocabularies, focus on competition, are thought to be open, house numerous interests, and are characterized by bargaining. Particularly at a time when no substantive common good seems to characterize the democratic polity, models that account for a plurality of understandings of the good and that recognize a variety of preferences seem to capture reality.[11] However, interest-group liberals who rely on Smithian metaphors or assumptions about rationality and economic markets omit critical parts of Smith's theory and, in the process, give us not merely an incomplete Smith but also a distorted Smith. As much as he emphasizes the importance of interests in explaining market behavior, Smith clearly wants to limit the pull of interests outside economic markets. And as much as he thinks instrumental rationality leads to optimizing private advantage in markets, he relies on the moral sentiments to explain ideal behavior in noneconomic social relations. Moreover, even though Smith believes that the pursuit of self-interests in economic markets generates social benefits, he warns that such interests are too often driven by deceits that serve our vanities and lead to our own unhappiness.[12] If this is so, interest-group liberalism has less to recommend it than we might have previously suspected.

Libertarian Debts

Libertarianism has come to mean support for a highly limited state, an unobstructed market, and negative liberty. Although a purist position would give the state little permission to act, a view advanced by Robert Nozick,[13] many supporters of the negative state, open markets, and a protective view of traditional rights cluster around the kind of position advanced by Friedrich Hayek, who rejects Nozick's minimal state.[14] In this section, I use Hayek to represent a modified libertarian view because he has elaborated a coherent, comprehensive argument since the Second World War. Hayek has advanced the claim that the good society is based on a spontaneous order where the domain of negative liberty is extensive, the market robust, and the walls separating civil society from the state are thick and high. Hayek's modified libertarianism is reflected in his consistent attack on the welfare state, which he finds takes us down the road to serfdom, his stress on individual over social ends, his assault on interest-group politics, his argument that democratic majorities are unrestrained,[15] and his celebration of a competitive economy.

Hayek often approvingly refers to Mill, and, to a lesser extent, Locke, but his major debt is to Smith.[16] There is the obvious affinity to Smithian markets and a limited state, but more important to Hayek's argument, Smith is the forerunner of the literature on liberty.[17] He finds that Smithian markets give rise to a "spontaneous order" that replaces the "artificial rules" that had been earlier imposed by powerful individuals or groups and stifled liberty. Hayek's liberalism

> derives from the discovery of a self-generating or spontaneous order in social affairs. . . . The central concept of liberalism is that under the enforcement of universal rules of just conduct, protecting a recognizable private domain of individuals, a spontaneous order of human activities of much greater complexity will form itself.[18]

Hayek offers rules of just conduct, which include a commitment to the free market and to negative liberty, and he finds efforts to undermine or regulate them dangerous. Fearing modern voters have lost a sense of limits and moderation, he sees them relying on a short-term political instrumentalism to guide them in their search for private benefits exacted from the rest of society.[19] To counter these modern trends, Hayek asks us to return to a stable or slowly evolving tradition of settled law to restrain voters and move them away from instrumental rationality.[20] The traditions, conventions, and mores of society are "learnt rules of conduct which have not been 'invented' and whose functions the acting individuals usually do not understand."[21] For Hayek, these disciplinary rules once protected liberty, but over time we encounter a new "process of winnowing and shifting" that undermines self-restraint.[22] Even though Hayek's view of tradition relies heavily on self-restraint, he is no compatriot of traditionalists who blindly grasp ancient practices because of their age, even when it restrains liberty.

In the past few years, several political theorists have moved beyond concentrating on Adam Smith's economic theories and libertarian fragments. These theorists describe a noninstrumental Adam Smith concerned not only with markets and freedom but also with a moral life. This chapter builds on their scholarship, and I show why Smith is suspicious of interests, why Smithian politics cannot be market politics, and how market politics undermines his view of the good life for free men and women in the commercial republic. To do this, I turn to Smith's anxious liberalism to explain why interest-group liberalism and libertarian theories must be unfaithful to his moral project.

Adam Smith's Secular and Moral Agents

The prominence Smith gives to self-interest is widely known. In both *The Wealth of Nations* and *The Theory of Moral Sentiments*, he repeatedly argues that people have an interest in their own well-being and that they engage in activities that they think will promote it. He tells us, in a variety of ways, that "every man, therefore, is much more deeply interested in whatever immediately concerns himself than in what concerns any other man."[23] Even though we are primarily concerned about our happiness, Smith believes we often fail to achieve it because we deceive ourselves about what constitutes happiness. In his account, we are most happy when we are tranquil in body and mind.

In addition to self-interests, Smith credits people with carrying moral sentiments.[24] He sees our moral judgments coming from our internal capacities of "sense and feeling" which are the "natural sentiments of all mankind."[25] Rejecting Locke's claim that human beings come into the world with minds that are empty cabinets ready to be filled, Smith claims we come with natural endowments that enable us to make elementary moral judgments, to rejoice with the happiness of others, and to grieve at their misfortune. Smith's sentiments "superintend" our passions and desires and prompt us to be attentive to others. In this way, Smith challenges Hobbes's claim that we are ruled by our desires and passions and holds that we have internal principles to move us beyond our vanities. "How selfish soever man may be supposed, there are evidently some principles in his nature, which interest him in the fortune of others, and render their happiness necessary to him, though he derives nothing from it, except the pleasure of seeing it."[26]

Smithian sentiments lead us to create social bonds with others and to do this we must first dampen our ego.[27] According to Smith, our initial moral socialization is prompted by our desire to win the approval of others: "Nature, when she formed man for society, endowed him with an original desire to please, and an original aversion to offend his brethren."[28] Refuting some of their self-interested passions, Smithian agents become accepted in their society by learning its standards of good and evil, beauty and deformity.[29] For Smith, this minimal normative internalization is almost automatic.[30] However, it can lead merely to the outward appearance of accepting social standards while internally rejecting them. Smith claims that this is not what generally happens; few people wait for the opportunity to break standards when no one is looking. Not only would such a person be morally unreliable, but also the person would be unhappy. For Smith,

> Nature, accordingly, has endowed him not only with a desire of being approved of, but with a desire of being what ought to be approved of. . . . The first desire could only have made him wish to appear to be fit for society. The second was necessary in order to render him anxious to be really fit. The first could only have prompted him to the affectation of virtue, and to the concealment of vice. The second was necessary in order to inspire him with the real love of virtue and with the real abhorrence of vice. In every well-formed mind this second desire seems to be the strongest of the two.[31]

Smith realizes that when people are concerned only with how their conduct is judged by observers, they repress any semblance of an honest self, and we should expect to encounter apprehensive, vulnerable human beings who have no inner core. Smith, however, thinks that our deeply internalized standards of fairness and justice generally harmonize with our moral sentiments.[32] We not only want to appear to be good but actually to be good, not only "to be loved but to be lovely."[33] Acknowledging that vanity is sometimes more potent than the moral sentiments, Smith wants to show that self-interests can, nevertheless, be tamed. It turns out that some settings are much more conducive to the expression of the sentiments than others and some institutional practices lessen the tug of self-referential considerations more than others.

Natural Rights and Acquired Rights

According to Smith's principles of natural jurisprudence, law fulfills its highest purpose when it safeguards "natural rights." He holds that everyone has the "right . . . to the free use of his person and in a word to do what he has a mind to when it does not prove detrimental to any other person."[34] In this sense, Smith's understanding of natural rights embodies the principles of negative liberty and is violated by self-serving intentional acts that harm others. He argues, "To hurt in any degree the interest of any one order of citizens, for no other purpose than to promote that of some other, is evidently contrary to that justice and equality of treatment which the sovereign owes to all . . . of his subjects."[35] Injury can occur when an agent's physical person is violated or when someone is deprived of such rights as "the right to free commerce and the right to freedom in marriage."

When Smith identifies basic natural rights, he does not include property rights as one of them.[36] To be sure, he argues that the product of a person's labor naturally belongs to the laborer, but he does not make a blanket justification for all private property as a natural right and never claims that mere personal possession of property provides a valid title under the rules of natural jurisprudence.[37] Some forms of private property are simply contrary to the rules of natural jurisprudence, such as property in slaves in a slave-owning society.[38] Smith also holds that certain forms of property are best held in common, "must continue common by the rules of equity," and ought not be converted into private property.[39]

What kind of a right is a property right? Holding that some forms of private property are simply antithetical to natural jurisprudence, such as private property that is unearned and unrelated to the owner's labor, Smith finds that property historically requires its own special justification as a right.[40] For the most part, he sees it as an "acquired" rather than a natural right.[41]

> The origin of natural rights is quite evident. That a person has a right to have his body free from injury, and his liberty free from infringement unless there be a proper cause, no body doubts. But acquired rights such as property require more explanation. Property and civil government very much depend on one another. The preservation of property and inequality of possession first formed it, and the state of property must always vary with the form of government.[42]

Property, ideally obtained through a person's honest labor, is also often acquired by guile, force, tricks or interference with the labor of others. However obtained, those with property desire to protect it and call on government to give blanket protections to their property, covering both morally defensible and indefensible claims.[43] Given his penchant for order and security, Smith is willing to accept various forms of property, but he never attempts to legitimize those that rest on suspect grounds, hoping that over time, the market will favor property based on individual labor and dismantle other forms of property.

The Origins of Government

His argument about a society without government sounds Hobbesian; for Smith, "civil society would become a scene of bloodshed and disorder, every man revenging himself at his own hand whenever he fancied he was injured."[44] While neither Smith nor Hobbes hold that people are inherently aggressive, cruel, or disorderly, Smith parts company from Hobbes's argument that the psychological states or desires of diverse people in the context of perfect freedom and equality lead to inevitable conflict. Smith's reasoning about social conflict and a consequent need for government resembles Locke's. The critical factor that Smith believes introduces intense conflict is private, fixed property because it expands and intensifies the natural inclination of people to look after their own interests.

In the earliest stage of history where the meager possessions of the hunters and gatherers never "exceeds the value of two or three days labor," Smith finds no need for government. "Men who have no property can injure one another only in persons or reputations." But Smith does not think these latter injuries pose a serious threat in the earliest stage of history; even murder is not seen as a problem because murderers would receive "no benefit." In this early period, "men may live together in society with some tolerable degree of security, though there is no civil magistrate to protect them from the injustice of those passions."[45]

Fixed property, "the grand fund of all disputes," changes all of this.[46]

Desires are altered and people want more than can be possessed and consumed in a few days time. With the advent of fixed property, Smith imagines people now find that they can benefit from hurting others. The "avarice and ambition in the rich, in the poor the hatred of labour and the love of present ease and enjoyment are the passions that prompt to invade property." Smith reasons that because the "affluence of the rich supposes the indigence of the many," a volatile brew of resentment and greed pervades society and suspicion and insecurity are the patterns of everyday life. Like the wealthy in Rousseau's late state of nature,[47] Smith's property owner

> is at all times surrounded by unknown enemies, whom, though he never provoked, he can never appease, and from whose injustice he can be protected only by the powerful arms of civil magistrate continually held up to chastise it. The acquisition of valuable and extensive property, therefore, necessarily requires the establishment of civil government.[48]

Smith sees government arising not out of some inherent human need or defect but to protect private, fixed property, which disables the harmony and tranquillity that come when individuals live and work within their natural limits. The government Smith imagines is not neutral. With property comes government and with government comes "subordination . . . which naturally . . . [gives] some men some superiority over the greater part of their number."[49] What began as economic inequality expands to political inequality with government justifying the acquired rights of those with great wealth.

If it were not for fixed, private property, we would have no need for government. For Smith, government arises not to protect natural rights or the market but to protect the acquired rights of the powerful. What describes the origins of government historically repeats itself until challenged by commerce. Like his near-contemporary Rousseau, Smith finds government is originally designed to protect the wealthy few from the impoverished many and enforces undeserved inequalities and subordination.[50] But the parallels with Rousseau soon fade, and Smith leads us to claims about the emancipatory power of markets to destroy the dependencies marring human history. There is a paradox to Smith's account of the origins of government when read through libertarian lenses: the government libertarians fear because it can undermine negative liberty would never have arrived if there were no fixed property. In Smith's writings, we find that in the earliest societies, people are all equal, labor only for themselves, can satisfy their daily needs, and require no government. From Smith's perspective, when government emerges, it is likely to favor existing forms of property, even if undeserved and at the expense of the natural rights of others.

Dependence and Independence

Smith finds that when one person or a few people hold the preponderance of power and wealth in society, they can be counted on to use these goods to serve their interests, not the interests of those dependent on them for a living and security. Smith repeatedly argues that when wealth and power are combined, the greatest social cost comes from the loss of independence of those who are excluded. This can be seen in the case of the Tartar chief who creates dependencies that serve his own good, and his subordinates feel compelled to act at his behest.[51] He directs, because he defines, their interests in ways they would not have necessarily chosen for themselves. Meeting the interests of the Tartar chief becomes their interest. They obey him because they believe that it is in their interest to do so. When subordinates please the Tartar chief, they safeguard whatever rights they have acquired from the chief.

Smith reasons that because people are concerned about their own welfare, when they are confronted with the choice between their wellbeing and security and a principled stand, they ordinarily choose the former, usually without thinking about it. For this reason, he holds "Nothing tends so much to corrupt and enervate and debase the mind as dependency, and nothing gives such noble and generous notions of probity and freedom as independency."[52]

It turns out that historically, most people in most societies have been dependent on others or found themselves in positions where their choices were highly constricted. The way we make a living, the vulnerabilities that follow us, the opportunities that await us, the acquired rights we enjoy, and the responsibilities assigned to us are, in Smith's view, contingencies we have not always chosen for ourselves, and not just in precommercial societies. This can be seen in his comparison of the philosopher and the street porter. For Smith, each of them has roughly the same capacities and talents until about the age of six when their very different contingent attributes make a profound difference. One becomes learned and respected, the other remains unlettered and neglected. Who is who is not explained by the superior virtue, wisdom, or abilities of the former over the latter but by the enabling and disabling attributes attached to each.[53]

Because people are deeply embedded in their social location, Smith thinks they frequently identify some of their attributes for their "real" selves. They seek to protect their livelihood as well as safeguard their acquired rights. He frequently talks about serfs in feudal society, workers in modern industry, and women in any society. Who they are, in substantial measure, follows from their contingent properties as serfs, workers or women. The fact that some people are serfs, workers, or women does not determine everything about them: they may be virtuous or vicious, and, Smith holds, these qualities are independent of a person's background.[54] However, the social location of serfs, workers, or women in the institutional arrangements of their society profoundly influences the way they understand themselves, what is important to them, what is expected of them, and what they think they deserve. Their contingent attributes delineate their interests and opportunities not only in the broad sense that they cannot do what barons, employers, or men do, but in two other critical ways as well. In order to protect themselves, Smith thinks they often suppress the honest, open expression of their moral sentiments when they think it will hurt them in their assigned positions. Second, they accept the many layers of deceptions housed in their society that legitimize their subordination and dependency.

The distorting effects Smith attaches to dependency can be seen in his historical account of why the Reformation occurred when it did. As he understands it, the peasants had long known that the Catholic Church was corrupt, but their interests held their moral sense in check. The vast property holdings of the Church along with its hospitality and charity made the peasants dependent on the clergy and interested in pleasing them. However, these dependencies were severed when the clergy sold much of its land and suspended its public charities in its quest for luxury. Only when they were no longer dependent on the clergy, Smith argues, were the peasants free to rebel and honestly follow their moral sentiments.[55] The peasants, like other people, changed because their situation changed; interests that once seemed central to their well-being become superfluous or even obstacles to what now is important to them.[56] Equipped with new understandings of themselves and their rights, Smith's feudal peasants reorder their interests, are free for the first time to express their sincere religious beliefs, and rebel.

Smith's account of the peasant's reluctance to challenge the Church is not a critique of the inherent weakness of people but rather of the importance of distributions of power and wealth. He takes their behavior to demonstrate how institutional arrangements can create heavy penalties or open promising opportunities for the honest expression of the sentiments. He is optimistic about his own times, in part because he sees a growing independence that greatly reduces the risks of honestly expressing our commitments and thereby enhances our moral autonomy. However, Smith never holds a utopian view that the best social and economic conditions produce painless choices. He understands that morally difficult situations continually confront men and women if for no other reason than they often deceive themselves about the nature of their happiness and allow their vanity to smother their sentiments. But this is a much different problem than that created by dependencies where honesty is routinely penalized.

Smith also finds that dependencies exist in a perverse way when there is acute scarcity and insecurity. Imagining life during the earliest historical period, Smith finds every small community faces constant dangers from others who seek its meager resources. Its members depend on the cooperation, bravery, and self-discipline of one another for their mutual protection. In the process, they repress their own individual feelings. Dependency makes honest choices difficult as people are forced to choose between their own survival and their moral sentiments. As Smith sees it, security and prosperity change this and offer us the opportunity to define our interests in new ways and express our moral sentiments honestly, without fear of reprisal.

The importance Smith credits to the disabling effects of constant danger and acute economic scarcities emerges in his account of "savage" societies. In his account, pervasive insecurities and scarcities require a strict self-discipline in order to maintain the survival of the group. For Smith's "savages," pain is a constant companion that is borne silently. Control over their bodies and emotions are standards that he imagines "savages" learn from their earliest experiences because that is what is honored and honorable in societies of pervasive scarcity and insecurity. Smith's "savage"

> is inured to every sort of hardship. He is in continual danger: he is often exposed to the greatest extremities of hunger, and frequently dies of pure want. His circumstances not only habituate him to every sort of distress but teach him to give way to none of the passions which that distress is apt to excite. He can expect from his countrymen no sympathy or indulgence for such weakness. Before we can feel much for others, we must in some measure be at ease ourselves. If our own misery pinches us very severely, we have no leisure to attend to that of our neighbor: and all savages are too much occupied with their own wants and necessities to give much attention to those of another person. A savage, therefore, whatever be the nature of his distress, expects no

sympathy from those about him, and disdains upon that account to expose himself, by allowing the least weakness to escape him.[57]

Smith sees the dishonesty of the "savage" as something that is not volitional but institutionally required. Where danger and poverty are constant companions, people do not feel free to express their own pains and agony or sympathize with the suffering of their fellows. To cry out is to humiliate oneself and earn the contempt of one's fellows who see weak, self-regarding persons endangering the safety of the entire community. For this reason, Smith thinks "savages," "being obliged to smother and conceal the appearance of every passion, necessarily acquire the habits of falsehood and dissimulation."[58]

When people are preoccupied with physical existence, Smith argues, they do not think of others. Even when they come to marry, partners are not drawn together by love or intimacy but by the prospects that their union will enhance their physical protection. Hence, Smith's "savages," surrounded by danger and scarcity, may be hardy and courageous but are not generous to others or honest to their moral sentiments.[59] One of the great benefits Smith attributes to commerce is its promise that scarcities that previously spawned a thick dependency on the group for security will be eliminated. For this reason, efforts to emphasize that Smith prizes commerce to dismantle the supervisory state captures only a part of his argument. He also insists that people must escape the dependencies created by acute scarcity and insecurity if they are to be autonomous. Smith plays no favorites in criticizing dependencies: whether it is an oppressive government or acute scarcity and insecurity, each form subverts autonomy, none can be exonerated, and all restrict the honest expression of the sentiments.

Smith is troubled by dependencies because they rob people of choice. To act contrary to standards defined by dependency relations is to risk one's maintenance and security. In this sense, dependency relations serve to integrate people into their particular social status because that is what protects them at the time. It would be incorrect, from Smith's perspective, to complain that people are deceived about their "real" interests within dependency situations. In their current situation, people are not deceived about what will immediately help or hurt them. They attempt to preserve what they believe is in their best interests, given the opportunities and constraints of the situation in which they find themselves at that time.

Smith also emphasizes that those who have become dependent rationalize their status: in accepting conventional relationships as legitimate and in deferring to wealth and status as appropriate justifications for inequality, individuals implicate themselves in their own situation. We all care about our well-being, and we all have interests in maintaining what we possess. Smith posits that because we are risk averse, our conservatism clouds our vision about what we are due and brings us to accept our own subordination.

With the elimination of dependency relations, Smith detects both new opportunities and dangers. The dismantling of many of the historic restrictions that hindered choice frees individuals to act on their own understanding of what will make them happy, and they, not some superior, are responsible for deciding what is best for them. From Smith's perspective, commercial society is said to approach the standards of natural jurisprudence better than earlier political arrangements, although he does not take this to mean it embodies perfect justice. However, there is always the possibility that people will squander their freedom on choices that are driven by self-deceptions and illusive goals.[60]

Interests and Markets

Interests need homes, and economic markets provide appropriate ones for Smith. Why he thinks markets, not politics, make a perfect setting for interests reveals the role of interests in his broader theory. For Smith, people naturally want to better their current situation. When he tells us that it is natural for people to barter and truck, he assumes that most people are continually restless with their present situation and desire to improve it. We trade when we think we will be better off because of the trade, but that is not what we tell the other party. When we try to interest someone to trade with us, "we address ourselves, not to their humanity but to their self-love, and never talk to them of our own necessities but of their advantages."[61]

One of the great advantages Smith attributes to the introduction of market transactions in the late feudal period is that it dismantles concentrated wealth and power and thereby widens the domain of freedom for more people. The rich and powerful release their hold on those below them and surrender their advantages when their interests change; and their interests change because of extrinsic factors, particularly the growth of commerce.[62] For Smith, it is commerce, not the virtue or generosity of the powerful, that frees men and women and opens new opportunities to the honest expression of their sentiments because commerce ruptures the connection between economic wealth and political power.

There is another characteristic Smith assigns to markets. He believes that unlike other forms of social relations, perfect markets discipline interests through the law of supply and demand. As much as merchants might want to raise their prices and thus increase their profits at the cost to the consumer, they must always be concerned about their competitors in a free market. The merchant's interests are not served by raising prices and losing customers to competitors.[63] The preferences of the merchant for high prices and easy profits have to give way to Smith's invisible hand, which, through the law of supply and demand, guides the merchant to make instrumental decisions about what will work in the market. In Smith's theory, market prices reflect the activities of countless participants with no single party dominating because of the disciplinary properties of the invisible hand. Whether economic markets work the way Smith thinks is not the issue I want to pursue here. He believes that he has discovered the proper venue for self-interests in economic markets where they can be disciplined by impersonal forces.

In considering the issue of self-interests, Smith makes a well-known argument for independent, unobstructed action in economic markets, holding that the state ought not to interfere with the lives of citizens except for compelling reasons. But he does not hold that what is appropriate for economic markets can be transported to politics. In Smith's economic market, a just price is determined by the law of supply and demand, something that flows from each participant, regardless of his or her capital resources. Outside of economic markets, Smith sees differences in resources counting for very much and detects no internal, impersonal mechanism disciplining those with more resources. He fears that in politics, the stronger side prevails. Introducing more participants does not necessarily change this. With more citizens active, we find that power and interest recombine, not as the replica of the old Tartar chief but as strategic winning coalitions that distinguish new winners from losers.

For Smith, instrumental rationality, so decisive in economic exchanges, is often self-defeating elsewhere, and he wants to quarantine it to economic markets.[64] In his rendition of early human history, shepherds give up their liberty in order to attend their flocks. They focus on the short-term benefits of these economic choices because their reason is too fragile and limited to forewarn them of the consequences of instrumental advantages. Many commentators use his argument about the fragile nature of knowledge and inherent inability to control outcomes in complex situations to warn against the positive state.[65] What also needs to be noticed is that Smith employs this same argument to caution individuals not to roam beyond their own limited capacities and to rely on their instrumental reason to control events they think will rebound to their happiness.

Moreover, market activities, as secular activities, carry no theory of citizenship and require no special virtues except those related to prudence and perseverance. Economic behavior is driven by interests and directed by instrumental rationality, but Smith expects more from politics, as his discussion of justice and natural rights indicates, even if it does not lead him to embrace a positive state. Though he hardly offers a robust theory of citizenship, he nevertheless wants people to carry a respect for their constitutional regime, a much different orientation than he finds in economic markets where, he argues, merchants have no country.[66] Smith also holds that if the bargaining that characterizes markets enters politics, participants will behave instrumentally and, to repeat his appraisal of motivation and behavior in bargaining, appeal "not to their humanity but to their self-love."[67] But more than that, the discipline Smith requires in economic markets to assure a just price is simply unavailable in political markets where there is no invisible hand but only power to sort out contending interests.[68]

The Deception of Wealth

Smith assumes the moral equality of everyone, and he also believes that everyone has the same capacity to become happy, whether king or beggar, rich or poor. But most people are not content to accept the lot of the beggar or the poor and believe that more personal wealth and power will bring them happiness. This is one of history's great and continuing deceptions, one that Smith believes powerfully competes with the moral sentiments which call on us to be concerned about others. For Smith, this deception is neither class selective nor historically bound. Both the powerful and the poor are liable to the deception that wealth brings happiness and often act in ways that thwart their desire to become contented. I do not mean to argue that there is a hidden text in Smith that opposes wealth. Smith sees wealth giving us the ability to make choices to do things we could not have made without it. However, he finds wealth becomes dangerous to us when we allow it to define our character.

Economists have commonly emphasized the unintended benefits Smith sees coming to strangers who become free when the rich and powerful deceive themselves about their own self interests.[69] Here, I want to follow his argument about the ways ambitious people hurt themselves with their deceptions in the commercial republic as well as feudal society. Smith's positive accounts of economic success emphasize individuals who marginally improve and do not make quantum jumps in fortune or rank. When Smith introduces us to those who have earned vast fortunes, such as the poor man's son who has worked arduously and accumulated great wealth, we encounter people who find that tranquillity has eluded them.[70] The lesson Smith wants us to draw from these stories is that there are limits to the happiness that economic advancement can promote. By his telling, to move too far too fast carries a moral and psychological price for the successful whose lives are barren except for their insecurity and anxiety.[71] Like the poor man's son who rises too high, too quickly, they find their "wealth and greatness are mere trinkets of frivolous utility, no more adapted for procuring ease of body or tranquility of mind, than the Tweezer-cases of the lover of toys."[72] When vanity is coupled with the deception that wealth will make us happy, people are snared into thinking that they can control their destiny and future happiness through their own labors and the wealth and power they acquire. In pursuing their ambition, they write a set of rules for themselves that turns out to deprive them of the very happiness they so desperately covet.

Smith's explanation of the collapse of feudalism pivots around his premise that the feudal barons deceive themselves into thinking that the pursuit of luxury will make them happy. To raise money for consumption, they sell their lands and unwittingly make their tenants independent of them. Displaying a consummate misunderstanding of their interests, they unwittingly squander "their birth-right," ignore "the serious pursuits of men," and undermine their power in their search for luxury.[73] Smith clearly welcomes the deception of the feudal barons because it stimulates trade and dismantles existing dependencies. But he also uses the feudal barons to serve as a cautionary tale about people overreaching their natural limits.

The barons are not the only ones Smith sees deceiving themselves about wealth. Usually seen as a champion of increasing national income, Smith nevertheless fears that when national wealth passes a critical point and luxury becomes widespread, the consequences are usually disastrous. In many ways paralleling the strong republican warning about the paradox of abundance, Smith fears that during prosperous times, individuals lose a sense of their limits and refuse to do what is necessary to retain their freedom. He develops this theme in his discussion of the fall of Rome where he sees affluence undermining the sense of civic duty that previously secured the freedom of its citizens. When wealth becomes their preoccupation, the Romans neglect to attend to the basis of their prosperity and liberty, namely their readiness to defend themselves. With growing "domestic luxury," the Romans

> become less fond of going out to war, and besides the government finds that it would hurt its revenue to send out those employed in manufacture. If barbarous nations be in the neighborhood, they can employ them as soldiers at an easier rate, and at the same time not hurt their own industry. . . . The barbarous chieftain, at the head of his own men, possessed the whole military authority of the people for whom he fought, and whenever the government in the least offended him, he could turn his arms against those who employed him, and make himself master of their country.[74]

Smith does not use this and similar passages to call for a return to civic virtue but to warn that prosperity leads people individually and collectively to deceive themselves about what is really important to their happiness in the long run.[75] In pressing their own immediate interests, they do not secure their long-term welfare but rather buy a little time for their current enjoyment only, in the end, to become dependent on those who care little about them. What is arresting in Smith's argument is his concern over how excessive individualism undermines itself. His own famous celebration of individualism is bounded and cautious, and he warns about personal and social costs when moderation and prudence are ignored. Even though Smith believes that the commercial republic repeals many of the civic requirements of earlier regimes, he holds that self-restraint remains necessary for people who wish to retain their freedom.

Internalizing Limits: The Deception of Deference

Running parallel to the deception that wealth brings happiness is the deception of deference, namely that those who possess great wealth and honor deserve our admiration and respect as well as their extraordinary prizes which, Smith believes, are beyond the reach of ordinary people.[76] We are deferential because we believe the rich and famous possess something we think meritorious and we honor them, even blindly, for their success, accepting the current pattern of inequalities of wealth and power without question or hesitation. According to Smith, the deception of deference "of mankind to go along with all the passions of the rich and the powerful, is founded on the distinction of ranks and the order of society."[77] For him, this deception is "the great and most universal cause of the corruption of our moral sentiments." The deception of deference is so strong in Smith's account that people fail to use rational standards when they assign legitimacy to their regime or react to all but the most flagrant abuses of power. When we are deferential, we excuse our "superiors," even when our moral sense would direct otherwise. Standing in awe of wealth and power, we not only ignore the wise and virtuous, but we also despise and "neglect persons of poor and mean condition."[78]

As with many topics he treats, Smith finds the deception of deference carries mixed moral consequences. It turns us away from concern for the most disadvantaged and vulnerable and thereby subverts the expression of our moral sentiments. At the same time, he thinks it constrains a dangerous and expansive ambition in us which, if expressed, would bring unhappiness to the agent and instability to society. In this sense, Smithian deference moderates politics and serves as a gatekeeper, limiting the issues and interests that appear in politics.

Accepting the proposition that what the rich and famous possess is not likely to be within our reach, ordinary people are spared embarking on a barren journey filled with disappointments and avoiding a life of perpetual envy and resentment.[79] By deferring to the rich and powerful, we tacitly accept gross political and economic inequalities. In breaking the force of envy, deference invites us to work within our present condition, satisfied with incremental advancements rather than striving to reach the rarefied heights where the rich and famous live. Moreover, Smith finds that deference contributes to the legitimization of a regime, its practices, and the inequalities it protects and exonerates.[80]

From Smith's perspective, deference is built on a deception, there being nothing natural, justifiable, or convincingly explicable to account for the great inequalities that mark different people in society. But he believes people come to accept these distributions; credit them with being natural, justifiable, and explicable; and accept their own "subordination" without question. In this way, Smithian politics rests on a nonrational foundation to moderate interests, explain disappointments, and promote self-restraint. This heavy reliance on the mythological can be traced to his view that much that we find in the world, including social and economic inequalities and political subordination, is inexplicable and, like Smith's stoic, we would be better off accepting our situation. When we roam away from the mythical, Smith wants it to be to economic markets, but even there, we are at the mercy of an inexplicable, invisible hand.

The Dangers of a Demythologized Politics

Smith simultaneously expects the continued expansion of economic markets alongside a relatively stable mode of politics and regime.[81] For him, the great institutional transformations introduced by economic markets that overturned the old feudal order have spent themselves, and radically new institutional changes are no longer necessary to Smith's project.[82] Indeed, drastic social changes are harmful because they threaten to weaken deference and erode the legitimacy of the regime. The changes that Smith welcomes concern the steady extension of the market to include more and more people who, he believes, will not only become independent but economically secure as well.[83]

The danger in Smith's commercial society does not come from a revolutionary class consciousness but from something mundane, that is, people using their instrumental rationality to judge politics. When interests and instrumental rationality direct popular government, politics is demythologized and secularized, something that Smith believes is happening among the merchants of his generation who, in their search for profits, no longer have a home in their own country and who use politics for their personal gain. He alerts his fellow citizens not only to the dangers that merchants pose but also to the dangers of instrumental politics. Should self-interested calculations so central to economic markets inundate politics, Smith fears that the foundations of legitimacy will be seriously disturbed and not apt to be replaced by something more solid and stable.[84] Moreover, he does not expect that a politics based on new interests will necessarily correspond any better to the principles of natural jurisprudence than what had preceded it. Once the fragile foundation of deference is exposed, people have nothing but instrumental rationality and self-interests to guide them when they make political judgments.[85]

There is an ironic twist in Smith's argument. The instrumental reason serving self-interest in economic markets is only partially reliable for him elsewhere. He holds that it helps us get much that we think is important and it is particularly useful when applied within the disciplinary framework of economic markets. But if we are armed only with deceptions about wealth but none of the restraints attached to deference and convention, Smith sees dire consequences for both the individual and society. At the personal level, he fears, we will either descend into a morass of self-pity and envy or allow our vanity and ambition to carry us to a world that is, in his eyes, as make believe for us as it is for the poor man's son. At the political level, he sees the politics of merchants who have attachments only to their trade and profits and not to natural jurisprudence.

Smith's social and political equilibrium departs radically from the version offered by strong republicans, but it shares two important features with theirs. In each case, the actual distributions of power and wealth in society are buttressed by convention, tradition, and deference, which bestow legitimacy on a regime and, as in Machiavelli's republicanism, justify inequalities. Moreover, each version of the good society is jeopardized by sweeping change. Acknowledging that many of the liberating effects he attributes to commercial society have yet to work their ways throughout society, Smith underestimated the magnitude of changes awaiting commercial society. These changes would not only introduce new interests but also lessen the coherence that he believes his contemporaries detect in their regime. More important to Smith's project, the accumulative, unsettling effects of economic growth serve to demythologize the very restraints that he thinks are necessary for a flourishing, autonomous life and for political legitimacy.

Politics and the Corruption of Interests

The invasion of interests into politics is critical to Smith on several counts, some of which have already been discussed. When power and wealth are combined, winners have the capacity to compel others to obey rules that benefit the politically successful even at a heavy cost to the losers. Normally, this is taken to apply to closed societies. But I want to expand Smith's argument and show why Smith thinks the political expression of interests can be as dangerous to autonomy in a free, democratic society as in any other. Like Mill, Smith sees no logical relationship between democratic government and a respect for liberty. Majorities have interests just as kings, clergy, and nobles, and whatever their source, politics becomes dangerous when driven by interests. For Smith, it is a mistake to think that in a democracy, morality displaces or transforms interests any more than in any other form of government. The infusion of popular participation does not necessarily humanize interests or bestow a moral cast on them simply because they are interests of a majority.

Smith examines the issue of interests in a democracy in his discussion of slavery, which he takes to be wrong whether it is practiced by a few chiefs or the free citizens of Greece, Rome or America. According to him, "the freer the [citizens] the more miserable are the slaves; in a democracy they are more miserable than in any other" because those with power have an interest in preserving the institution.[86]

> In a free government the members would never make a law so hurtful to their interest, as they might think the abolishing of slavery would be. In a monarchy there is a better chance for its being abolished, because one single person is lawgiver and the law will not extend to him nor diminish his power, tho' it may diminish that of his vassals. In a despotic government slaves may be better treated than in a free government, where every law is made by their masters, who will never pass any thing prejudicial to themselves.[87]

Smith's critique of slavery in free governments reflects his constant fear that closely held interests that can be maintained through superior power corrupt the expression of the moral sentiments as well as destroy natural jurisprudence. People do not sacrifice their interests because they win political power; on the contrary, they use their power to protect and enhance those interests. In his critique of interests, he borrows much from the civic humanist argument about what constitutes a corrupt politics. But the republican optimism that interests can be tamed by institutions and civic virtue is not shared by Smith, whose solution is to break the bond between power and interests. In this way, he departs profoundly from interest-group liberals who find the intersection of interests, markets, and politics epitomizes an open, competitive system where none dominates and all are invited to participate. For Smith, there is a constant need to expose interests in politics for what they are: efforts to employ public power on behalf of private advantage. Running parallel to this argument is Smith's admonition to distinguish natural rights from ascribed ones, knowing full well that many claims to rights, including property rights, are not earned but stand because they are sanctioned by power.

Taxes and the New Civic Duty

Nozick succinctly summarizes a common libertarian position on taxes: "Taxation of earnings from labor is on a par with forced labor."[88] He reaches this conclusion with his highly individualistic reading of what people deserve, his indifference to the ways that environmental conditions contribute significantly to success (or failure), his belief that we owe nothing to others except to refrain from harming them, and his view that whenever government acts, it is usually contrary to the negative freedom of individuals.

Smith takes a much different view of taxes. Acknowledging a relatively inactive government reduces public spending and taxes, Smith assigns the state a legitimate need for income. His position on taxation is important because of its practical effects on funding security and other projects he deems necessary, and because he attaches moral meaning both to the payment of taxes and the rates of taxation. He appreciates that the civic bond is weakened in economies of specialization and complexity. One way to maintain a civic attachment, and one that Smith roundly rejects, would be to substitute intense civic participation and service for taxes. Personal activity in public affairs cannot be substituted with taxes, according to Rousseau, who sees them as a way of purchasing personal time and energy to serve one's own interests at the expense of the community. But Smith believes the payment of taxes carries its own important moral and political benefits. "Every tax, however, is to the person who pays it a badge, not of slavery, but of liberty. It denotes that he is a subject to government, indeed, but that, as he has some property, he cannot himself be the property of a master."[89]

In Smith's account, taxes add a new dimension to the civic self: people carry an obligation to the regime because they benefit from it. When political conditions secure rights, including rights to property, every beneficiary "is bound to contribute to the support of the sovereign."[90] Smith's individualism and independence are not free gifts or separate from society. The opportunities that await citizens, the successes they enjoy, the security they take for granted, and the venues in which they express their sentiments are not their personal inventions or constructions. For Smith, government and its laws provide "the main pillar that upholds the whole edifice. If it is removed, the great, the immense fabric of human society . . . must in a moment crumble into atoms."[91] In this reading, everyone derives a benefit from government, which attempts to reduce chance in the lives of its citizens and provide them with a manageable environment where they make choices that would not otherwise be available to them. However, those with property enjoy especially greater advantages and, therefore, a correspondingly greater duty to support government.

Holding that, like other forms of law, revenue law should accord with the rules of natural jurisprudence, Smith reasons that taxes serve justice when they are levied proportionally to the ability to pay and do not disturb economic growth or harm labor. According to Smith, the subjects of every state ought to contribute towards the support of the government, as nearly as possible, in proportion to their respective abilities, that is, in proportion to the revenue which they respectively enjoy under the protection of the state. . . . In the observation or neglect of this maxim consists what is called the equality or inequality of taxation[92]

And when Smith turns to the subject of taxing the poor, he relies on his fairness standard to reject any tax on "the necessities of life," although he would allow taxes on luxuries because they "have no tendency to raise the price of any other commodities except that on the commodities taxed."[93] For Smith, taxes are a sign of liberty, and to say that someone is free does not and cannot mean that the person is free from the duties of natural jurisprudence. Smith's desire to defend and nourish the free institutions of the commercial republic hardly qualifies as a republican remedy but he attempts to subvert a pure individualistic view that people can define their own relationship and responsibility to their regime.

Reading Smith Today

The foundational principles of Smithian politics are found in both his normative and empirical theories. His normative theory revolves around natural jurisprudence, which he takes to provide a standard for identifying and honoring the natural rights of everyone and securing the independence of autonomous agents. His empirical theory emphasizes interests and instrumental reason in economic markets.

In Hayek we find a contemporary effort to employ Smithian empirical theories to draw normative conclusions, most notably that markets are absolutely essential to liberty and that efforts to regulate the market undermine freedom. With Hayek, we are offered negative liberty and a negative state. How closely connected are his conclusions to Smith's? Clearly, both are committed to economic markets and are skeptical of the hyperactive state. Nevertheless, we cannot leave the issue here but rather need to consider Smith's larger project, which centers on the integrity of autonomous agents. His good society is characterized by more than markets, diffused power, and freedom. It is a place where acute insecurities and scarcities have been overcome, where politics is not instrumental, and where culture promotes a sense of limits and deference. If any of these latter characteristics are weak or missing and if the negative state and unregulated markets do not appear to meet the requirements originally assigned to them by Smith, it is not at all clear that Smith would automatically opt for the negative state and unrestricted markets, particularly if they contribute to misery and poverty.[94] Unlike libertarians who are stuck with negative liberty, Smith is also concerned about the concentration of private power and the pattern of hierarchy and subordination that evolves within civil society, knowing that people can be dependent on private concentrations of power as well as public ones.[95] Moreover, libertarians lack Smith's environmentalism, which acknowledges that background makes the most profound difference in the chances and choices available to people and restricts the autonomy of many in commercial society.

But even if one is reluctant to accept these arguments about why Smith cannot be a libertarian today, there is another telling argument that goes to the core of Smith's theory. He expects people to pursue their interests in economic markets and to be deferential and stoic when they view politics. One problem with a libertarian solution is that the genie of interests is out of the bottle. Interests cannot be easily capped today, diverse identities are not readily forgotten, and any legitimate democracy must somehow respond to the expectations of the public for a state that must be much more active than Hayek allows. Finally, one wonders about the little attention given to moral autonomy in the libertarian account. The reduction of state intrusion and the protection of robust markets are not sufficient structural requirements for Smithian autonomy, however much he thinks these are important, contributory elements to the good life. Smithian agents must also be able to overcome necessity and insecurity if they are honestly to express their moral sentiments.

Smith's political solutions have not worked as he intended. Deference is no longer the sturdy political buttress he expected; distributive issues are central in contemporary political life; more and more people judge politics instrumentally; economic markets have not operated as benignly as Smith expected but have rather been marked by concentrations of economic power; and if government is not controlled by interests, it is closely tied to many of them. It would appear that the politics of restraint have been replaced by political markets where interest-group liberalism thrives. Such a solution represents a problem for Smith who finds that political interests are undisciplined by invisible hands, elude substantive efforts to legitimize them, and—when effectively joined with power—perpetuate existing dependencies or create new ones.[96] For these reasons, Smith would be highly suspicious of efforts to transport markets to politics. One of the central features of Smithian politics that is absent in political market models is a culture that supports political restraint.

Smith's critique of interests in politics goes beyond his recognition that they deplete social relations of moral substance and sanction instrumental rationality. He is particularly concerned about those transactions that do not carry mutual benefits for the parties. Smith's account of history emphasizes that dominant parties force advantages for themselves at the cost of others. Although he condemns such actions, he also finds it natural for ambition to run wild if left untethered. The one place where ambition can harmlessly roam, according to Smith, is in economic markets which are said to discipline participants through the law of supply and demand. But Smith cannot imagine effective ways of disciplining political interests in markets.

One should also notice that Smithian markets are secular. Its members are not driven by considerations of the common good, benevolence, or natural jurisprudence. Within its boundaries, participants are valued because of the market-worth of their services or products. When secularized markets are transferred to democratic vistas, we get something quite unexpected. To the extent that markets do not depend on theories of citizenship or the good, we are provided with a model of politics that is incapable of saying much about some very basic political principles, except negative liberty and efficiency.[97] But political markets do not necessarily even produce efficiency or negative liberty. For that to occur, the disciplinary properties of Smith's invisible hand that are said to work in economic markets must be transportable to political markets. If these properties cannot be transferred, we have no real political markets and we risk having a political system where power becomes self-justifying and self-legitimizing.

One reason Smith remains politically important today stems from his serious concern about interests in politics. Although he provides no neat solution to this problem in contemporary politics, what he finds remains important to us; interests are not self-justifying, often rest on deceptions, disable citizenship, and disfigure natural jurisprudence. For this reason, Smith, parting company with interest-group liberals, seeks to confront political interests rather than optimize them. He also reminds us that neither interests nor markets speak to justice.

Efforts to repair the damage to liberal democratic politics with a return to some variation of the negative state are as likely to end in failure as Smith's own effort did. Legitimacy for a highly limited state has eroded before the complexity of modern life and the pervasiveness of interests in public life. Whether the reason for the malaise in liberal democracies today stems from its broken promises[98], secular-ism and rationalization,[99] or the contradictions of capitalism,[100] they are facts of modern democratic society. The important defeat for Smithian politics comes not just with the expansion of state activity but more especially when once-stable forms of mystification are replaced by interests and instrumentalism in political life. Smith's challenge is not to force us to think about ways of reviving deference to act as a sturdy brace for legitimacy or finding a way to cleanse politics of economic issues. The real challenge posed by Smith is how we think about the things that matter most to both Smith and us, an autonomy that reflects the principles of human dignity and promotes an honesty to the self but that can be thwarted by institutional arrangements, acute scarcities and insecurities as well as our own self-deceptions.

Any Smithian account of contemporary politics has to recognize the demystification of the modern state along with an impatience with a wide range of inequalities. In this sense, a Smithian critique of politics today would not focus simply on the state but also on other sources of power and privilege that subvert the rules of what he calls natural jurisprudence, that is, that protect, to use Smith's language, the acquired rights of some at the expense of the natural rights of others. To move to an inclusive autonomy requires, for Smith, a politics that exposes infractions of natural jurisprudence and seeks to diminish the dependencies associated with scarcity, necessity and a paternalistic state.

Notes

1. For a succinct review of liberal democratic politics as a market, see Jon Elster ("The Market and the Forum," in *Foundations in Social Choice*, edited by J. Elster and A. Hylland [Cambridge: Cambridge University Press, 1986]) and Joseph Schumpeter, *Capitalism, Socialism, Democracy* (New York: Harper & Brothers, 1942), 103–5. On the purported openness of the pluralist system, see Robert Dahl, *Who Governs?* (New Haven: Yale University Press, 1961), 380. On the propensity for citizens to rank-order their political preferences in ways analogous to economic models of rank-ordering, see Robert Dahl, *After the Revolution* (New Haven: Yale University Press, 1970), 3–56, and Elster, "The Market and the Forum."

2. David Truman denies it is helpful to consider interests as "selfish." Judgments about "selfish" interests "have no value for a scientific understanding of government or the operation of society" (*The Governmental Process* [New York: Knopf, 1951], 38). For Arthur Bentley, a group interest "is first, last, and all the time strictly empirical" and should not be subjected to normative interpretations when they are analyzed as part of the political process

(*The Process of Government* [Evanston: Principia Press, 1908] 214–15).

3. For a representative pluralist position, see Dahl, *Who Governs?* and his *Dilemmas of Pluralist Democracy* (New Haven: Yale University Press, 1982). For a representative economic analysis of democracy, see Anthony Downs, "An Economic Theory of Democracy," *Journal of Political Economy* 64 (1957): 135–52. For a rational choice position, see William Riker, *Liberalism against Populism* (San Francisco: W. H. Freeman, 1982). See Schumpeter's argument that the democratic process has become rationalized in ways characteristic of market transactions (*Capitalism*, 121–22). Also see Max Weber, "Politics as a Vocation," *From Max Weber*, edited by H. H. Gerth and C. W. Mills (New York: Oxford University Press, 1958).

4. Bentley, *Process*, 215.

5. Dahl argues that in nonpluralist systems, "political resources were marked by cumulative inequality: when one individual was much better off than another in one resource, such as wealth, he was usually better off in almost every other resource." In his reading of pluralism, resources are widely dispersed and no one group can dominate (*Who Governs?*, 85).

6. Schumpeter, *Capitalism* 270–71; see also Downs, "Economic Theory," 137.

7. Dahl, *Who Governs?*

8. Truman talks about the "tendency to maintain or revert to equilibrium" by individual groups as well as the political system at large (*Governmental Process*, 27). For an extended treatment of equilibrium, see his discussion "The Equilibrium of Institutionalized Groups," (*Governmental Process*, 26–33). Reflecting an equilibrium perspective, Bentley holds that government "is the organization of forces, of pressures" (*Process*, 453). Downs announces that he will offer a "theory of political action of democracy" in the context of "a single general equilibrium theory" ("Economic Theory," 135).

9. Interest-group liberals find that citizens or consumers pursue their preferences or interests within the constraints of scarce resources such as money or time (see Downs, "Economic Theory;" Dahl, *After the Revolution*).

10. Milton Myers, *The Soul of Economic Man* (Chicago: University of Chicago Press, 1983).

11. The pervasive role of interests in explaining contemporary democratic politics has recently been challenged by Jane Mansbridge, "Self Interest in Political Life," *Political Theory* 18 (Feb. 1990): 132–53, and others who show that political behavior is often better explained by motivations that are not narrowly self-interested.

12. I show later in this chapter that Smith argues that the successful pursuit of political interests commonly leads to the loss of the independence of others.

13. Nozick's libertarianism owes its debt to Locke (see his *Anarchy, State, and Utopia* [New York: Basic Books, 1974], 9–18; 131–38; 174–8) and not to Smith. Nozick's Locke is drawn exclusively from the *Second Treatise,* and

the part Nozick finds most appealing is Locke's rendition of the state of nature, that idyllic time when individual effort is rewarded and there is no government. Nozick also briefly turns to Locke's views on civil society and parental duties. For a discussion of Nozick as a libertarian, see Will Kymlicka, *Contemporary Political Philosophy* (Oxford: Oxford University Press, 1990), 95–159.

14. Friedrich Hayek denies Nozick's position that a person is free only under a minimal state. Hayek argues that "far from advocating such a 'minimal state,' we find it unquestionable that in an advanced society government ought to use its power of raising funds by taxation to provide a number of services which for various reasons cannot be provided, or cannot be provided adequately, by the market" (*Political Order of a Free People* [Chicago: University of Chicago Press, 1979], 41).

15. Hayek, *Rules and Order* (Chicago: University of Chicago Press, 1973) 44–5. See also Hayek, *Political Order*, 9–17, 129, and 3–8.

16. Alan Haworth, a staunch critic of libertarian thought, finds it "has a serious side . . . and can claim, with at least some justification, a distinguished ancestry in the work of John Locke and Adam Smith, among others" (*Anti-Libertarianism* [London: Routledge, 1994], 4).

17. According to Hayek, "The foundation of modern civilization was first understood by Adam Smith" (*Political Order*, 158).

18. *Studies in Philosophy, Politics, and Economics* (London: Routledge & Kegan Paul, 1967), 162.

19. Hayek is one of the most unrelenting critics of interest-group liberalism. He finds modern voters "will normally merely agree to something being given to others about whom they know little, and usually at the expense of third groups, as the price of having their own wishes met, without any thought whether these various demands are just. . . . The result of the process will correspond to nobody's opinion of what is right, and to no principles; it will not be based on a judgment of merit but on political expediency" (*Political Order*, 9).

20. For Hayek, instrumental rationality leads to chaos. For a discussion of Hayek's views on this topic, see John Gray, *Hayek on Liberty* (Oxford: Basil Blackwell, 1984), 50–51.

21. *Political Order*, 154–55.

22. *Political Order*, 159–60.

23. Adam Smith, *The Theory of Moral Sentiments*, edited by D. D. Raphael and A. L. Macfie (Oxford: Oxford University Press, 1976), II.ii.2.1; hereafter referred to as *TMS*.

24. Smith works with theories of the moral sentiments that enjoyed considerable popularity in intellectual circles in Scotland in the eighteenth century. The Scottish school democratized the sentiments by making them universally accessible and in this way departed from earlier renditions that required individuals to cultivate the sentiments through special training.

25. *TMS*, VII.iii.2.7 and *TMS*, II.iii.29.

26. *TMS*, I.i.1.

27. *TMS*, III.2.31–32. For Smith, the pure ego not only makes a person unfit for society, but also puts happiness out of the reach of such a person.
28. *TMS*, II.V.1.
29. See D. D. Raphael, *Adam Smith* (Oxford: Oxford University Press, 1985), chap. 3.
30. Smith holds that our disposition to care about others is not dependent on formal learning and is accessible to everyone who lives in society.
31. *TMS*, III.ii.6–7.
32. At first glance, Smithian agents appear to internalize the norms of their culture in the deepest way and do not appear to have the resources to separate themselves from it. However, this is not a problem for Smith who believes that the norms embedded in most cultures "coincide with the natural principles of right and wrong" in important respects and do not contradict the moral sentiments (*TMS*, V.2.2).
33. *TMS*, III.2.1.
34. Adam Smith, *Lectures on Jurisprudence* (Oxford: Oxford University Press, 1978), 8.
35. Adam Smith, *An Inquiry into the Nature and Causes of the Wealth of Nations* (Oxford: Oxford University Press, 1976), IV.viii.30.
36. See *Lectures*, first manuscript, bk 1, for Smith's argument that the way property is acquired reflects social conditions.
37. *Lectures*, pt. 1, esp. 19.
38. *Lectures*, 401.
39. An example of a breach of this rule is provided by the prohibition on the commoners from hunting on the lands of the kings or nobles. According to Smith, game was considered common in the ancient constitution because it could not be permanently attached to any person's private holdings, and "this certainly is what is more agreeable to reason." However, the power and greed of the feudal kings and lords converted what had been common property into an acquired right for themselves. In this and other examples, Smith draws attention to "encroachment made on the rights of the lower rank of people" by the rich and powerful (*Lectures*, 23–25). In his arguments on behalf of property rights held in common, Smith lays the basis for environmental regulation within the liberal language of rights, even if his vernacular of rights is less individualist than usually supposed.
40. See *Lectures*, 9–19; 399–400.
41. See *Lectures*, 105.
42. *Lectures*, 401; see also 13.
43. In *Lectures*, Smith defines crime as "always the violation of some right, natural or acquired" (476).
44. *TMS*, II.ii.2.
45. *Wealth*, V.i.b.2.
46. *Lectures*, 200.
47. J. J. Rousseau, *A Discourse on the Origins of Inequality* (London: Dent, 1983), 87–89.
48. *Wealth*, V.i.b.2.

49. *Wealth*, V.i.b.2–4.

50. Civil government is in reality instituted for the defense of the rich against the poor, or of those who have some property against those who have none at all (*Wealth*, V.i.b.12).

51. See *Wealth*, V.ii.1.

52. *Lectures*, 333.

53. *Wealth*, I.ii.4–5.

54. For a discussion of Smith's view of the way these groups are subordinated and accept their subordination, see *Lectures*, 143–153 and 438–43, concerning women; *Lectures*, 451–55 regarding slaves; and *Wealth*, I.vii.13 and I.x.c.58–59, regarding workers.

55. *Wealth*, V.i.3.

56. Smith denies that principled positions lead to broad social change. For him, individual moral conduct leads to personal happiness not social justice.

57. *TMS*, V.ii.9.

58. *TMS*, V.ii.11.

59. TMS, V.ii.9–11.

60. See *TMS*, IV.1.6–9.

61. *Wealth*, I.ii.2.

62. See *Wealth*, V.i.

63. Nor are they served by putting a religious or other ascriptive test on potential customers, which would only contract the merchant's market. This is an argument of some libertarians for open markets and a negative state as the best way to deal with discrimination.

64. Smith works with a commonplace assumption of his time when he holds that self-interest can be contained within economic markets. For him, individuals can segment their lives not only into discrete roles but also into very different modes of thinking appropriate to each role. From this perspective, there need not be any seepage from one modal way of thinking to another. In one way, he is probably correct. We do not engage in instrumental reason in our intimate relations. But in another way, he is mistaken. We have come to employ instrumental reason in our political roles as voters and members of interest groups. By the nineteenth century, Smith's optimistic assessments will be replaced by worry, and sometimes despair, that instrumental rationality has overwhelmed politics. Weber's argument about a disenchanted world that has become rationalistic best captures this shift.

65. This can be found in Hayek's arguments for the negative state and negative liberty.

66. Smith also thinks the merchant class, one of the great beneficiaries of markets, wants to subvert the market. For him, "people of the same trade seldom meet together, even for merriment and diversion, but the conversation ends in a conspiracy against the public, or in some contrivance to raise prices" (*Wealth*, I.x.c.27).

67. *Wealth*, I.ii.2.

68. Lowi makes the point that interest-group liberalism is "unable to come

to terms with the problem of imperfect competition" (Theodore Lowi, *The End of Liberalism* [New York: Norton, 1969] 295). See Elster ("Market and the Forum") for a discussion of markets as an inadequate metaphor for politics.

69. See Milton Friedman, *Capitalism and Freedom* (Chicago: University of Chicago Press, 1963); Albert Hirschman, *The Passions and the Interests* (Princeton: Princeton University Press, 1977); and Myers, *Soul of Modern Economic Man*.

70. *TMS*, IV.I.8.
71. See *TMS*, IV.1.8.
72. *TMS*, IV.1.7.
73. *Wealth*, III.iv.1–5.
74. *Lectures*, 414–15.
75. For a reading that emphasizes Smith's civic-humanist concerns, see Donald Winch, *Adam Smith's Politics* (Cambridge: Cambridge University Press). For a dissenting view, see Edward Harpham, "Liberalism, Civic Humanism, and the Case of Adam Smith," *American Political Science Review* 78 (1984): 764–74.
76. *TMS*, I.iii.2.
77. *TMS*, I.iii.3.1.
78. *TMS*, I.iii.3.1.
79. *TMS*, III.iii.
80. The wealthy and powerful hold their place not only because of secular deceptions but also, by Smith's account, because of the trust that ordinary people put in God's justice. Their faith tempers any inclination for secular justice or retribution when the rich and famous overstep moral boundaries. Smith holds that most people believe that God will punish the likes of the knave and any temporal reward for vanity or injustice will eventually be corrected by God. Sometimes the knaves are punished in this life and their victims are rewarded here, but when this does not happen, most people are assured, according to Smith, that God will punish the guilty with eternal damnation (*TMS*, III.5.10). But in a secular society, we do not wait for the last judgment. Rather, we impatiently wait for the next election, hurry to lobby officials, or try to influence policy. For someone like Smith, to defer to God is not to call on the divine to validate our position in this world, but to allow God to act without our active intervention. This is one of the very few instances when Smith resorts to religion to explain behavior, and his analysis rests on a sociology of religion rather than theology.

81. Also see Schumpeter, *Capitalism*; Fred Hirsch, *The Social Limits to Growth* (Cambridge: Harvard University Press, 1976); Daniel Bell, *The Cultural Contradictions of Capitalism* (New York: Basic Books, 1976); and John Dunn, *John Locke* (Cambridge: Cambridge University Press, 1984).

82. According to Smith, stable social and economic arrangements "though [they] may sometimes be unjust, may not . . . be useless It checks the spirit of innovation. It tends to preserve whatever is the established balance among the different orders and societies into which the state is divided; and while it

sometimes appears to obstruct some alterations of government that may be fashionable and popular at the time, it contributes in reality to the stability and permanency of the whole system" (*TMS*, VI.ii.2.10).

83. This is what Smith finds so attractive in North America. See *Wealth*, III.iv.19; see also David McNally, *Against the Market* (London: Verso, 1993).

84. *TMS*, VI.ii.2.10.

85. Smith finds the interests of "merchants and master manufacturers . . . [are] always in some respects different from, and even opposite to, that of the public." They "have generally an interest to deceive and even to oppress the public, and . . . accordingly have, upon many occasions, both deceived and oppressed it" (*Wealth*, I.xi).

86. *Lectures*, 185.

87. *Lectures*, 453. Smith also theorizes that slavery is harsher in countries that are economically prosperous. He imagines that in poorer societies, master and slave work side by side, and because the investment the master has in his few slaves represents a large part of his wealth, Smith speculates the master is careful not to mistreat his slaves (*Lectures*, 183–84). Moreover, Smith imagines a proximity of condition between the poor master and his slave who work together. Through their daily, similar contact, Smith expects that the former will see his slave as human (*Lectures*, 184). Any readiness to recognize the humanity of slaves grows weaker when the master is socially and physically distant and, accordingly, calls on no rules of impartiality to examine his own conduct. For these reasons, Smith concludes the very liberty and prosperity that normally are welcome for humanity at large are morally suspect when allotted to only a few: "Freedom and opulence contribute to the misery of the slaves. The perfection of freedom" for citizens is for the slaves "their greatest bondage. And as they are the most numerous part of mankind, no human person will wish for liberty in a country where this institution is established" (*Lectures*, 453).

88. Nozick, *Anarchy*, 169. Hayek parts company from Nozick on this issue, finding that the idea of taxation in advanced societies is defensible (*Political Order*, 41). The issues for Hayek are how government taxes (he is opposed to progressivity), how much it taxes, and the uses for which tax revenue are appropriated.

89. *Wealth*, V.ii.g.11.

90. *Wealth*, IV.viii.31.

91. *TMS*, II.ii.3.4.

92. *Wealth*, V.ii.b.3.

93. *Wealth*, V.ii.k.5–6.

94. Smith argues, "No society can surely be flourishing and happy of which the far greater part of the members are poor and miserable. It is but equity, besides, that they who feed, clothe, and lodge the whole body of the people, should have such a share of the produce of their own labour as to be themselves tolerably well fed, clothed, and lodged" (*TMS*, I.8.36).

95. This can be seen in Smith's treatment of organized religion in feudal Europe, slave owning in any society, the status of women throughout history, and the intrigues of merchants in the commercial republic.

96. Lowi holds that "interest-group liberalism tend[s] to create and maintain privilege; and it is a type of privilege particularly hard to bear or combat because it is touched with a symbolism of the state" (*End of Liberalism*, 87-88).

97. According to Smith, "He is not a citizen who is not disposed to respect the laws and to obey the civil magistrate; and he is certainly not a good citizen who does not wish to promote, by every means in his power, the welfare of the whole society of his fellow-citizens" (*TMS*, VI.ii.2.11).

98. Noberto Bobbio, *The Future of Democracy* (London: Polity Press, 1987).

99. See Max Weber, *From Max Weber* and Schumpeter, *Capitalism*.

100. Claus Offe, *The Cultural Contradictions of the Welfare State* (Cambridge: MIT Press, 1984).

Chapter Seven

The Languages of American Politics

The current debate between American liberals and communitarians is more than an academic controversy about the history of ideas. It is also about how we should think and act politically. Both sides have laid claims that they represent what is best in the nation and carry the necessary materials to meet its present needs. Communitarians find the country's original political language patriotic, civic, participatory, and consensual while procedural liberals hold it to be about rights and equality of opportunity. Others have found that Americans have frequently spoken both republican and liberal languages in their history and find no need to pit one language against the other. In this chapter, I consider the role of liberalism and republicanism during the country's founding and in Lincoln's political language in order to show that the nation's dominant political language is liberal and that Americans have employed a republican idiom to prod and correct the narrow individualism that often comes to define liberalism.

Echoes of republicanism are heard during both of these periods, but they are never strong enough to replace the clear, persistent sounds of individualism, equality of opportunity, and mobility in America. Nor do the republican echoes ever clearly carry many of the central concerns of continental republicans, who are preoccupied with stability and suspicious of many of the goods Americans value.[1] What we get in American republicanism are fragments that disclose the dangers of corruption, celebrate a civic life, and search for a common good. These republican fragments often fit comfortably into the country's political rhetoric because they do not deny the validity of the liberal goods Americans prize. In employing republican idioms as they do, Americans amend, modify, and distill selected republican categories for a politics suited to their needs and aspirations, leaving behind earlier republican conceptions of property and deference and carrying none of the republican suspicion of change and mobility.

Continental Republicanism: A Reprise

Historians and political theorists have returned to the American founding to determine the principles that animate the revolution and the federal constitution. Some of what is at stake in the debate has contemporary relevance and is used as a way of understanding politics today. If the nation's origins can be shown to be primarily republican, we need to ask whether the legacy is valuable, and if it is, whether we can return to it.

What has become known as the ideological school of Bernard Bailyn, Gordon Wood, and J. G. A. Pocock holds that civic humanism or republicanism—not a Lockean, liberal consensus—moved the colonists to revolution. They introduce us to Americans in the 1760s and 1770s who are committed to freedom and virtue but are deeply troubled by the signs of growing corruption and licentiousness, which they associate with British rule.[2] However, the republicanism that emerges in America during the eighteenth century is a strange breed and departs from earlier, continental versions. Although much of the rhetoric and many of the principles of the earlier accounts of European republicanism remain, there are important additions and omissions, and it is helpful to recollect some salient features of continental republicanism.

For republicans such as Machiavelli and Rousseau, the good republic is continually haunted by decay and, if its citizens are wise, they recognize their own inherent vulnerabilities. In addition to the problem of an internally generated corruption, republican vitality is also vulnerable to sweeping economic and social changes that undermine its foundational principles and institutional practices. Disturbing once-settled equilibria and quickening the pace of individualism, widespread change is particularly dangerous to the European reading of the good republic. New situations often leave people unsettled and dissatisfied, and their institutions no longer speak to them convincingly about a common good, civic virtue, and public service. Frequently, change leaves some citizens better off and some worse off, and the advantages that some citizens win for themselves are seen by other citizens as coming at their expense. In addition, change disturbs the accepted patterns of deference that most continental republicans think are necessary for a politics of concord.

Stability is critical to continental republicans because it shields citizens from ambition and factional politics and enables them to practice civic virtue and honor their traditions. Long a staple of European republican thought, the concept of civic virtue emphasizes restraint, service, and duty. The character of its citizens makes the character of the republic because, in the last analysis, a free government is thought to reflect their strengths and weaknesses. Continental republicans hold that when character is marred by ambition, envy, licentiousness, and luxury, civic virtue vanishes, corruption enters, and politics becomes a prize that bestows advantages on the victorious faction at the cost of the rest. When civic virtue flourishes, continental republicans hold that order is natural, not imposed, and liberty is assured, not assaulted.

In the eighteenth-century American version of republicanism elaborated by Bailyn, Wood, and Pocock, we encounter an ideology that celebrates liberty, civic virtue, and the rule of law, and fears factions and corruption.[3] In this respect, American republicanism seems to be the offspring of continental republicanism. Unexpected from a republican perspective, Americans welcome change, prize equality of opportunity, alter the meaning of property, and increasingly lose their deference to authority.

The American Version of Republicanism

Bailyn, Wood, Pocock, and, more recently, Michael Lienesch have recounted the heady optimism that marks the beginning of the prerevolutionary period and the profound reassessments about virtue, character, self-interest, and corruption that characterize its end.[4] They show how, in the early period, Americans try to make a place for individual liberty, popular government, and civic virtue, but how, in the process, many of their assumptions become suspect and a plea for civic virtue gives way to sharp recriminations and deep cleavages. I want to show not only that the republican rhetoric of the early period diminishes by the 1780s but also that in the 1760s and 1770s, liberalism already occupies the center stage of American politics.

The republican revision of the American founding began inauspiciously enough with Bernard Bailyn's analysis of prerevolutionary colonial pamphlets. Although he finds Locke and his English contemporaries are read in the colonies, Bailyn argues that the discourse of the Revolutionary War period is largely shaped by "the heritage of classical antiquity."[5] The colonial pamphleteers look to republican Rome as an ideal and a warning; they applaud its virtue but lament its corruption; they praise Roman liberty but fear Roman tyranny. Even when the pamphleteers move to more recent times, they never forget Rome. When they turn to England, they see Rome, with its rise and fall. Like Rome, England has squandered its liberty, "from being the nursery of heroes, it became the residence of musicians, pimps, panderers, and catamites," forsaking constitutional government for "corruption, effeminacy, and languor."[6] Americans, according to Bailyn, view politics through the lens supplied by radical English Whigs, particularly the authors of Cato's letters, John Trenchard and Thomas Gordon, who on Bailyn's account, "more than any single group of writers . . . shaped the mind of the American Revolutionary generation."[7] The fear of Bailyn's colonial Americans centers on moral rather than political issues, and the major culprit is corruption.

Gordon Wood, who takes up the story where Bailyn left off, concentrates on the debates revolving around the Revolution, Confederacy, and Philadelphia convention. According to Wood, "the sacrifice of individual interests to the greater good of the whole" animates American politics during the revolutionary period.[8] This public good signifies more than independence from Britain; in Wood's account, citizens restrain their personal ambition for the good of the whole.[9] He approvingly cites a sermon which argues that in the good republic, "each citizen gives up all private interest that is not consistent with the general good, the interest of the whole body." Armed with this and similar passages, Wood claims, "ideally, republicanism obliterated the individual" in America.[10] In summarizing the American view of civic virtue in the 1770s, Wood writes about the "willingness of the individual to sacrifice his private interests for the good of the community."[11]

Pocock extends and expands the arguments of Bailyn and Wood, finding Americans are repeating history, or more especially are applying republican principles. Their "confrontation of virtue with corruption constitutes the Machiavellian moment" in America.[12] Pocock's Americans owe their outlooks to English Commonwealthmen, neo-Harringtonians, and Whigs who oppose the court's proclivity to favor commerce, financial speculation, public debt, and self-interest.[13] In structuring his argument as he does, Pocock offers us Americans who are primarily intent on resisting modernity and capitalism in order to protect their liberty.[14]

Recovering Liberalism

Two literatures have responded to the republican revisionists: one largely from historians who reexamine the texts and assumptions of the period and the other largely from political theorists who reassess the portrait of liberalism offered by Bailyn, Wood, and Pocock. Both approaches challenge the historical and theoretical assumptions of the ideological school. Isaac Kramnick and Joyce Appleby, for example, wonder why the pervasive American individualism, expressed in agrarian markets, is overlooked. Kramnick's Americans find "self-centered economic productivity, not public citizenship, [to be] the badge of the virtuous man."[15] If Pocock has trouble locating liberals in colonial America, Kramnick and Appleby have an equally hard time finding republicans in the period preceding and during the Revolution. Their Americans repudiate civic humanism and replace what they see "as corrupt political man with virtuous and productive economic man."[16]

Joyce Appleby has been a particularly helpful critic of what she calls the "Neo-Whig historians."[17] She finds the colonial period is marked by extensive economic changes, particularly the growth of "paper money, land banks, and credit extension [which] created opportunities, democratized competition, unleashed the acquisitive instinct, and encouraged personal ambition—all corrosives to a community order which valued continuity, solidarity, and stability."[18] What emerges in Appleby's account are not republicans resisting corruption but many Americans, whether among the successful or not, eagerly seeking to become beneficiaries of the new economy.

Appleby's Americans frequently speak in republican dialects as well as in the language of liberalism, but the way they use the two serves to strengthen liberalism and deplete republicanism of its moorings. This can be seen in the language Americans employ to describe the English threat to their freedom. Appleby observes they use the "imagery of subjugation, submission, and subordination."[19] In dichotomizing the sides, no unusual feature in a contest with high stakes, colonial Americans are not content to talk about corruption but contrast it with the image of slavery. Hamilton asks his fellow citizens if they are ready to be slaves; and Adams discovers "two sorts of men in the world, freeman and slaves," and he, for one, resists becoming a slave.[20] Appleby finds that the contrast between freedom and slavery gives the revolutionaries "an absolute value to freedom which it had not previously possessed, even in the intellectual tradition from which they drew."[21] In this way, Americans during the late colonial and revolutionary periods clearly embrace the liberal view that rights are an essential good and are independent of the sufferance of the state.

Appleby's Americans are primarily responding to changing social and economic conditions and finding a language that accurately captures their aspirations and fears. "Despite the austere truths of classical republicanism, American colonists from all walks of life were infected by new economic ambitions in the middle decades of the eighteenth century" and readily absorb individualism.[22] For Appleby, the American character has little of the republicanism that Bailyn, Wood, and Pocock discover. Along with Kramnick, she finds that Americans are much more individualistic in the colonial and revolutionary periods than allowed in the neo-Whig account.

Daniel Rogers has a different set of complaints with the republican paradigm: it simplifies what is complex. He criticizes revisionists who find a republican commitment behind every word and action in colonial and revolutionary America.[23] The revisionist reading of republicanism, he argues, "organized, structured, and empowered all the messy, emotional, frenzied, utopian, extra-Lockean stuff in the late eighteenth-century air."[24] Rogers sees the revisionist position providing a critique of contemporary American politics and presenting itself as an alternative to the shortcomings it associates with liberalism. The republican synthesis offers a "commitment to an active civic life (contra liberalism's obsession with immunities and rights), to explicit value commitments and deliberative justice (as opposed to liberalism's procedural neutrality), to public, common purposes (contra liberalism's inability to imagine politics as anything other than interest group politics)."[25] Questioning the reliability of the republican synthesis to weave the many pieces together, Rogers finds that its attraction to many scholars shows "how deeply responsive the interpretative disciplines are, not to evidence . . . but to their interpretive problematics."[26]

The neo-Whigs find no language of possessive individualism present at the origins of the American republic and conclude that Locke and liberalism are largely absent. They have been looking for a Locke who is hedonistic, possessive, individualist, and materialistic. This is the Locke as presented by Hartz, Macpherson, and Strauss and employed by communitarians in their current debate with liberals. A growing number of Locke scholars, primarily political theorists, have seen Locke as a liberal who is attentive to moral issues. As I indicated in my earlier discussion of Locke as an anxious liberal, he is concerned with the moral development of persons and he buttresses his arguments with appeals to reason and religion. Thomas Pangle, for one, sees Locke as an individualist but not the possessive individualist identified by the ideological school. The Locke that Pangle sees Americans reading synthesizes concerns about individual well-being with moral development, reason with law, and an accountable government based on legislative primacy with economic advancement.[27]

Several scholars find that Locke is widely read in America but he is read selectively and certainly not as a possessive individualist.[28]

Locke's readers of the *Second Treatise* apparently pass over his discussion of property (as a materialist, possessive individualist reading of Locke emphasizes) and turn to his chapter entitled "The Extent of the Legislative Power."[29] And, as Pangle observes, Americans also study Locke's pages on a variety of educational, moral, and legal issues. Locke makes sense because he writes about matters that genuinely concern the colonists. Deeply religious, they find Locke's formulation of individualism resting heavily on Protestant dissent with its emphasis on individual responsibility.[30] They are not striving for some civic ideal; they want to secure their rights and property as well as attend to their "eternal estate."[31] This leads John Dworetz to conclude "the theistic Locke is more historically appropriate than the Bourgeois Locke for a study of American Revolutionary thought."[32]

Critics of the neo-Whig reading of the American founding readily acknowledge a republican presence but challenge its pervasiveness and dominance; they find a formidable individualism in America, but not one indifferent to moral issues.[33] The Americans they survey are also deeply concerned with moral autonomy, and, as I propose to show, with political equality and equality of opportunity. These Americans seek their own popular government to secure liberty and protect economic opportunity; preserving the stability and civic virtue that continental republicans prize is far removed from their political or personal imagination.

Republican Deference and American Egalitarianism

Why did the republicanism that Bailyn, Wood and Pocock locate in America shrink in importance after the revolution? One reason neo-Whigs advance but do not pursue concerns the collapse of deference and the way ordinary Americans come to view themselves. Continuing social and economic change makes republicanism fragile in America.[34] The society in motion that alarms continental republicans suits Americans nicely, and the equilibrium that signals a citizenry satisfied with its standing and possessions quickly becomes alien to the American conception of the good society. Americans are more apt to prize mobility than stability; and they find something like equality of opportunity is the positive and distinguishing characteristic of their country. They want to protect it and take advantage of it.

To pursue these issues, it is helpful to follow Wood's discussion of how the cohesion, courage, self-restraint, and sacrifice that he sees marking the struggle of the Americans against entrenched British power quickly fade as some of the victors seek to employ their new freedoms in ways that make sense to them but that interfere with the freedoms of some of their fellow citizens. The short period between the Peace of Paris and the Philadelphia convention is a time when a consensus about what constitutes the common good dissolves and when talk about the lack of restraint abounds. Rather than regenerating Americans, victory divides them amidst the politics of interests.

For their part, the Federalists condemn the power and behavior of the state legislatures where local majorities are charged with governing on their own behalf at the expense of the rest. But the argument is not only political; it also hinges on a reading of a society that has become corrupt and a people growing licentious. In this setting, John Adams, for one, leaves his earlier optimism behind to observe that Americans in 1787 are "as incapable now of going through revolutions with temper and sobriety, with patience and prudence, or without fury and madness, as it was among the Greeks so long ago."[35]

To focus only on the clash of interests is to ignore the question of why interests should become so important at this time. Part of the answer is found in the changing status of deference in American politics. Continental republicans have historically relied heavily on deference in their political theories. They assume that most people voluntarily accept the rule of others who are said to be better prepared and qualified to govern and that there is something like a natural aristocracy based on virtue, civic duties, and patriotism and tied to education, training, and property.

Deference entails holding others in esteem or even awe and serves to legitimize place, both higher and lower ones. As such, deference domesticates ambition and envy, dispositions dangerous to the good republic. Republican citizens, then, are expected to be content with their assignment in society and accept the legitimacy of an equilibrium of liberties and obligations. If either political or social deference weakens, republican politics is in trouble. What citizens once shared fractures, and personal zeal cancels the common agreements that once tied republican citizens together.[36] For Pocock, the "decline of virtue [and deference is one of the virtues of Pocock's republican citizen] had as its logical corollary the rise of interest." Without "the conditions thought necessary to make [citizens] capable of perceiving the common good," he argues citizens only have their interests to guide them.[37]

Although deference is weaker in the American colonies than in

Europe prior to the revolution of 1776, Americans are nonetheless deferential to authority during the colonial period and the early years of the revolution. At the outbreak of the war, Wood finds that deference to authority is widespread, and the revolutionary leaders work strenuously to convince ordinary Americans "that they rightfully had a share in government."[38] America's natural aristocracy assumes the major roles in the revolution, supplying leadership and rhetoric to the cause, including appeals to ordinary Americans to quit their deference to the agents of the crown. As Wood clearly demonstrates, most Americans accept the invitation. However, the rhetoric of equality that is so effectively employed against the British during the conflict is turned on the American natural aristocracy after victory.[39] By the mid-1780s, the mystique of deference is in tatters. Many ordinary Americans increasingly formulate their own political positions and are no longer willing to wait for the prior approval of local notables before proceeding.

The decline of deference and the arrival of a newly secularized American politics comes from many sources; some aspire to "places of consequences but are made to feel their inferiority in innumerable, often subtle ways," some are resentful of "the 'authority of names' and 'the influence of the great,'" some no longer assume that an "organic social homogeneity" attends to their interests and insist on having their interests represented by themselves or people like them.[40] For their part, those who think of themselves as part of the natural aristocracy see this as a "threat to the very foundations of society."[41]

The changing attitude to deference owes less to liberalism and more to emerging theories of democracy and a modernizing economy. Given the social, political and economic changes that precede and accompany the revolution, it is not surprising to find that many Americans turn to the familiar political language of republicanism to express their concerns about freedom, political equality, and participation. However, the rhetoric of political equality undermines deference to a natural aristocracy and introduces new identities to people. It seems counterintuitive that in a society undergoing significant change, once-stable relationships, particularly those based on deference, will persist.

Tied to the collapse of deference is the evolving conception that everyone should have an opportunity to improve economically and socially. The growing emphasis on equality of opportunity would alarm Pocock's republicans. Equality of opportunity rests not only on assumptions about the openness of the economy and society but on several other premises that thwart continental republican requirements. For one, people are expected to be at least marginally dissatisfied with their present situation and to desire more (wealth, prestige, status, power), but this kind of personal discontent undermines foundational principles so critical to continental republicans. Second, equality of opportunity is unsettling to public regardingness and civic virtue; people see themselves, and not society, as responsible for their well-being and security. They believe that time once devoted to civic matters deflects them from their new quests; they find that their success sometimes comes from getting in the way of others. Finally, equality of opportunity fuels mobility, and once-stable, traditional ties give way to new social arrangements. In seeing themselves as the authors of their success, forget their connectedness with others and with their social institutions and assume that their success is related to their own talents and efforts. Republican appeals to the common good and the connectedness of citizens reminds liberal citizens that they are endangering the things they want most when they make individualism an end in itself. But the language of republicanism does not so much replace liberal goods in America as chasten them.

Republican Fragments and Reformulations: Stable Property or the Opportunity Society

That Americans frequently employ republican language during the period of the country's founding is beyond doubt. That they are full-fledged republicans is highly doubtful. When they talk about virtue, the common good, and corruption, Americans blur the meanings of earlier republicans and understand such terms in their own ways. Virtue has a civic caste to it, but not too civic. Many are busy making a living, caring for their families, and attending to their spiritual lives; politics enters their world incidentally. It is not the center that someone such as Pocock sees as the core of republican citizenship. Indeed, many Americans think they are helping both themselves and their country through their economic activities; for them, the badge of citizenship signals economic opportunity, and their achievements need not be spectacular to be satisfying.

The virtues required for this kind of success are not the same ones entailed in civic virtue.[42] Perseverance, labor, self-discipline, and other small virtues do them nicely. These are the kinds of virtues that not only promote individual success but are thought not to injure or interfere with others.[43] From this perspective, the common good arises not so much from self-conscious exertions or sacrifice but from staying out of the way of others as one attends to his or her own affairs. Equipped with this kind of innocence, many Americans (then as now) find that their civic obligations require little from them.[44]

Pocock and Skinner find the goal of republicanism is autonomy, which is achieved through the free institutions of the republic and the ownership of private, landed property. Earlier, I argued that strong republicans hold that private property provides citizens with stakes in the well-being of the republic and enables citizens to care about both themselves and their households. Landed property, central to Pocock's and Skinner's reading of republicanism, is much less important to Americans who find their stakes come with the opportunity society.[45] Sometimes, that opportunity comes with the land and agriculture; sometimes it comes with the petty commerce of merchants; sometimes it comes with finance or an emerging manufacturing sector. Whatever its source, opportunity is not found in fixed estates, except for southern planters. Property is mobile and becomes a commodity and not a patrimony; many farmers improve the land, sell it, and move on. With the spread of contracts and market relations, the stable society so important to republicans gives way to change and mobility and, in the process, unglues whatever vestiges of republicanism remain in the country. Gordon Wood has recently argued that the traditional republican understanding that considered property "as a source of independence, not productivity," did not survive long in America. As Wood sees it, even before the Revolution,

> commerce and trade were creating new forms of property that gave wealth and power to new sorts of people. The Revolution accelerated the creation of this kind of property. This new property was anything but static. . . . This was the property of businessmen and protobusinessmen—of commercial farmers, artisan-manufacturers, traders, shopkeepers, and all who labored for a living and produced and exchanged things, no matter how poor or wealthy they might be.
> Unlike proprietary wealth, this new kind of dynamic, fluid, and evanescent property could not create authority or identity. . . . Hence it could not be relied on as a source of independence.[46]

The American view of property retains only echoes of the characteristics assigned to it by Pocock and Skinner. It is never a sturdy bulwark that protects its owners against change or is indifferent to profit or productivity. The autonomy Americans seek is found in an opportunity society which is highly reliant on an economy of growth rather than a stable society. Americans believe that what gets in the way is sometimes an unaccountable government that favors some at the expense of the rest, and at other times concentrations of private power and wealth in civil society that block choices and movement in what should be an open, opportunity society.

Republicanism remains in the country as a rhetorical but not an organizing presence. In the formative period, Americans speak a liberal language as well as the languages of democracy and markets, giving political equality a new meaning and shelving deference and paternalism. For those who find opportunity is elusive and are left behind, calls for the common good, lamentations about corruption, and celebrations about civic virtue run parallel to rather than against arguments for unblocking economic opportunities and extending democracy. From this perspective, the common good is found in the opportunity society (however understood), corruption is detected in restricting markets and blocking opportunities, and civic virtue means taking care of oneself and not getting in the way of others. Even though republicanism does not take on a continental form in America, it retains its appeal for many who find it does something that the languages of liberalism, democracy, and markets can not. It provides a readily comprehensible language challenging the excesses of the dominant languages, asking people to resist the seductive appeals that material acquisition is the basis of happiness, reminding them that the common good sometimes means more than not harming others, and emphasizing that citizenship entails both rights and duties.

Reconstituting the Founding and Lincoln's Moral Impatience

In challenging slavery and conducting the civil war, Abraham Lincoln has variously been described as a republican, a Christian, and a liberal thinker. No respecter of linguistic boundaries, he sees his republic decaying because of its indifference to slavery. As with so many other Americans of his generation, he had once expected that slavery would wither away on its own accord, but, with growing agitation about extending slavery to the new territories, he finds that this expectation is jeopardized. Faced with the possibility that slavery will continue and possibly expand, Lincoln disturbs the republic's tranquillity and challenges his fellow citizens who seek to avoid conflict by ignoring the issue. In mounting his attack, he appeals to what he considers the founding standards of the country. Although Lincoln's founding principles obviously depart from those of Machiavelli and Rousseau, his, like theirs, represent the defining ideals and best aspirations of a nation. For Lincoln, this means the basic equality of all persons.

Lincoln's Civic and Religious Credentials

There is considerable controversy about the best way to understand Lincoln. John Diggins sees him as an American Christian while William Corlett sees him as an American civic humanist.[47] Their arguments about Lincoln reveal something important about the ways commentaries are constructed and how someone can fit comfortably into very different constructions. In the first place, Lincoln frequently appeals to foundational principles, sometimes to the Declaration of Independence, and sometimes to the Bible, as sources of moral guidance. Moreover, he relies heavily on the language of shame and guilt both to explain and move people, a language that occupies important positions in both Christianity and republicanism, even if the former relies more heavily on guilt and the latter on shame. Third, Lincoln offers a strong critique on the vulnerability and weakness of the human condition while at the same time arguing that people have the capacities to dedicate themselves to something beyond their passions. For Diggins, this reflects Lincoln's preoccupation with sin; for Corlett, Lincoln offers a view of the corruptibility of both individuals and society. Fourth, Lincoln calls for sacrifice and sees suffering as redemptive. This Diggins takes as the quintessential Christian conviction, and a strong republican position likens it to patriotism.

That Lincoln is guided by his strong sense of Augustinian Christianity in no way precludes his honest affinity to many of the principles of republicanism.[48] This can be seen in his view of the vulnerabilities attached to every person, namely an unbridled attention to the self. Pride is the great temptation and sin in Christian teaching while unchecked ambition signals the onslaught of corruption to republicans. Pride, a refusal to recognize one's own limits, entraps Adam and Eve who ate of the forbidden fruit in order to assume divine attributes. From an Augustinian perspective, the temptation of pride continually follows men and women through their worldly sojourn. Pride manifests itself in many ways, large and small, and, when Christians succumb, they ought to experience guilt. However, pride often pays its own worldly dividends and makes us feel even more confident in our own powers and gifts. Not feeling guilty at such times, we need to be reminded of our vulnerabilities and limits.

The danger of acute self-love is also a persistent theme in strong republicanism. The risks of self-indulgence, the tendency to privilege oneself over others, and the proclivity of people to see themselves as the authors of the good that visits them (rather than to acknowledge that in addition to their own best efforts, they owe a heavy debt to their society) thematically reside in republican texts. In this literature, passion and pride are neither dissipated with the founding of the republic nor tamed by its participatory institutions. Neither the republican founding nor politics is sufficiently authoritative over time to eliminate pride. But both represent powerful weapons in the contest with pride and can summon citizens to look beyond themselves. Lincoln reflects this outlook when he observes,

> May we not justly fear that the awful calamity of the Civil War, which now desolates the land, may be but a punishment, inflicted on us, for our presumptuous sins? . . . . We have been the recipients of the choicest bounties of Heaven. We have been preserved, these many years, in peace and prosperity. We have grown in numbers, wealth, and power, as no other nation has grown. But we have forgotten God. We have forgotten the gracious hand which preserved us in peace . . . and we have vainly imagined, in the deceitfulness of our hearts, that all these blessings were produced by some superior wisdom and virtue of our own. Intoxicated with unbroken success, we have become too self-sufficient.[49]

Lincoln's assault on the pride of his fellow citizens is clearly steeped in Christianity but carries republican echoes throughout. He finds that Americans have become preoccupied with their own individual welfare and have not looked beyond their own labor and perseverance to understand their success. They do not see that they are part of a larger undertaking, one that begins with the founding and its sacrifices. Lincoln fears that Americans have forgotten the original meaning of their republic and are neglecting to preserve it.

In this sense, Lincoln departs from the Madisonian settlement, which expects that interests can be constrained under the new constitution. Madison's confidence that interests and passions can remain localized does not work as expected, but this is not Lincoln's complaint. As Diggins points out, Lincoln is less interested in perpetuating American institutions than American ideals and less concerned about structural solutions to pride and ambition and more about the character of the American people. Lincoln also leaves behind the Madisonian view that the Constitution embodies the origins of the nation, and he looks to the Declaration of Independence as its foundation.

Lincoln's Two Liberalisms

Lincoln also carries liberal credentials with his emphasis on rights, his dedication to economic modernization,[50] and his commitment to expanding political citizenship without prior civic requirements.[51] David Greenstone offers us a liberal Lincoln and in doing so takes us away from a dispute between liberals and republicans.[52] For him, there are two families of liberals in America. One family reflects Jeffersonian commitments to individual autonomy. As "humanist liberals," they hold that "the satisfaction of self-determined preferences is central to well being."[53] The other liberal family, "reform liberalism," traces its lineage to the Puritans and John Adams. Greenstone's reform liberals believe

> individuals have an obligation—not just an option—to cultivate and develop their physical, intellectual, aesthetic, and moral faculties. Importantly, the obligation extends to helping others to do the same. . . . The exercise of their abilities allows individuals to become full human beings and fully participating members of particular communities.[54]

Greenstone's humanist liberals look very much like individualists who are preoccupied with their own well-being, not in the sense that they do whatever is necessary to advance themselves, but in the more restrictive sense that they overtly avoid harming others and want to be left alone. Reform liberals, on the other hand, see their own moral development intimately tied to the other members of society. It is not good enough to ignore others when they are denied their rights. Greenstone's reform liberals extend themselves into politics to assure an equal opportunity for everyone.

Greenstone's Lincoln combines both liberal commitments but is ultimately guided by the reform branch. He does not want people just to be left alone but to be free to develop, to care for themselves but also for their community. For Greenstone, the "Lincoln persuasion . . . was a very successful synthesis of both outlooks: and it provided the North with a politically viable and intellectually coherent stand on slavery, because it added humanistic features to a more complex and subtle reform liberalism understanding of the issue."[55] It turns out that Lincoln is more than Diggins's Christian theologian or Corlett's republican. Lincoln reaches into many political vocabularies to fashion a language of rights and obligation, of founding principles and practical necessity, and of warning about both personal pride and civic lethargy. In the following sections, I argue that for all his debts to Christianity and republicanism, Lincoln's commitments resemble the complex liberalism Greenstone describes. Lincoln continually challenges Stephen Douglas's narrow individualism and employs republican and biblical idioms to construct an enlarged, reformed liberalism.

Lincoln's American Founding

When Americans reflect on their country, the theme of American exceptionalism frequently appears, and Lincoln contributes to this literature. He finds the country endowed in many ways: in its land and opportunities but most especially in the freedom professed at its founding and in its ideals to universal equality. Like Machiavelli and Rousseau in very different contexts, he sees his country favored in its origins; but unlike them, he believes his republic is marred in a crucial way. Its beginnings are flawed by slavery, a contradiction of the nation's highest aspirations.

Lincoln's claim of equality as central to the founding conflicts with the Constitution's tacit acceptance of slavery as a legitimate institution. This presents no major obstacle to Lincoln because he makes Jefferson's Declaration of Independence the heart of American's moral experiment and affirmation. His continued return to the Declaration as the embodiment of the nation's founding principles, which must guide his contemporaries, not only touches republican concerns about founding principles but also introduces a clear and unequivocal commitment to the liberal theme of equal rights. Lincoln uses the Declaration and its moral principles to define what it takes to be an American, namely that we recognize that everyone is "created equal" and each person is entitled to be free.[56] For this reason, he finds the Dred Scott decision, which holds that slaves can be considered private property, contradicts the principles of

> our Declaration of Independence [which] was held sacred by all, and thought to include all; but now, to aid in making the bondage of the negro universal and eternal, it is assailed, and sneered at, and construed, and hawked at, and torn, till, if its framers could rise from their graves, they could not recognize it.[57]

Lincoln concludes his speech with a question: are Americans "really willing that the Declaration shall be thus twittered away? thus left no more at most, than an interesting memorial of the dead past? thus shorn of its vitality, and practical value; and left without the *germ* or even the *suggestion* of the individual rights of man in it?"[58]

Lincoln continually returns to the Declaration as the embodiment of the founding and the beacon, which should guide Americans in their most fundamental moral and political commitments. For him, the principle of equality is not a symbol, a formula, or a token but the creed that animated the republic in the past and should do so in the present. When Lincoln looks at recent immigrants from Europe, he sees people whose forbearers had not participated in the work of the revolution but who find that the language of the Declaration embodies their own highest aspirations and ideals. Lincoln's Declaration allows them to be included as full citizens because of their civic commitments, not because of their family backgrounds.

"We hold these truths to be self-evident, that all men are created equal" . . . that moral sentiment . . . that is the father of all moral principles in them, and that they have a right to claim it as though they were blood of the blood and flesh of the flesh of the men who wrote the Declaration, and so they are. This is the electric cord in the Declaration that links the hearts of patriotic and liberty-loving men together.[59]

Lincoln's Declaration not only is the principle that serves as the touchstone of the republic but also is the standard that he wants Americans to use to give them their identity as Americans; citizens are expected to care deeply about the free institutions of their republic as well as the essential equality of everyone in the country. Castigating Stephen Douglas for saying that he does not care whether slavery is voted up or down, Lincoln insists the American commitment to equality represents the bedrock of the republic and that neither convenience nor interests should shake it. For him, the standards of the founding celebrate the liberty Americans prize and provide them with criteria to judge public policies and current practices and then to act accordingly.

The Need for Renewal through Confrontation

In the *Lyceum Address*, arguably one of Lincoln's strongest republican statements, he calls on his fellow citizens to renew their traditions now that the last of the founding generation is dying off and the memory of its work is fading. He tells his audience that they live "under a government of a system of political institutions, conducing more essentially to the ends of civil and religious liberty than any of which former times tells us." His audience should remember they are not responsible for the "fundamental blessings," which is

a legacy bequeathed us by a *once* hardy, brave and patriotic, but *now* lamented and departed race of ancestors. Theirs was the *Task* (and nobly they performed it) to possess themselves and through themselves, us, of this goodly land; and to uprear upon its hills and its valleys, a political edifice of liberty and equal rights; is ours only, to transmit these, the former, unprofaned by the foot of an invader, the latter, undecayed by the lapse of time and untorn by usurpation, to the latest generation that fate shall permit the world to know. This task of gratitude to our fathers, justice to ourselves, duty to posterity, and love for our species in general, all imperatively require us faithfully to perform.[60]

Dismissing the possibility of a foreign occupation, Lincoln insists that the danger to this legacy "must spring up amongst us. . . . If destruction be our lot, we must ourselves be its author and finisher.

As a nation of freemen, we must live through all time, or die by suicide."[61] For him, the process of self destruction comes not only from a neglect of founding principles but also from a rampant lawlessness, directed particularly against Negroes but also against others who fall into displeasure, such as gamblers and strangers. The problem with vigilantism for Lincoln is that it invites people to become a law unto themselves. "Having ever regarded Government as their deadliest bane, they make a jubilee of the suspension of its operations; and pray for nothing so much as its total annihilation."[62]

For Lincoln, the founding principles of the Declaration were once nourished by patriotic citizens. Today, however "Mammon, . . . ambition, . . . philosophy, . . . [and even] the Theology of the day" conspire to undo the principles on which the nation was founded.[63] Rather than challenging narrow interests, even religion, Lincoln despairs, becomes politically instrumental. He returns to the theme that Americans have become civically lethargic and morally indifferent in his last debate with Douglas in 1858. Lincoln criticizes the view that

> you must not say any thing about . . . [slavery] in the free states *because it is not there*. You must not say anything about it in the slave states, *because it is there*. You must not say any thing about it from the pulpit, because that is religion and has nothing to do with it. You must not say any thing about it in politics, *because that will disturb the security of "my place."*[64]

Lincoln finds the republic is in jeopardy at this time, because the once-solid buttresses supplied by the founding generation "are now decayed and crumbled away." Earlier generations were not certain the republican experiment would succeed and they worked for its success: the leaders of the founding generation linked their own ambition and destiny inseparably with the experiment of self-government. "Now it is understood to be a successful one" but, paradoxically, success threatens to undermine it. The reason, Lincoln argues, is that talented people will not abandon their ambitions for success but will find no "gratification . . . in supporting an edifice that has been erected by others."[65] Paralleling Machiavelli and Rousseau, he sees ambition as pervasive and ubiquitous and fears that some talented, ambitious Americans will use their considerable rhetorical and political abilities to advance themselves at the expense of the republic. Their appeals to the passions and interests of voters as well as the desire of citizens to favor their own tranquillity and prosperity serve to subvert the republic's principled origins. Unlike the patriots of the founding era who experience the dangers and corruption of nonrepublican government, succeeding generations have only a faulty memory to remind them why republican government is necessary. The meaning and principles of the revolution "*cannot be* so universally known, nor so vividly felt, as they were by the generation just gone to rest." The passions that move the earlier generation are no longer reliable and, in their place, Lincoln offers "reason, cold, calculating, unimpassioned reason," which is molded into "a *sound morality* and, in particular, a *reverence for the constitution and laws.*"[66]

> Let every man remember that to violate the law is to trample on the blood of his father, and to tear the charter of his own, and his children's liberty. Let reverence to the law be breathed by every American mother to the lisping babe . . . preached from the pulpit, proclaimed in legislative halls, and enforced in courts of justice. And, in short, let it become the *political religion* of the nation; and let the old and the young, the rich and the poor, the grave and the gay, of all sexes and tongues, and colors and conditions, sacrifice unceasingly upon its altars.[67]

For Lincoln, neither the political institutions of a free society nor the fading memory of a sacred cause are sufficient to sustain the republic. Liberty, in Lincoln's hands, retains its strong republican paradox: many of the very things we seek, such as peace and prosperity, undermine our commitments to foundational principles and practices on which the republic rests. However much the founding generation is central to Lincoln's republic, the work of present-day citizens remains equally important. Summoning "cold, calculating, unimpassioned reason" and reverence to the law to sustain liberty, he invites his fellow citizens to uncouple themselves from their interests and security when foundational principles are at stake and to protect what is general and hallowed. He wants his fellow citizens to look beyond their narrow, instrumental advantages and realize their liberty depends on the vitality of the free institutions of the republic. He also reminds Americans that freedom is not a grant to some but the right of every citizen. If a free people are to keep their freedom they must recognize their own vulnerabilities, their own susceptibility to pride and passivity, and their own need to sacrifice. And for Lincoln, sacrifice does not so much mean relinquishing something (except complacency and apathy); it means doing something politically. At the time of his Lyceum address, Lincoln sees no civil war approaching, but he is prepared to oppose mob rule and the spread of slavery and is ready to invite political discord. Indeed, he demands it.

For all their agreements, there is a critical difference between the noisy republican account of conflict and Lincoln's. The former believe there is a rough harmony between the republic's foundational principles and its actual practices and institutions. For Machiavelli and Rousseau, good citizens consider the social arrangements of the republic to be fair and accept the apportionment of the liberties, duties, and advantages assigned to them. This view rests on the presumption that after noisy politics, most citizens will be satisfied to return to the traditional equilibrium or at least a close approximation to it.

Lincoln sees a contradiction between the standards of equality embodied in the Declaration and the institution of slavery. The resolution of the conflict cannot lead to the restoration of the old equilibrium because it is deeply flawed, and Lincoln seeks to refound the American republic with a commitment to the basic rights of all citizens. But this raises serious political problems because any refounding is unlikely to be accepted by everyone; some winners and/or losers can be counted on to consider the new settlement unfair or inadequate. Refounding the republic committed to equal rights in a society whose members disagree about what this means in theory and practice means continued conflict. Rather than finding the harmony and reinforcements that Machiavelli and Rousseau locate in foundational standards and current practices in the good republic, Lincoln seeks to reconstruct the founding, that is, he works for the elimination of slavery to confirm the Declaration's ideals. But losers will not be content, and Lincoln (and liberals in general) can expect no stable equilibrium to follow conflict as strong republicans do.[68]

Lincoln's commitments to equal rights show him as a liberal—not as a possessive individualist, but as one who fits into Greenstone's reform branch. At the same time, Lincoln comfortably employs republican fragments to remind his fellow citizens about the importance of their own founding and that their own good is inexorably tied to a common good that also speaks to the rights of all citizens. He calls up an Augustinian Christianity to talk about human frailty, pride, and redemption. Lincoln draws on the religious and secular commitments of his fellow citizens to convince his northern audience that it must break from a political and moral lethargy and embark on a noisy politics. In these and other ways, Lincoln shows how liberal commitments can be extended and emboldened by religious and republican principles.

American Rhetorics

Some communitarians return to the nation's past to demonstrate that we do not need to embrace something new or alien to relieve us of our discontents but rather should retrieve the valuable parts of our own lost heritage. But what the revisionists retrieve from their reading of the country's formative period is curiously decontexualized. We are usually offered collections of patriotic appeals directed at individualistic Americans to be civic. What is particularly arresting about most invocations to community and civic virtue in communitarian rhetoric is the lack of proposals to change the basic structures of politics, society, or the economy in order to provide institutional arrangements that dampen individualism or materialism or, to put it less politely, to challenge the institutions that are seen as most likely to corrupt citizens. When that challenge comes, it is from Lincoln who wants to make the country more liberal, not more republican.

In asking us to return to our roots, the revisionists challenge the thesis of a monolithic liberalism in order to show us a domestic alternative. Often allied to this argument is John Pocock's claim that republicanism can surmount the peculiarities of its earlier formulations and practices and be transported across time and space to other, quite different settings. The founding generation of Americans borrows abundantly from historic republican rhetoric, but it is never as pure as Pocock thinks. This generation employs terms assigned to republicanism to challenge both the crown and a narrow individualism and to talk about a common good that always embodies strong commitments to individual rights, a readiness to embrace change, and a dedication to equality of opportunity. For his part, Lincoln comfortably calls on his religious principles and the founding principles of the Declaration of Independence to fortify and extend his liberal commitments to the equality of all persons.

Several factors explain the fragility of republicanism in the United States, and one of the most important is the privileged status of equality of opportunity in American political discourse. While it is easy enough to recognize that opportunities are often more confined than the myth would allow, the myth is powerful and pervasive.[69] What makes equality of opportunity so attractive to Americans is what makes it dangerous to continental republicans. To Americans, categories such as occupation, status, or income should reflect merit, not birthright. By the standard account of equality of opportunity, our successes and failures should reflect our individual talents and efforts and not an assignment made by powerful authorities or inert traditions. From this perspective, we have a responsibility for our own well-being as well as a responsibility for not harming others. This position is developed in Greenstone's discussion of humanist liberalism. But, as Greenstone amply demonstrates, reform liberalism can challenge a narrower conception of liberalism, not to destroy it but to direct liberals to a concern about their fellow citizens.

Communitarian claims notwithstanding, the dominant language of American politics is the liberal language of rights. This is not to deny that republican themes frequently appear in American political discourse and theorizing, particularly efforts to claim a common good or warn about the corrupting influence of possessive individualism. It turns out that the first language of Americans is liberalism but many also accept the idea that they require a republican idiom, not to replace liberalism but to chasten it. From this perspective, American politics and theory reflect both agreement and dissonance as well as commitment and compromise in a world of flux.

Notes

1. I have in mind not only Aristotle, Machiavelli, and Rousseau but also Cicero, James Harrington, Algernon Sydney, and John Trenchard and Thomas Gordon.

2. In this account, what ultimately moves the colonists to break with the crown is not politics but morality. According to Gordon Wood, "It was more than Europe that the Americans rejected in 1776. It was the whole world as it had been, and indeed it was themselves as they had been" (*The Creation of the American Republic* [New York: Scribners, 1969], 113). He claims that "many Americans" seek "to realize the traditional Commonwealth ideal of a corporate society, in which the common good would be the only objective of government" (*Creation*, 54).

For a critique of the failure of the revolution to solidify a genuinely participatory democracy, see Benjamin Barber, *Strong Democracy* (Berkeley: University of California Press, 1984).

3. For a recent discussion of the neo-Whigs, see Michael Zuckert, *Natural Rights and the New Republicanism* (Princeton: Princeton University Press, 1994), chap. 6, and Daniel Rogers, "Republicanism: The Career of a Concept," *Journal of American History*, 79 (1992): 11–38.

4. Wood, *Creation*; Bernard Bailyn, *Ideological Origins of the American Revolution* (Cambridge: Harvard University Press, 1976); J. G. A. Pocock, *The Machiavellian Moment* (Princeton: Princeton University Press, 1971); and Michael Lienesch, *New Order of the Ages: Time, the Constitution, and the Making of Modern American Political Thought* (Princeton: Princeton University Press, 1988).

5. Bailyn, *Origins*, 23.
6. Bailyn, *Origins*, 136.
7. Bailyn, *Origins*, 35.
8. Wood, *Creation*, 53.
9. Wood, *Creation*, 60–61.
10. Wood, *Creation*, 60–61.
11. Wood, *Creation*, 68.
12. Pocock, *Moment*, 546–47.

13. *Moment*, 468, 487. Pocock goes to great lengths to show that credit is expanding in the late seventeenth century, that [some] republicans speak against it, and [some] members of the court favor it. He then shows how a life built on credit could be taken to be a corrupt life, one disdainful of work (*Moment*, 177–78). What is puzzling in Pocock's reading is that he concludes that the colonist's revulsion to credit, particularly by the crown, should make them into republicans. Writers of the time usually identified as liberals, such as Benjamin Franklin, have no trouble regaling against credit. See Isaac Kramnick for a discussion of the opposition of English "liberals" to credit (*Republicanism and Bourgeois Radicalism* [Ithaca: Cornell University Press, 1990]).

14. According to Pocock, growing economic specialization in America menaces republican values because "specialists became servants to others. . . . Specialization . . . was a prime cause of corruption; only the citizen as amateur, propertied, independent, and willing to perform in his own person all functions essential to the polis, could be said to practice virtue" (*Moment*, 499).

15. Kramnick, *Republicanism*, 196.
16. Kramnick, *Republicanism*, 197.

17. Even though she believes the republican critique hides more than it reveals, Joyce Appleby credits it with emphasizing the ideological basis of American politics. The revisionists invite us to examine "liberalism as a cultural artifact" and she observes that both self-interests and civic virtue are "social constructions of reality" (*Liberalism and Republicanism in the Historical Imagination* [Cambridge: Harvard University Press, 1992], 141).

18. *Liberalism*, 150.
19. *Liberalism*, 155.
20. *Liberalism*, 158.
21. *Liberalism*, 158.
22. *Liberalism*, 177.

23. Rogers argues, "this investing of the revolutionary mind in the texts of a handful of English publicists was clearly wrong. It squeezed out massive domains of culture—religion, law, political economy, ideas of patriarchy, family, and gender, ideas of race and slavery, class and nationalism, nature and reason—that everyone knew to be profoundly tangled in the revolutionary impulse . . . . [With the revisionist version] eighteenth century history was simplified and secularized, repackaged along linear lines of influence that had long given political theory a bad name . . . . [With] the republican synthesis

[it appeared] as if the revolutionary mind had come across the Atlantic in one or another late eighteenth-century sailing vessel, packed as tract and pamphlet, to be grafted onto a headless social body" ("Republicanism," 18–19).

24. "Republicanism," 22.
25. "Republicanism," 33.
26. "Republicanism," 38.
27. Thomas Pangle, *The Spirit of Modern Republicanism* (Chicago: University of Chicago Press, 1988). Also see Richard Sinopoli, *The Foundations of American Citizenship* (New York: Oxford University Press, 1992); Michael Zukert, *Natural Rights and the New Republicanism*, and Jermone Huyler, *Locke in America* (Lawrence: University Press of Kansas, 1995).
28. Kramnick demonstrates a strong Lockean presence in the colonies. Pangle, Sinopoli, and Zuckert also provide ample materials to show that Locke was widely read before, during, and after the Revolution, and not as a possessive individualist.
29. John Dworetz, *The Unvarnished Doctrine: Locke, Liberalism, and the American Revolution* (Durham: Duke University Press, 1990), 70.
30. Dworetz finds that many Americans who never read Locke came to know some of his basic arguments through sermons. Donald Lutz has shown that many Americans were acquainted with Locke through political pamphlets published during the period.
31. Dworetz, *Unvarnished Doctrine*, 71.
32. Dworetz, *Unvarnished Doctrine*, 132.
33. Appleby, for one, complains that "once having been identified, [republicanism] can be found everywhere" (*Liberalism*, 277).
34. Among the characteristics of what he calls classical republican thought, Benjamin Barber lists "a distrust of rapid change" (*Strong*, 44).
35. Lienesch, *New Order*, 73.
36. The importance attached to deference in republicanism is provided by Pocock who finds that "in Harrington as in every other republican classic, it was unequivocally stated that the alternative to a hereditary, entrenched, or artificial aristocracy was a natural aristocracy—an elite of persons distinguished by natural superiority of talent, but also by contingent material advantages such as property, leisure, and learning, as possessing the qualities of mind required by the classical Few. It was assumed that a supply of such persons was guaranteed by nature, and part of the case against artificially established aristocracies was the true elite were naturally recognizable by the many. The democracy could discover the aristocracy by using its own modes of discernment, and there was no need to legislate its choice in advance; a theory of deference was usually invoked in order to democratize the polity" (*Moment*, 515; also see 485).
37. *Moment*, 521.
38. Wood, *Creation*, 90.
39. Bernard Bailyn writes, "Americans of 1760 continued to assume, as had their predecessors for generations before, that a healthy society was a

hierarchical society, in which it was natural for some to be rich and some poor, some honored and some obscure, some powerful and some weak. And it was believed that superiority was unitary, that the attributes of the favored—wealth, wisdom, power—had a natural affinity to each other, and hence political leadership would naturally rest in the hands of the social leaders. . . . "Circumstances" particularly the call for disobedience to the crown "had pressed harshly against such assumptions" (*Origins*, 302–4).

40. Wood, *Creation*, 488, 490, 491–92.

41. Wood, *Creation*, 497. Adam Smith is not far off the target when he observes, "The leading men of America, we may believe, wish to continue to be the principal people in their own country" (cited in J. W. Gettridge, "Adam Smith on the American Revolution: An Unpublished Memorial, *American Historical Review* 38 [1933]: 714–20).

42. For a contrary view, William Sullivan who finds earlier generations of Americans seek "to promote civic virtue through an active life" (*Reconstructing Political Philosophy* [Berkeley: University of California Press, 1982], 12).

43. See Lienesch, *New Order*, 34, 44; Martin Diamond, "Ethics and Politics: The American Way," in *The Moral Foundations of the American Republic*, edited by Robert Horwitz (Charlottesville: University Press of Virginia, 1986), 107–8.

44. See Hector St. John de Crevecour, *Letters from an American Farmer* (New York: Doubleday, 1961).

45. For Pocock, "An infinite supply of land, ready for occupation by an armed and self-directing yeomanry, meant an infinite supply of virtue" (*Moment*, 535).

46. Gordon Wood, *Radicalism of the American Revolution* (New York: Knopf, 1992), 711.

47. John Diggins, *The Lost Soul of American Politics* (New York: Basic Books, 1984), and William Corlett, "The Availability of Lincoln's Civil Religion," *Political Theory* 10 (1982): 520–40.

48. Diggins continually contrasts his Christian Lincoln with the Machiavelli of the *Prince* in order to show the distance that separates Lincoln from republicanism. What is curious in this strategy is that Diggins fails to make comparisons with other parts of Machiavelli's texts or his civic humanism and offers us a Machiavelli that neither Pocock nor Skinner would recognize.

49. Cited in Diggins, *Lost Soul*, 330.

50. During his political career, he also supported a national bank, tariffs to protect a developing domestic market, a state university system, and a national transportation system. The classical republican predilection for economic stability and suspicion about sweeping changes do not describe Lincoln's views.

51. Lincoln rejects the appeals of some Republicans to support nativist movements, such as the Know-Nothings, and runs on a platform in 1860 that opposes efforts to restrict the rights of immigrants. Also see his speech to German-Americans, *The Collected Works of Abraham Lincoln*, vol. 4, edited

by Roy Basler (New Brunswick: Rutgers University Press, 1953), February 12, 1861, 201–3.

52. David Greenstone, *The Lincoln Persuasion* (Princeton: Princeton University Press, 1993.

53. *Lincoln Persuasion*, 54. This is exemplified in the humanistic view of individual responsibility and a commitment to a society that is open to the best efforts of everyone. Lincoln recalls that he "was a hired laborer. The hired labor of yesterday labors on his own account today, and will hire others to labor for him tomorrow. Advancement—improvement in conditions—is the order of things in a society of equals" (Lincoln, *Collected Works*, 2. 221).

54. *Lincoln Persuasion*, 59.

55. *Lincoln Persuasion*, 7; also see 244.

56. According to Lincoln's revisionist account of the meaning of the federal constitution, slavery was an embarrassment to the framers, and he interprets the prohibition of the slave trade as a conscious effort to hasten its end. In a variety of ways, Lincoln imputes antislavery positions to people and laws that are, at best, conjectural, and he later admits that some of his interpretations had been made in haste. The important issue here, however, is not how faithful Lincoln is to the historical record in his reading of the framers and the constitution but his antislavery reading of the American founding.

57. Speech at Springfield, June 26, 1857, vol. 2, 404.

58. Speech at Springfield, 407.

59. Speech at Chicago, July 10, 1858, vol. 2, 499–500.

60. Speech at Springfield, January 27, 1838, vol. 1, 108.

61. Speech at Springfield, 109.

62. Speech at Springfield, 109. He goes on to argue that if "the laws be continually despised and disregarded. . . . the alienation of their affections [of good citizens] from the Government is the natural consequence" (Springfield, 112).

63. Speech at Springfield, June 26, 1857, vol. 2, 404.

64. *The Lincoln-Douglas Debates of 1858*, edited by Robert Johannsen (New York: Oxford University Press, 1965), 318.

65. Speech at Springfield, January 27, 1838, vol. 1, 114.

66. *Lincoln-Douglas Debates*, 125.

67. *Lincoln-Douglas Debates*, 21–22.

68. One of the marks of Lincoln's liberalism is that there is little of the preoccupation of strong republicans about distributional arrangements. He can avoid this discussion because of what he takes to be the exceptional promise of reward in an economy of opportunity and growth.

69. See Appleby, *Liberalism*; Fred Hirsch, *The Social Limits to Growth* (Cambridge: MIT Press, 1976); and John Schaar, "Equality of Opportunity and Beyond," in *Equality, NOMOS,* vol. 9, edited by R. Pennock and John Chapman (New York: Atherton, 1967).

Chapter Eight

Paradoxes and Anxieties for Politics Today

Appearances and rhetoric notwithstanding, the debate between contemporary liberals and communitarians is not essentially a contest between good and evil but rather a serious and important clash between two very valuable goods. In presenting some of the neglected fragments of strong republicanism and anxious liberalism, I have not aimed at reconciling the two positions because each contains its own distinctive good. Nor do I claim that strong republicanism or anxious liberalism carry the authentic core of their respective traditions. I have argued that both strong republicans and anxious liberals offer us something valuable that we lose if we are unnecessarily forced to choose between rigid constructions of the two traditions and that we do not always have to choose. One reason is that the concerns of republicans and liberals often overlap. Both talk about virtue and are concerned about the self; both warn about the abuses of power and about self-deception; and both celebrate the autonomous life.

The need for contemporary liberals to enrich their language is particularly pressing since liberalism is the nation's dominant political language. Because it sometimes exaggerates what proceduralism can accomplish and is intolerant of goods other than rights, it needs internal resources to call attention to some of the important goods it neglects. However, even an enriched liberalism will not always be able to chastise itself, and then it needs to be challenged by alternative, independent principles, such as those found in communitarianism. To be effective, such alternatives need themselves to be flexible and expansive rather than rigid and narrow.

Reconsidering the Two-Language Paradigm

In the preceding chapters, I showed that some linguistic constructions we find among contemporary liberals and communitarians depart remarkably from what we find among anxious liberals and strong republicans. Anxious liberals, for example, are heavily steeped in moral language and strong republicans continually acknowledge the importance of the self. Moreover, strong republicans and anxious liberals often share many of the same goods: each, for example, talks about liberty and a moral life. It might appear, then, that we do not have two distinctive, warring languages but a single one. From this perspective, we should be able to blend liberalism and republicanism into a common political language that acknowledges the importance of both the free person and the coherent community.[1]

However, it is a mistake to discard the two-language paradigm. The most important reason is that it acknowledges something important about politics: any solution is subject to decay or abuse and therefore is provisional. The liberty we seek can degenerate into chaos and conflict; the unity we pursue can become oppressive. There are times when community becomes overbearing and restrictive and its demands stifle individual autonomy. There are other times when individualism traverses the boundaries of self-restraint and threatens the common institutions that secure the autonomy of all citizens. When the first is the issue, the language of liberalism is appropriate and the language of republicanism seems suited to the second danger.[2] The two-language paradigm acknowledges that for some, the pressing issue of the day is how those who have been neglected or dominated in our society's historical and contemporary practices require liberal principles that speak to the ideal of full and equal treatment. For others, our condition is fragmented, our sense of connectedness is weak, and our moral coherence is shattered. The language of communitarianism reminds us of what we risk losing or have already lost but might recover. To blend the two languages means we often mute conflicts over important but distinct principles.[3]

Who is right? The question is worth asking, not because it leads us to the answer that convinces and satisfies everyone. Rather, it calls attention to the importance of the issues at stake. It enables us to recognize that different positions can be held by honest advocates who observe the same phenomena. America today is, after all, both inegalitarian and materialist; it is both racist and incoherent. Some will see the nation's greatest dangers one way and others will point another way. Nothing I write (or, I suspect, others write) will convince those who are told their concerns are really secondary to change their position. If we take both positions as principled and valuable in a free society, friends will seek to enrich and extend their respective positions, rather than reinforce narrowness and rigidity. Nor will they try to blend them and pretend that nothing important is lost in the new amalgam.

Returning to Republican Roots

Strong republicans as opposed to nostalgic communitarians realize the importance of people caring about themselves and recognize that they do not suspend their concern about themselves because they are good citizens. Indeed, one of the reasons they value their republic is that it respects the important, multiple needs of citizens. They see their own good depends not only on their own exertions but also on the vitality of their republic and its free institutions. In the good republic, citizens also attach themselves to its basic principles, particularly those embedded in its founding. What makes civic attachments credible to republican citizens is not merely remembrance, ritual, and renewal but also the repeated experiences and satisfactions that validate their personal investment in the continued well-being of the republic.

However much strong republicans try to resist certain kinds of change, they know the republic is not frozen in time and its citizens are not fixed in their dedication to the republic. Not only can extrinsic factors disturb the republican settlement; more especially, some citizens can be expected to become dissatisfied with that settlement and breach it to satisfy their own ambitions. Strong republicans appreciate that pride and vanity follow everyone, and some republican citizens are likely to understand themselves apart from their republican attachments and use their resources and opportunities to attend to their interests at the expense of their republican responsibilities. For such citizens, stable stakes and robust traditions are insufficient to restrain ambition. To challenge ambition, Machiavelli and Rousseau appeal to noisy citizens to come to the fore, defending not only their own individual stakes but also the republic that remains important to them. These patriotic citizens are thought to have a clear understanding of the founding principles of the republic and work to return the republic to its original ideals.

More dangerous to the republic than ambitious citizens who can be confronted and resisted by patriotic citizens is the tendency of any citizen to take liberty for granted and to retreat from politics. The most perilous moment in the life of the republic occurs when it appears most successful: when its citizens enjoy peace and security. Then, the interdependence between the political and the private is forgotten, the connection between the well-being of their particular households and their stakes in the good republic is ignored, and the bond between maintaining past traditions and enjoying present-day life is discounted. When this happens, a new pride invades the precincts of the republic. It is not the pride of overwhelming ambition that prompts a few to seek much more for themselves. It is the small pride that comes from believing that one can be sufficient without attending to the vitality of the republic. Machiavelli and Rousseau see this infection creating a vacuum in republican space that threatens to be filled with the politics of corruption with its rampant dissatisfaction and ambition.

This paradox of republican politics, that its greatest success breeds its greatest danger, is unavoidable in the accounts I have been detailing. But its inevitability does not mean its immanence. The corrupting perils of self-interest can be avoided, sometimes through renewal and remembrance and sometimes through adjustments of the equilibrium. Sometimes, the tempo of decay can be delayed with measures that seem stark and uninviting. Machiavelli offers us "necessity," those moments of crisis that shake us from our lethargy and remind us in the most compelling ways that our republic is important to us and requires our dedication and service.

Strong republicans call our attention to a dark future that awaits any good regime in order to warn us not to surrender to an inevitable decay and to caution us that the good republic can be prolonged only through our political attentiveness and commitment. A difficulty for those who want to carry on the republican tradition today comes with the inadequacy of the foundational principles to satisfy everyone about its fairness. To understand the nature of this republican difficulty, it is necessary to untangle several of the terms used in this formulation, because each is important and all are interrelated. The founding tells us what is good, possible, and natural and contributes to our own identity and to our ideas about what we are due and what we owe others, including the collectivity. The myth of the founding accomplishes these tasks by explaining that the inequalities and subordinations that mark any society are natural, that it would be impossible for things to be otherwise, and that our society, for all of its disappointments, is a good society. To the extent that citizens accept this reading, they agree to their own place in society as well as the places of others, both above and below, as essentially appropriate. The equilibrium that evolves out of the republic's founding is both normative and structural. As I indicated earlier, this solution works for strong republicans because the settlement is tied to concrete stakes that citizens see as including secure places for their own household as well as the good of the whole. Second, the distributions are accepted as fair and equitable, whether in a one-class society or a society divided by classes. However, when the scope of citizenship enlarges, ultimately including all adult members of society, many are without concrete stakes, and the inequalities and diversities that are now housed in the republic are often wide and deep. For many, the republic's founding settlement does not speak to them.

Why not? Envy and resentment take us only a short distance in understanding the dilemma facing the inclusive republic. What nostalgic communitarians repeatedly forget is that the stakes-carrying citizens of the strong republic are not only normatively attached to but also institutionally integrated into the life of the republic. Today, the gap between substantive inclusion and formal inclusion is extensive and the ability of many citizens to pursue the good within current institutional settings is constrained. What strikes stakes-carrying citizens of the strong republic as good, natural, and necessary does not cover many citizens in the enlarged republic today. In the transformed milieu of the extended polity, we encounter demands that cannot easily be accommodated within the traditional equilibrium, particularly its institutional pattern of rewards and protections. Not surprisingly, we find a new politics in the inclusive republic, with some citizens demanding something like stakes and some other citizens fearing that accommodation to these demands will destabilize the current equilibrium and endanger their own stakes. In this cauldron, the politics of assertion (by would-be stakes-carriers) and the politics of resentment (by current stakes-holders) clash and what commonalities they share are frequently lost.

Even to begin to develop a serious case for their position, sooner or later communitarians need to demonstrate that they can address the structural and distributional disequilibrium in the late modern world. It is not good enough to search for a public morality, not because we do not need one or that liberalism has been unable to generate a public morality. If we want to avoid a community that is sustained only by moralisms or that becomes another name for the tyranny of the majority, we need to ask what sustains the kind of community where everyone is treated as a full citizen. It is not sufficient to cull through the remains of our past to discover what general principles we share, salutary as that exercise may be. It is also necessary to ask what ought to be the requisites for full citizenship and what ought to define citizens, not just in the sense of their obligations and responsibilities, but also whether (and which) substantive and procedural stakes are attached to citizenship. Many communitarians neglect the concerns of strong republicans in critical ways and unwittingly borrow one of the features of liberalism that they most criticize. Liberalism is said to leave people lonely and unsituated in a world that is fragmented and incoherent. But nostalgic appeals to citizenship that ignore the settings in which people live their daily lives, fashion their identity, and carry out their responsibilities ask persons to transcend their insecurities, vulnerabilities, and disabilities and, through an act of their will, join around some minimal historical and normative commonalities.

The Lives of Ordinary Liberals

The liberal self is hardly a fixed self. Anxious liberals believe individuals have the moral capacities to challenge instincts, contingency, convention, and manipulation. In this sense, agents are open to redefining themselves by their reflective choices. For anxious liberals, moral agents can never evade responsibility for their choices, and grounded moral standards provide the materials for choice. Clearly, anxious liberals disagree among themselves about the precise content of those standards; but whether they are found in religion, the family, or philosophy, there is a continued reliance on principled standards to provide the basis for understanding society as well as oneself. Many anxious liberals go on to argue that the chances of failure are particularly pressing in an environment of growing freedom where men and women are not tethered by the institutional obstacles that once reduced their choices.

Warnings about confusing happiness with pleasure and about knowing the limits of our ability to become happy are not meant to deny the naturalness or importance of interests. Albert Hirschman's discussion of interests shows one reason they are attractive to many liberals is that they reduce violent conflict. He finds that by the seventeenth century, a general agreement emerged that neither a philosophical nor religious consensus could "be trusted with restraining the destructive passions of men."[4] Hirschman charts the fall of the socially disruptive virtue of glory that is won in war and its replacement by ostensibly tamer, socially quieter economic interests, which are pursued in impersonal markets. By his reading, liberal, and especially market, values become justified as an escape from the turbulence of war and as a place where ambition can be contained.

Even so, anxious liberals such as Smith who advance the cause of interests as a counterweight to the passions see a potential dark side to this solution at the individual level. To the extent that people are free to pursue their interests, they are also free to misunderstand or exaggerate them at the expense of some other, valuable goods. Indeed, much of John Locke's argument in *The Essay on Human Understanding* is about such confusions and his fear that many people act in ways that lead to their own unhappiness. Similar themes are sounded in the next century by David Hume and Adam Smith, no hostile observers of interests. The liberating effects that Smith attributes to commerce do not keep him from claiming that many interests in his generation rest on self-deceptions that not only distort what he takes to be the natural principles of justice but that can also be self-destructive. Mill's later, blistering indictment of motivation and conduct in commercial society amplifies many of these anxious liberal themes and applies them to an increasingly democratic society. At this point, it is helpful to consider two issues in the critique of liberalism, namely the morality or amorality of liberal agents and their authenticity or artificiality. Although there is no unified position among anxious liberals regarding these issues, a pattern emerges about what it means to be a liberal agent.

Critics charge that liberalism leaves agents amoral as they grope for meaning and direction amidst the materialistic, relativistic standards of their society. Anxious liberals attempt not only to equip agents with grounded standards to build a coherent moral life but also to challenge the efficiencies of their day while making agents responsible for their own moral character and happiness. Moreover, anxious liberals see money, fixed property, or commercial society carrying special obstacles to moral development, although none of the authors surveyed here wants to return to some earlier age where these features are missing.

Recognizing the innumerable opportunities and temptations people face, Locke, Smith, and Mill assign individuals the responsibility for flourishing or succumbing. Locke and Smith see moral standards learned at home as the best way to respond to the challenges facing agents, not efforts to cleanse society or introduce a misplaced perfectionism. Even though Mill thinks its structure and practices are defective in many important respects, the family remains important to him as the initial teacher of moral principles. However, he fears that commercialism has invaded the precincts of the household. This is one reason for his frontal assault on the commercial norms of his society, which, he argues, are destroying independent standards ordinary men and women use to judge themselves and their society. By promoting local participatory settings, Mill hopes to extend the attachments of agents and provide them with materials for an expanded social and moral autonomy. Anxious liberals appreciate that what we make of our attachments deeply matters to us and we need a moral framework to understand them. Some extend and enlarge us, some are debasing, and some mislead us. Anxious liberals seek not only to remove those obstacles that come from an arbitrary state, but also to challenge the array of social norms and practices that we unreflectively accept and that often retard our development. To mount the necessary challenge, they insist we require a firm, moral grounding when making choices.

With some readings of liberalism, the liberal self is contrived and other-directed and, therefore, unauthentic. Ironically, this also captures the way in which Locke, Smith, and Mill think that people can be "artificial." For them, an artificial person is someone who is created by external factors and whose choices are not referenced to the agent's own moral standards. In a very important sense, the anxious liberals I have been discussing believe that the natural self is not the self they see in their own generation because the context for the development of the self has changed.

For Locke, the innocence, goodwill, and peace of the early state of nature evaporate with the invention of money and the accumulation of acquired desires. The issue for him is not how we return to the uncomplicated but poor beginnings of human history but how the constructed self can be morally self-assured and alert to the opportunities as well as the dangers that are housed in a free society. Smith also sees the natural self as innocent and peaceful. When the historical process opens opportunities to acquire more possessions, then deceit enters, inequalities explode, liberty flees, subordination is institutionalized, and government falls under the control of the powerful. With commercial society, Smith argues, individuals can morally construct themselves in ways that lead to their own happiness. This Smithian self is expected to be honest to the sentiments and know the limits of reason. Mill's view of the natural self, departing from these earlier optimistic premises, is dark and foreboding. For him, the natural self is understood in terms of its passions, which produce someone whom Mill sees as cruel and selfish. He assigns civilization the task of providing developmental models for the self which introduce ways for agents to express their unique sensibilities, feelings, tradition, and reason. Within diverse settings, Mill holds out a self that is able to reconstruct itself through participation.

Anxious liberals, then, challenge a fatalism that holds that because we cannot control everything that happens to us, we do not have responsibility for our choices and conduct. In their own distinctive ways, Locke, Smith, and Mill hold that the liberty necessary for human flourishing also opens the possibility of human failure but individuals are not ill equipped to meet the challenge. They can take the materials that reside in their traditions and are taught in their families to develop morally.

Enlarging the Debate for Communitarians

The most pronounced feature of the internal debate among communitarians concerns which standards should describe the good community. Some, such as MacIntyre and Bloom, favor conservative solutions while Barber, Taylor, Sullivan, and Sandel tend to cluster on the opposite side. Important as it is, this is not the internal debate I want to encourage. Rather, I want to consider two other issues. The first is embedded in the arguments of strong republicans concerning the necessity for stakes and politics while the second involves protecting local communities in the late-modern world.

If many liberals mistake procedural stakes for the core of citizenship today, many communitarians mistake morality for its center. These communitarians need to make a place for the substantive stakes of citizens. However much the character of stakes in the late-modern world differs from earlier renditions, there are features in the concept of stakes that remain important today, particularly that all citizens have overcome necessity and are able to meet their multiple needs. In disregarding stakes, communitarians ignore the recurring expectation of strong republicans that good citizens care not only about their regime and its free institutions but also about themselves. Strong republicans do not expect people to become good citizens when their lives are preoccupied with matters distant from a common civic life and they lack incentives to attach themselves to the ideals of the republic which seem remote from their everyday lives.

Today, many citizens are without minimal stakes and carry only weak substantive attachments to the good republic. Yet, most still think of themselves as part of the republic where they desire to be full citizens. In such a situation, we should expect communitarians to speak on their behalf as well as encourage them to make noise when they are not treated as full citizens. The language they collectively employ need not be (and in many cases ought not be) the language of rights but vocabularies familiar to communitarians such as citizenship, participation, community, and shared responsibilities.

There is another issue that communitarians need to address much more seriously than they do now. The late modern world is one which has been dangerous for local communities, especially the most local of all, the family. Bureaucracies, the mass media, megainstitutions, an intrusive government, impersonal corporations, accelerating mobilities, and economic restructuring are not always hostile to local communities or families but they are seldom friendly and often dangerous. When valuable local communities are under attack, it is both practical and beneficial to call attention to what is endangered in order to know better what we risk losing. But that hardly completes the project, and communitarians need to ask what is necessary for vibrant local communities and flourishing families.

The incoherence we find in the United States or Canada, for example, is poorly explained by the argument that each country houses more self-consciously diverse groups than it did a century ago or that some new group identities carry distinctive understandings of the good that are incommensurate with traditional ones. More salient in explaining our incoherence is that our institutional life is fragmented, not merely in the sense that we are separated from each other by Weberian-style bureaucracies but also that our personal lives are fractured by competing institutional demands and practices.

Consider the stress that describes much modern family life, a challenge to both liberals as well as to communitarians. Those who fear the weakening of the family will not understand the causes of their discontent if they concentrate on those who offer alternative modes of thinking about marriage, gender, and the household. The modern family is buffeted by a variety of intrusions and is battered by internal factors that problematize earlier family practices in the most profound way. Child rearing is shared with the mass media, advertizing, and a variety of other agents. Mobility scatters its members to far-off places. Most women working outside the household do so as much for economic reasons as for emancipatory ones, and parental care has been augmented with day care, usually of an institutional variety, for a large part of the work week. Moreover, with both parents working, what was once discretionary time is now crowded with meeting myriad obligations, leaving less time for the members to share with one another or their community.

To address this kind of incoherence seriously means talking about institutional design of the most sweeping nature, one that addresses the demands of the family and the economy, that reduces the tension between the private and the public, that seeks inclusion while recognizing difference, and that challenges the pervasiveness of consumerism. Such an undertaking has enormous implications and reminds us why strong republicans are concerned with the institutional and distributional character of civil society: it is not possible to maintain the good republic when its professed ideals are discordant with the practices that are actually rewarded.[5] In neglecting the ways that modern institutions shelter some and leave others vulnerable and fracture families and communities, many nostalgic communitarians forget that the way society is organized counts in the most profound ways. For this reason, communitarians need to debate among themselves on how our social practices reflect the patterns of rewards, neglect, and penalties embedded in our institutions.[6] When they find that institutional practices fracture and fragment, communitarians need to challenge them politically.

Enlarging the Debate for Contemporary Liberals

The academic debate among liberals generally focuses on which rule or principle best covers the rights due to equal persons, typified by the arguments between Rawls and some of his fellow liberals. The major political disagreement among liberals concerns the proper relationship between negative rights (such as free speech) and property rights, on the one hand, and positive or social rights (such as affirmative action) on the other hand. Although it is clearly an important and pressing issue, I want to turn to three other problems that deserve the attention of liberals today: the moral socialization of children, the role of duties in a theory of rights, and the conflict of rights-claims among the most vulnerable. The first two flow from the tradition of anxious liberalism while the latter addresses the status of rights in a world that is very different from the one Locke, Smith, and Mill knew.

In taking up these issues, procedural liberals need to expand their moral and political vocabulary to include the concerns of anxious liberals about the ways that people use their freedom. Procedural liberals also should be prepared to listen to grammars other than the language of rights and acknowledge that rights cannot cover everything. Isaiah Berlin's famous essay on liberty is helpful here.[7] Best known as a defense of negative liberty, the piece goes on to claim that there are some principled conflicts between rights and other goods, and we ought not have one or another kind of liberty trump every other good. Rather, we should acknowledge that sometimes we want a particular good, such as justice, and that rights-claims subvert it.

When this happens, Berlin warns us against enlarging the concept of rights in order to make rights cover something that is better addressed by other standards of the good. From his perspective, we need to avoid a language of rights that is so broad that it addresses all of our concerns, vetoes all competitors, and silences all critics.[8]

With this in mind, let me turn to the first debate I would like to encourage among liberals. Liberals today need to acknowledge that their tradition relies heavily on the moral socialization of children, which, in turn, depends on a robust, credible culture. This is a pressing issue for anxious liberals because of their understanding of freedom. They repeatedly announce that liberty does not mean license and many of the external restraints imposed by the state need to be replaced by an internal self-discipline. The materials for our self-discipline initially come to us when we are children and ought to be carefully nourished, not randomly or haphazardly delivered.

Anxious liberals are extraordinarily preoccupied with the education of children. Locke and Smith are particularly attentive to moral socialization to provide children with standards of the good, which they are expected to apply as future citizens, regardless of their status or station.[9] However, Locke and Smith fail to anticipate the sweeping changes that penetrate what they take to be invincible walls protecting the private lives of family members from public menace. The challenge to the family that is so disturbing to liberalism comes not from the state but from within civil society, which is becoming increasingly secularized, commercialized, and bureaucratized. Today, the socialization of fewer and fewer children is adequately described as occurring behind the thick walls that Locke and Smith think will insulate families. Because the walls that remain around families today are more porous and transparent than Locke and Smith require, what anxious liberals take to be benign approaches to moral socialization no longer suffice. For this reason, liberals today need to ask themselves many of the same tough questions communitarians need to raise regarding the family and its ability to perform its educative and socializing goals. Any application of this principle in a demystified, post-Weberian world is bound to be contentious, but the need to provide children with a moral compass remains as important today as it did earlier.[10]

The second debate I wish to encourage concerns the status of duties in contemporary liberal democracies. For anxious liberals, rights are accompanied with duties, particularly the duty to avoid harming others. However, many critics of liberalism fear that in its emphasis on rights, duties soon evaporate. The issue here is not that most liberals have no conception of responsibilities or refuse to carry out a panoply of duties today. In their roles at home, in the family, and at work and in their myriad memberships and charities, liberal citizens continually perform duties, frequently of a demanding sort. The complaints about the lack of duties today are usually of a different sort. One concerns the issue of whether society and its nonvulnerable members owe duties to its vulnerable members. The second asks whether the recipients of any enlarged conception of rights have duties attached to these rights. Each of these issues signals a shift from earlier liberal versions of duties, which are tied to negative liberty. However, in the modern era, many rights require positive action, usually from the state, not just noninterference in the lives of others. This shift makes the performance of duties complicated, often nonlinear, and seldom reciprocal. For this reason, relying exclusively on the language of rights often adds unnecessary complications to the problem.

Many efforts to address the enlarged domain of rights-claims require state action in terms of funding and regulation. In practice, this means that if one person has a right to a particular good, then government should do what is necessary to deliver that right and citizens should pay the necessary taxes or accept the required regulations to achieve the goal. In theory, those who are thus taxed or regulated will see this as an expression of their duties. But many citizens dispute this position, denying that certain claims qualify as valid rights-claims and finding increased taxation and regulation intrude into what they take to be their own valid rights. At this point, the liberal language of rights pits some rights-claims against others, leading to the spectacle of liberals arguing over which rights-claims have priority. Whether the issue is taxes that fund projects for the vulnerable, incommensurable understandings of equality of opportunity, or regulating the environment or protecting jobs, diverse liberals tend to fortify their respective positions with the language of rights. But, as Weber noticed, this trivializes the language of rights, and liberal rhetoric becomes a way of legitimizing policies that favor whoever has the greater political power at a particular moment.[11] For these reasons, liberals need to ask what we owe one another not simply as rights-carriers but also as citizens who are engaged in common projects. At this point, it is helpful to return to Berlin's essay and ask what other kinds of goods we seek besides rights and what our obligations are to achieving those goods.

The limits of an exclusive use of the language of rights to guide our moral and political judgments can also be seen in the third issue liberals need to address today. This concerns the internal conflict of rights-claims among the most vulnerable members of society. Procedural liberals are not very good at sorting out and then ranking claims among the neglected, the discriminated, or the least well-off members of society. When we look at the claims of people who are vulnerable, we quickly realize that there are many vulnerabilities, and efforts to address all of them simultaneously lead to a politics of tragic choices. If we want to say that children have a right to a quality education independent of their parent's resources, that the physically or psychologically disabled have a right to certain claims, that the medically indigent have a right to health care, that the elderly have a right to a secure old age, that the hungry have a right to food, and that the homeless have a right to shelter, then we are enumerating claims that most would recognize as meritorious.[12] A problem arises when we make all such claims into rights and then attempt to deliver on each of them. Each is dependent on government spending but there are insufficient funds available to meet all of the rights-claims.[13]

The contest among the rights-claimants who are vulnerable is not the same kind of conflict that characterizes many other debates in modern society. The intense disagreements between supporters of the right to choice and the right to life concern incommensurable moral positions about which rights-claim should be honored and which not. However, we do not encounter arguments that the many different rights-claims of the vulnerable are theoretically incommensurable. We do not want to say that the elderly have a stronger rights-claim than the young or that the homeless have a superior rights-claim over the disabled. In practice, however, some of these claims are more likely to be honored (funded) in the budgetary process than others, and we need to ask how we should respond to this. It turns out that however harmonious a general theory of rights might be advanced on behalf of the vulnerable, in practice the claims attached to different vulnerabilities become irreconcilable.

Do we want to say that it is wrong to choose between valid rights-claims? Or do we want to argue that some rights-claimants need to wait their turn until other rights-claims are met? Or do we want to hold that all claims have the same status as a right but that whichever can muster greater support in the democratic process deserves to succeed? If we accept the position implicit in the first question that some rights ought not be discounted for other rights, we are simply avoiding the issue. A sorting process follows, whether we want to acknowledge it or not. An affirmative answer to the second question is also contrary to theories of rights that deny that one person's rights are more meritorious than someone else's. When we say that someone deserves a right, we mean that the right is attached to the person and must be acknowledged and defended. That I deserve a right does not mean that my right overrides your right or that you must wait in line for some period of time while the rest of us attend to our rights-claims. The position implicit in the third question relates the dynamics of budgetary politics with the delivery of rights-claims, but it does not provide us with standards to judge the worth of various claims. Rather, it recognizes that the side that is better organized and mobilized gains benefits while the other receives little or nothing.

If we stick with the language of rights or neutral proceduralism, we will continue to pit the vulnerable against each other. Liberals need to expand their language repertoire to make room for other considerations, such as how advantages and costs are shared throughout society; how particular policies favor justice; what is required for citizenship; how practices validate, ignore, or deny the founding principle of the community; and how various claims affect a community, not merely in its shared moral understandings but also in its substantive and institutional dimensions. In relying exclusively on a language of rights, procedural liberals often uncritically contradict their own commitment to respect the dignity and worth of all persons because, in practice, they discount the rights-claims of some persons, including those they most want to assist, the vulnerable. Any language embedded in universalism and proceduralism will continue to force hard choices between the competing claims of the vulnerable.

Welcoming Politics Back to Theory

For some, the pressing issue of our times is how we acknowledge the full rights of everyone, particularly those who have been denied them in the past. For others, the imperative is to replace a society that is fragmented and incoherent and whose members are isolated from one another with a vibrant community. Is one of these critiques mistaken? I think not. Both identify crucial problems and if either is to be addressed effectively, each will have to acknowledge what it ignores in its own tradition. In moving beyond rigid constructions of what ails us, contemporary liberals and communitarians need to see politics as less amenable to coherence and more problematic than they do now.

The communitarian response to liberalism must be more than lamentation; but in the end, it offers us no good reason to believe that if only people share the same moral outlooks, all will be well. For someone such as Hegel, this would be an incomplete project. He sees us becoming estranged not merely when we are distanced from others but also when the institutions of our society are incongruent with our expectations about them and about ourselves. When institutions promote practices that are contrary to the ideals of citizens, we should not be surprised to encounter a society that is incoherent and unintelligible. For its part, the liberal response must move beyond the claim that if everyone is treated according to a uniform proceduralism, society will take care of itself and every agent will find a satisfying and coherent life.

If we remain within the language of communitarian restrictiveness, we minimize the prospects of autonomy because we may be too ready to reject claims that diverge from our own conceptions of the good. But when procedural liberals decline to evaluate divergent rights-claims for fear of abandoning its neutrality principle, we often introduce standards that are incommensurate with one another and a proceduralism that leaves individuals fragmented and frustrated. When contemporary liberals pass over the importance of moral standards we use to judge, they assign the task of developing a principled life to isolated individuals operating in a world of randomness and accident.

Both liberals and communitarians need to talk about the family, with liberals focusing on the moral socialization of children and communitarians thinking about the stakes that are required for both full citizenship in the late-modern world as well as for the security and integrity of family units. Moreover, each side in the debate needs to acknowledge that many institutions today reward self-involvement and penalize cooperative action, thereby often promoting a defensive corruption on the part of many households. For these reasons, both liberals and communitarians need to ask whether our institutional practices harmonize or contradict their ideals.

In attempting to address these and related issues, it is necessary to move beyond a search for strict coherence, as if the logic embedded in one single paradigm will solve all our problems and heal all of our discontents. The rigidity that characterizes much of the debate between liberals and communitarians today results in each position ignoring both what it shares with the other and materials in its own tradition that are not readily accommodated within the logic of its reigning paradigm. The rigid commitments of each side today often lead its advocates to ignore what is problematic in their own positions and should be fluid and argumentative in politics. Enriched positions promote a politics that extends and enlarges debate because each side recognizes that in accommodating many (but not all) goods it had previously neglected, it is forced to address the multiple needs of ordinary men and women in a complex, changing world.

What is often forgotten in the current debate is that politics is invariably steeped in paradox and irony and that political theory is rich when it moves beyond rigidities and acknowledges the inevitable complexity of political life. The politics of a free people who are attached to their regime cannot escape disagreements; in the best polity, citizens embrace politics rather than neglect it. In the process, we want to acknowledge that in a world where ordinary people have multiple needs, fixity ignores too much that is good and even risks harming much that is good.

A democratic regime cannot escape tension and fluidity. However, the impulse for coherence eliminates tensions, makes talk among citizens formalistic rather than discursive, and transforms politics into the administration of procedures or custom. The tension necessary for democracy comes from an appreciation that the common life of citizens is not meant to stifle their individual conceptions of normative and substantive goods. Citizens settle their differences, not by finding some theoretical formula that covers everything but by privileging a speech that discloses problems, respects the autonomy of different citizens, and admits that any resolution of their differences is, at best, an interlude that will soon again be punctuated by new disagreements. Democracy is greatly diminished when tensions are banished. Any static solution, directed by a single, coherent logic, is blind to the many different principled aspirations and agonizing vulnerabilities of ordinary people. Politics would be enhanced today if we recognized the paradoxes that reside in our own conceptions of the good, and if we carried anxieties not only about our own opponents but also about our own best efforts to achieve the good.

Notes

1. Finding political language more porous and fluid and less adversarial than the two-language paradigm allows, several commentators urge us to seek a common political language. Forest McDonald's American founders are "able to speak in the diverse languages of Locke, the classical republican, Hume, and many others, depending upon what seemed rhetorically appropriate to the argument at hand" and are "multilingual" (see *Novous Ordo Seclorum* [Lawrence. University Press of Kansas, 1989], 9).

Taking up the theme of indistinguishable languages during the formative years of the United States, Jerome Huyler sees no "separate 'paradigmatic' language, but merely several levels or layers of discourse." His republicans and Lockean liberals "addressed a single 'problematic' (the just organization of civil government and society) but come at it from two distinct but related paths." For this reason, "the liberal reading of the American founding can be right without rendering the revisionists wrong" (*Locke in America* [Lawrence: University Press of Kansas, 1995], 27–28). The blending James Kloppenberg finds in eighteenth-century discourse can be seen in the title of his article, "The Virtues of Liberalism: Christianity, Republicanism, and Ethics in Early American Political Discourse," *Journal of American History,* 74 (1987): 1245–57.

2. With this in mind, Norberto Bobbio finds "two great antitheses dominate political thought: oppression-freedom and anarchy-unity" (*Thomas Hobbes and the Natural Law Tradition* [Chicago: University of Chicago Press, 1993], 29).

3. Lyle Downing and Robert Thigpen argue, "The liberal emphasis on the right of individuals to evaluate shared understandings cannot be reconciled with a communitarianism in which persons must seek their good totally within existing roles and institutions" ("Communitarian Theory and Domination," paper presented at the Annual Meetings of the American Political Science Association [1985], 15).

4. Albert Hirschman. *The Passions and the Interests* (Princeton: Princeton University Press, 1977), 15.

5. One of the ironies in the current debate is that communitarians have neglected what should have been central to their position; the argument for just distributions in a good regime lies with a liberal, John Rawls, who seeks to pattern benefits in society with an eye to justice.

6. Local communities are under siege not just from big government but also from an economy that values profits and efficiency even if it means disrupting local communities when it moves to more lucrative locales. Sandel has discussed this issue, but his contribution needs to be elaborated into a larger theoretical language that connects the economy with other aspects of civil society and links them in ways that serve to enrich citizenship rather than deplete it.

7. Isaiah Berlin. *Four Essays on Liberty* (Oxford: Oxford University Press, 1969).

8. Ronald Terchek. "The Fruits of Success and the Crisis of Liberalism," in *Liberals on Liberalism,* edited by Alfonso Damico (Totowa, N.J.: Rowman & Littlefield, 1986).

9. Even though Mill takes a very different view of the conventional family from Locke and Smith, he still relies on it for the moral socialization of children to prepare them for their lives as adults in an open society where they freely decide to retain or modify their earlier understandings of the good or reject them in favor of a new plan of life.

10. On the issue of moral education in liberalism, see William Galston, *Liberal Purposes* (Cambridge: Cambridge University Press, 1991). For a discussion of democratic education, see Amy Gutmann *Democratic Education* (Princeton: Princeton University Press, 1987).

11. One way of expanding our political language is to ask what is required for an inclusive democratic society. Anne Norton's discussion of the rhetoric of the New Deal is helpful. She dismisses the usual explanation of its success as an exercise in coalition building and concentrates on Franklin Roosevelt's language of community and justice. She writes, "The inclusion of the poor, of blacks, of women, and of the handicapped had once served as gestures signifying the [Democratic] party's representation of the nation by signifying its representation of those liminal groups on its farthest borders" (*Republic of Signs* [Chicago: University of Chicago Press, 1993], 111).

12. I do not hold that all procedural liberals acknowledge each claim is a valid rights-claim. I only want to argue that many liberals have seen these claims as rights and often employ the language of rights to advance their position. For an expansive view of rights, see Charles Reich, "Individual Rights and Social Welfare: The Emerging Legal Issues," *Yale Law Journal* 74 (1965): 1245–57.

13. This is discussed as the conflict of good causes in Terchek, "The Fruits of Success."

Bibliography

Ackerman, Bruce. *Social Justice and the Liberal State.* New Haven: Yale University Press, 1980.
Alford, C. Fred. *The Self in Social Theory.* New Haven: Yale University Press, 1991.
Appleby, Joyce. *Capitalism and a New Social Order.* New York: New York University Press, 1984
———. *Liberalism and Republicanism in the Historical Imagination.* Cambridge: Harvard University Press, 1992.
Arendt, Hannah. *The Human Condition.* New York: Doubleday, 1958.
———. *On Revolution.* New York: Penguin Books, 1977.
———. *The Life of the Mind.* New York: Harcourt Brace Jovanovich, 1978.
Aristotle. *The Politics.* Chicago: University of Chicago Press, 1984.
———. *Nicomachean Ethics.* Indianapolis: Hackett Publishing Company, 1985.
———. *On Rhetoric.* New York: Oxford University Press, 1991.
Ashcraft, Richard. *Revolutionary Politics and Locke's Two Treatises.* Princeton: Princeton University Press, 1986.
Augustine. *City of God.* New York: Random House, 1950.
Bailyn, Bernard. *Ideological Origins of the American Revolution.* Cambridge: Harvard University Press, 1967.
Banning, Lance. "The Republican Interpretation." In *The Republican Synthesis Revisited,* edited by Milton Klein et al. Worcester, Mass.: American Antiquarian Society, 1992.
Barber, Benjamin. *Strong Democracy.* Berkeley: University of California Press, 1984.
Baumgold, Deborah. *Hobbes' Political Theory.* New York: Cambridge University Press, 1988.
———. "Political Commentary on the History of Political Theory." *American Political Science Review* 75 (1981): 928–40.

Beiner, Ronald. *What's Wrong with Liberalism?* Berkeley: University of California Press, 1992.

Beitz, Charles. *Political Equality.* Princeton: Princeton University Press, 1989.

Bell, Daniel. *The Cultural Contradictions of Capitalism.* New York: Basic Books, 1976.

Bellah, Robert N. "Civil Religion in America." *Daedalus* 96 (1967): 1-21.

———, et al. *Habits of the Heart: Individualism and Commitment in American Life.* Berkeley: University of California Press, 1985.

Benn, Stanley. *A Theory of Freedom.* Cambridge: Cambridge University Press, 1988.

Bentley, Arthur. *The Process of Government.* Evanston: Principia Press, 1908.

Berger, Peter. "On the Obsolescence of the Concept of Honour." *European Journal of Sociology* 11 (1970): 339-47.

Berlin, Isaiah. "The Originality of Machiavelli." In *Against the Current: Essays in the History of Ideas,* edited by Henry Hardy. New York: Viking, 1980.

———. *Four Essays on Liberty.* Oxford: Oxford University Press, 1969.

Bloom, Allan. *The Closing of the American Mind.* New York: Simon and Schuster, 1987.

Bobbio, Norberto. *The Future of Democracy: A Defence of the Rules of the Game.* London: Polity Press, 1987.

———. *Thomas Hobbes and the Natural Law Tradition.* Chicago: University of Chicago Press, 1993.

Bock, Gisela. "Civil Discord in Machiavelli's *Istorie Florentine.*" In *Machiavelli and Republicanism,* edited by Gisela Bock, et al. Cambridge: Cambridge University Press, 1990.

Booth, William J. "The New Household Economy." *American Political Science Review* 85 (1991): 59-75.

Brint, Michael. *Tragedy and Denial.* Boulder: Westview Press, 1991.

Caney, Simon. "Liberalism and Communitarianism: A Misconceived Debate." *Political Studies* 40 (1992): 273-89.

Chapman, John. *Rousseau: Totalitarian or Liberal?* New York: Columbia University Press, 1956.

Clark, Paul. *Citizenship.* London: Pluto Press, 1994.

Colman, John. *John Locke's Moral Philosophy.* Edinburgh: Edinburgh University Press, 1983.

Connolly, William E. *Appearance and Reality in Politics.* Cambridge: Cambridge University Press, 1981.

———. *Political Theory and Modernity.* London: Basil Blackwell, 1988.
Corlett, William. "The Availability of Lincoln's Civil Religion." *Political Theory,* 10 (1982): 520–40.
Coser, Lewis. *The Functions of Social Conflict.* New York: Free Press, 1956.
Crevecoeur, J. Hector St. John de. *Letters From an American Farmer.* New York: Doubleday, 1961.
Crick, Bernard. *In Defense of Politics.* Chicago: University of Chicago Press, 1962.
Crittenden, Jack. *Beyond Individualism: Reconstituting the Self.* New York: Oxford, 1993.
Cropsey, Joseph. *Polity and Political Economy.* The Hague: Nijhoff, 1957.
Cunningham, Frank. *Democratic Theory and Socialism.* Cambridge: Cambridge University Press, 1987.
Dahl, Robert. *Who Governs?* New Haven: Yale University Press, 1961.
———. *After the Revolution.* New Haven: Yale University Press, 1970.
———. *Dilemmas of Pluralist Democracy.* New Haven: Yale University Press, 1982.
———. *Democracy and Its Critics.* New Haven: Yale University Press, 1989.
Dahrendorf, Ralf. *Class and Class Conflict in Industrial Society.* Stanford: Stanford University Press, 1957.
Damico, Alfonso. "The Democratic Consequences of Liberalism." In *Liberals on Liberalism,* edited by Alfonso Damico. Totowa, N. J.: Rowman and Littlefield, 1988.
Diamond, Martin. 1986. "Ethics and Politics: The American Way." In *The Moral Foundations of the American Republic,* edited by Robert Horwitz. 3rd ed. Charlottesville: University Press of Virginia, 1986.
Diggins, John. *The Lost Soul of American Politics.* New York: Basic Books, 1984.
Donner, Wendy. *The Liberal Self.* Ithaca: Cornell University Press, 1991.
Douglas, R. Bruce, et al. *Liberalism and the Good.* New York: Routledge, 1990.
Downing, Lyle A. and Robert Thigpen. "Communitarian Theory and Domination." Paper presented at the annual meeting of the American Political Science Association, 1985.
Downs, Anthony. "An Economic Theory of Democracy." *Journal of Political Economy* 64 (1957): 135–52.

Duncan, Graeme, ed. *Democracy and the Capitalist State*. New York: Cambridge University Press, 1989.

Dunn, John. *The Political Thought of John Locke*. Cambridge: Cambridge University Press, 1969.

———. *Locke*. Oxford: Oxford University Press, 1984.

Dworetz, Steven. *The Unvarnished Doctrine: Locke, Liberalism, and the American Revolution*. Durham: Duke University Press, 1990.

Dworkin, Gerald. "Moral Autonomy." In *Morals, Science, and Sociality* edited by H. T. Englehard, Jr. and Daniel Callahan. New York: Hastings Center, 1978.

———. *The Theory and Practice of Autonomy*. Cambridge: Cambridge University Press, 1988.

Dworkin, Ronald. "Liberalism." In *Public and Private Morality*, edited by Stuart Hampshire. Cambridge: Cambridge University Press, 1978.

———. *Taking Rights Seriously*. Cambridge: Harvard University Press, 1978.

———. Review of Michael Walzer's *Spheres of Justice*. *New York Review of Books,* April 1983.

Eisenach, Eldon. *Two Worlds of Liberalism*. Chicago: University of Chicago Press, 1981.

Elster, Jon. "The Market and the Forum." In *Foundations in Social Choice,* edited by J. Elster and A. Hylland. Cambridge: University of Cambridge Press, 1986.

Euben, J. Peter. *The Tragedy of Political Theory: The Road Not Taken*. Princeton: Princeton University Press, 1990.

Feinberg, Joel. *Harm to Self*. Oxford: Oxford University Press, 1986.

Fishskin, James. *Justice, Equality of Opportunity, and the Family*. New Haven: Yale University Press, 1983.

Flathman, Richard E. *Thomas Hobbes: Skepticism, Individuality, and Chastened Politics*. Newbury Park: Sage, 1993.

Fowler, Robert. *The Dance with Community*. Lawrence: University Press of Kansas, 1991.

Fox Bourne, H. R. *The Life of John Locke,* vol. 1. New York: Harper & Brothers, 1876.

Frankfurt, Harry. *The Importance of What We Care About*. New York: Cambridge University Press, 1988.

Friedman, Milton. *Capitalism and Freedom*. Chicago: University of Chicago Press, 1963.

Galston, William. *Justice and the Human Good*. Chicago: University of Chicago Press, 1980.

———. "Defending Liberalism." *American Political Science Review* 76 (1982), 621–629.
———. *Liberal Purposes: Goals, Virtues, and Diversity in the Liberal State.* Cambridge: Cambridge University Press, 1991.
———. "Moral Personality and Liberal Theory." *Political Theory* 10 (1982): 492–519.
Garforth, F. W. *John Stuart Mill's Theory of Education.* New York: Barnes and Noble, 1979.
Gettridge, G. H. "Adam Smith on the American Revolution: An Unpublished Memorial." *American Historical Review* 38 (1933): 714–20.
Glendon, Mary. *Abortion and Divorce in Western Law.* Cambridge: Harvard University Press, 1987.
———. *Rights Talk: The Impoverishment of Political Discourse.* New York: Free Press, 1991.
Gobetti, Daniela. *Public and Private.* New York: Routledge, 1992.
Graeme, Duncan. *Democracy and the Capitalist State.* Cambridge: Cambridge University Press, 1989.
Gramsci, Antonio. *Letters from Prison.* New York: Harper & Row, 1973.
Grant, Ruth. *John Locke's Liberalism.* Chicago: University of Chicago Press, 1987.
Gray, John. "Political Power, Social Theory, and Essential Contestability." In *The Nature of Political Theory,* edited by D. Miller and L. Siedentop. Oxford: Oxford University Press, 1983.
———. *Hayek on Liberty.* Oxford: Basil Blackwell, 1984.
———. *Liberalisms.* London: Routledge, 1989.
Greenstone, J. David. *The Lincoln Persuasion: Remaking American Liberalism.* Princeton: Princeton University Press, 1993.
Gunnell, John. 1978. "The Myth of Tradition." *American Political Science Association* 72 (1978): 122–34.
———. *Between Philosophy and Politics.* Amherst: University of Massachusetts Press, 1986.
Gutmann, Amy. "Communitarian Critics of Liberalism." *Philosophy and Public Affairs* 14 (1985): 308–22.
———. *Democratic Education.* Princeton: Princeton University Press, 1987.
Habermas, Jurgen. *Legitimation Crisis.* Boston: Beacon, 1976.
Haksar, Vinit. *Equality, Liberty and Perfectionism.* Oxford: Oxford University Press, 1979.
Harpham, Edward "Liberalism, Civic Humanism, and the Case of Adam Smith." *American Political Science Review* 78 (1984): 764–74.

———, ed. *John Locke's Two Treatises of Government.* Lawrence: University Press of Kansas, 1992.

Harrington, James. *The Commonwealth of Oceana and a System of Politics,* edited by J. G. A. Pocock. Cambridge: Cambridge University Press, 1992.

Hartz, Louis. *The Liberal Tradition in America.* New York: Harcourt, Brace and World, 1985.

Haworth, Alan. *Anti–Libertarianism.* London: Routledge, 1994.

Hayek, Friedrich A. *Road to Serfdom.* Chicago: University of Chicago Press, 1944.

———. *Studies in Philosophy, Politics, and Economics.* London: Routledge, 1967.

———. *Rules and Order.* Chicago: University of Chicago Press, 1973.

———. *The Political Order of a Free People.* Chicago: University of Chicago Press, 1979.

Held, David. *Models of Democracy.* Stanford: Stanford University Press, 1987.

Himmelfarb. Gertrude. *On Liberty and Liberalism: The Case of John Stuart Mill.* New York: Knopf, 1974.

Hirsch, Fred. *Social Limits to Growth.* Cambridge: Harvard University Press, 1976.

Hirschman, Albert O. *The Passions and the Interests.* Princeton: Princeton University Press, 1977.

Hobbes, Thomas. *Leviathan,* edited by C. B. Macpherson. Harmondsworth, Middlesex: Penguin, 1968.

Hobsbawm. E. J. *The Age of Revolution.* New York: New American Library, 1962.

———. and Terence Ranger. *The Invention of Tradition* (New York: Cambridge, 1983).

Holmes, Stephen. *Anatomy of Antiliberalism.* Cambridge: Harvard University Press, 1993.

———. *Passions and Constraints: On the Theory of Liberal Democracy.* Chicago: University of Chicago Press, 1995.

Horne, Thomas. *Property Rights and Poverty: Political Argument in Britain, 1605–1834.* Chapel Hill: University of North Carolina Press, 1990.

Houston, Alan Craig. *Algernon Sidney and the Republican Heritage in England and America.* Princeton: Princeton University Press, 1991.

———. "'A Way of Settlement': The Levellers, Monopolies, and the Public Interest." Paper presented to the annual meeting of the American Political Science Association, 1993.

Hurka, Thomas. *Perfectionism*. New York: Oxford University Press, 1993.
Huyler, Jerome. *Locke in America*. Lawrence: University Press of Kansas, 1995.
Ignatieff, Michael. *The Needs of Strangers*. New York: Penguin, 1985.
Isaac, Jeffrey. "Republicanism vs Liberalism? A Reconsideration." *History of Political Thought* 9 (1988): 349–77.
Jacobitti, Suzanne. "The Public, the Private, the Moral: Hannah Arendt and Political Morality." *International Political Science Review* 12 (1988): 281–93.
Justman, Stewart. *The Hidden Text of Mill's Liberty*. Savage, Md.: Rowman & Littlefield, 1991.
Kendall, Willmoore. *John Locke and the Doctrine of Majority Rule*. Urbana: University of Illinois Press, 1941.
Kloppenberg, James. "The Virtues of Liberalism: Christianity, Republicanism, and Ethics in Early American Discourse." *Journal of American History* 74 (1987): 1245–57.
Kramnick, Isaac. *Republicanism and Bourgeois Radicalism*. Ithaca: Cornell University Press, 1990.
Kraus, Pamela. "Locke's Negative Hedonism." *Locke Newsletter* 15 (1984), 43–63.
Kress, Paul F. "Against Epistemology: Apostate Musings." *Journal of Politics* 41 (1979): 526–42.
Kristol, Irving. *Two Cheers for Capitalism*. New York: Macmillan, 1977.
Kymlicka, Will. "Liberalism and Communitarianism." *Canadian Journal of Philosophy* 18 (1988): 181–203.
———. *Liberalism, Community, and Culture*. Oxford: Oxford University Press, 1989.
———. *Contemporary Political Philosophy*. Oxford: Oxford University Press, 1990.
Lane, Robert. *Political Ideologies*. New York: Free Press, 1962.
Lasch, Christopher. *Haven in a Heartless World: The Family Besieged*. New York: Basic Books, 1977.
———. *Culture of Narcissism*. New York: Warner Books, 1979.
Lienesch, Michael. *New Order of the Ages: Time, the Constitution, and the Making of Modern American Political Thought*. Princeton: Princeton University Press, 1988.
Lincoln, Abraham. *The Collected Works of Abraham Lincoln*, edited by Roy P. Basler. New Brunswick: Rutgers University Press, 1953.
———. *Lincoln–Douglas Debates of 1855*, edited by Robert Johannsen. New York: Oxford University Press, 1965.

Lindblom, Charles E. *Politics and Markets*. New York: Basic Books, 1972.

Lindley, Richard. *Autonomy*. Atlantic Highlands: Humanities Press, 1986.

Locke, John. *The Conduct of Understanding*. London: Tegg, 1823.

———. *The Reasonableness of Christianity*. London: Tegg, 1823.

———. *Some Thoughts Concerning Education* in *The Educational Writings of John Locke*, edited by James L. Axell. Cambridge: Cambridge University Press, 1968.

———. *An Essay Concerning Human Understanding*, edited by Peter Midditch. Oxford: Oxford University Press, 1979.

———. *Two Treatises of Government*, edited by Peter Laslett. Oxford: Oxford University Press, 1988.

Lowi, Theodore J. *The End of Liberalism*. New York: Norton, 1969.

Lukes, Steven. "Making Sense of Moral Conflict." In *Liberalism and the Moral Life*, edited by Nancy Rosenblum. Cambridge: Harvard University Press, 1989.

Lutz, Donald. "The Relative Influence of European Writers on Late Eighteenth Century American Political Thought." *American Political Science Review* 78 (1984): 189–97.

McDonald, Forest. *Novus Ordo Seclorum: The Intellectual Origins of the Constitution*. Lawrence: University Press of Kansas, 1985.

———. "The Intellectual World of the Founding Fathers." In *Requiem*, edited by F. McDonald and Ellen Shapiro McDonald. Lawrence: University Press of Kansas, 1988.

Machiavelli, N. *Discourses*. New York: Random House, 1940.

———. *The Prince*. New York: Random House, 1940.

———. *The Art of War*. Indianapolis: Library of Liberal Arts Press, 1965.

———. *History of Florence*. London: Dent, 1975.

MacIntyre, Alasdair. *After Virtue*. Notre Dame: Notre Dame University Press, 1981.

———. *Whose Justice? Which Rationality?* Notre Dame: University of Notre Dame Press, 1988.

Macpherson, C. B. *The Political Theory of Possessive Individualism*. Oxford: Oxford University Press, 1962.

Madison, James, Alexander Hamilton, and John Jay. *The Federalist Papers*, edited by Isaac Kramnick. Middlesex: Penguin, 1987.

Mansbridge, Jane. "Self-Interest in Political Life." *Political Theory* 18 (February 1990): 132–53.

———. *Beyond Adversary Democracy*. Chicago: University of Chicago Press, 1983.

Marquand, David. *The Unprincipled Society.* London: Fantana, 1987.
Masters, Roger. *The Political Philosophy of Rousseau.* Princeton: Princeton University Press, 1968.
McNally, David. *Against The Market.* London: Verso, 1993.
McPherson, James M. *Abraham Lincoln and the Second American Revolution.* Oxford: Oxford University Press, 1991.
McWilliams, Wilson Carey. *The Idea of Fraternity in America.* Berkeley: University of California Press, 1974.
Mehta, Uday Singh. *The Anxiety of Freedom.* Ithaca: Cornell University Press, 1992.
Meyers, Marvin. *The Jacksonian Persuasion.* New York: Vintage Books, 1963.
Michelman, Frank. "Law's Republic." *The Yale Law Journal* 97 (1983): 1493–1537.
Mill, J. S. *Autobiography.* In *Collected Works,* vol. 1. Toronto: University of Toronto Press, 1981.
———. *Civilization.* In *Collected Works,* vol. 18. Toronto: University of Toronto Press, 1977.
———. "De Tocqueville." In *Collected Works,* vol. 18. Toronto: University of Toronto Press, 1977.
———. *Considerations on Representative Government.* In *Collected Works,* vol. 19. Toronto: University of Toronto Press, 1977.
———. *On Liberty.* In *Collected Works,* vol. 18. Toronto: University of Toronto Press, 1977.
———. *Late Letters.* In *Collected Works,* vols. 15 and 16. Toronto: University of Toronto Press, 1977.
———. *Principles of Political Economy.* In *Collected Works,* vols. 2 and 3. Toronto: University of Toronto Press, 1965.
———. *A System of Logic.* In *Collected Works,* vols. 7 and 8. Toronto: University of Toronto Press, 1974.
———. *Utilitarianism.* In *Collected Works,* vol. 10. Toronto: University of Toronto Press, 1969.
———. "Colderidge." In *Collected Works,* vol. 10. Toronto, University of Toronto Press, 1969.
Moon, J. Donald. *Constructing Community.* Princeton: Princeton University Press, 1993.
Moore, Margaret. *Foundations of Liberalism.* Oxford: Clarendon Press, 1993.
Myers, Milton. *The Soul of Modern Economic Man.* Chicago: University of Chicago Press, 1957.
Nedelsky, Jennifer. *Private Property and the Limits of American Constitutionalism.* Chicago: University of Chicago Press, 1990.

Niebuhr, Reinhold. *Moral Man and Immoral Society.* New York: Scribners, 1932.
Nietzsche, Frederick. *Thus Spoke Zarathustra.* In *The Portable Nietzsche,* edited by Walter Kaufmann. New York: Viking, 1954.
Nisbet, Robert. *The Present Age: Progress and Anarchy in Modern America.* New York: Harper and Row, 1988.
Norton, Anne. *Republic of Signs.* Chicago: University of Chicago Press, 1993.
Nozick, Robert. *Anarchy, State, and Utopia.* New York: Basic Books, 1974.
Nussbaum, Martha. *The Fragility of Goodness: Luck and Ethics in Greek Tragedy and Philosophy.* New York: Cambridge University Press, 1986.
Oakeshott, Michael. *Rationalism in Politics and Other Essays.* Indianapolis: Liberty Press, 1962.
———. *On Human Conduct.* Oxford: Oxford University Press, 1975.
Ober, Josiah. "Aristotle's Political Sociology: Class Status and Order in the *Politics.*" *Essays on the Foundations of Aristotelian Political Science,* edited by Carnes Lord and David O'Connor, Berkeley: University of California Press, 1991.
Offe, Claus. *The Contradictions of the Welfare State.* Cambridge: MIT Press, 1984.
Okin, Susan. *Justice, Gender, and the Family.* New York: Basic Books, 1989.
Pangle, L. S., and Pangle, Thomas P. *The Learning of Liberty.* Lawrence: University Press of Kansas, 1993.
Pangle, Thomas. *The Spirit of Modern Republicanism.* Chicago: University of Chicago Press, 1988.
Pateman, Carole. *Participation and Democratic Theory.* Cambridge: Cambridge University Press, 1970.
———. *Sexual Contract.* Stanford: Stanford University Press, 1988.
Pettit, Philip. *The Common Mind: An Essay on Psychology, Society, and Politics.* New York: Oxford, 1993.
Phillips, Derek. *Looking Backward: A Critical Appraisal of Communitarian Thought.* Princeton: Princeton University Press, 1993.
Plamenatz, John. *Man and Society.* New York: McGraw Hill, 1963.
Pocock, J. G. A. "Civic Humanism and Its Role in Anglo-American Thought." In *Politics, Language, and Time* edited by J. G. A. Pocock. New York: Atheneum, 1971.
———. *The Machiavellian Moment.* Princeton: Princeton University Press, 1975.

---. *Virtue, Commerce, and History.* Cambridge: Cambridge University Press, 1985.
Preus, J. Samuel. "Machiavelli's Functional Analysis of Religion: Context and Object." *Journal of the History of Ideas*, 40 (April-June 1979): 179–90.
Raphael, D. D. *Adam Smith.* Oxford: Oxford University Press, 1985.
Rawls, John. *A Theory of Justice.* Cambridge: Harvard University Press, 1971.
---. "Justice as Fairness: Political not Metaphysical." *Philosophy and Public Affairs* 14 (1985): 223–57.
---. "The Priority of Right and Ideas of the Good." *Philosophy and Public Affairs* 17 (1988): 251–76.
---. *Political Liberalism.* New York: Columbia University Press, 1993.
Raz, Joseph. *The Morality of Freedom.* Oxford: Clarendon, 1986.
Reich, Charles. "Individual Rights and Social Welfare." *Yale Law Journal* 74 (1965): 1245–57.
Reid, John. *The Concept of Liberty in the Age of the American Revolution.* Chicago: University of Chicago Press, 1988.
Reisman, David. *Adam Smith's Sociological Economics.* London: Croom Helm, 1976.
Riker, William. *Liberalism against Populism: A Confrontation between the Theory of Democracy and the Theory of Social Choice.* San Francisco: W. H. Freeman, 1982.
Robertson, John. "The Scottish Enlightenment at the Limits of the Civic Tradition." In *Wealth and Virtue,* edited by L. Hont and M. Ignatieff. Cambridge: Cambridge University Press, 1983.
Robson, John. *The Improvement of Mankind.* Toronto: University of Toronto Press, 1968.
Rogers, Daniel. "Republicanism: The Career of a Concept." *Journal of American History* 79 (1992): 11–38.
Rorty, Richard. *Contingency, Irony, and Solidarity.* Cambridge: Cambridge University Press, 1989.
Rosenblum, Nancy. *Another Liberalism: Romanticism and the Reconstruction of Liberal Thought.* Cambridge: Harvard University Press, 1987.
Rousseau, J. J. *A Discourse on the Origin of Inequality.* London: Dent, 1983.
---. *A Discourse on Political Economy.* London: Dent, 1983.
---. *The Social Contract.* London: Dent, 1983.
---. *The Government of Poland.* Indianapolis: Library of Liberal Arts, 1972.

Ryan, Alan. *J. S. Mill*. London: Routledge and Kegan Paul, 1974.

———. *Property and Political Theory*. London: Basil Blackwell, 1984.

Said, Edward W. *Orientalism*. New York: Pantheon Books, 1978.

Salkever, Stephen. *Finding the Mean*. Princeton: Princeton University Press, 1990.

Sandel, Michael. *Liberalism and the Limits of Justice*. New York: Cambridge University Press, 1982.

———. "The Procedural Republic and the Unencumbered Self." *Political Theory* 12 (1984): 81–96.

Schaar, John. "Equality of Opportunity and Beyond." In *Equality. NOMOS,* vol. 9, edited by J. R. Pennock and John Chapman. New York: Atherton, 1967.

Schumpeter, Joseph A. *Capitalism, Socialism, Democracy*. New York: Harper & Brothers, 1942.

Semmel, Bernard. *John Stuart Mill and the Pursuit of Virtue*. New Haven: Yale University Press, 1984.

Shapiro, Ian. *The Evolution of Rights in Liberal Theory*. Cambridge: Cambridge University Press, 1986.

———. "J. G. A. Pocock's Republicanism and Political Theory." *Critical Review* 4 (1990): 433–71.

Shapiro, Michael J. *Reading "Adam Smith": Desire, History and Value*. Newbury Park: Sage, 1993.

Shklar, Judith. *Men and Citizens: A Study of Rousseau's Social Theory*. Cambridge: Cambridge University Press, 1969.

Simmel, Georg. *Conflict and the Web of Group-Affiliations*. Translated and with an introduction by K. H. Wolff. Glencoe: Free Press, 1951.

Sinopoli, Richard. *The Foundations of American Citizenship*. New York: Oxford University Press, 1992.

Skinner, Quentin. *The Foundations of Modern Political Thought*. Vol. 1. Cambridge: Cambridge University Press, 1978.

———. "The Paradoxes of Political Liberty." In *Tanner Lectures on Human Values,* edited by S. McMurrin. Salt Lake City: University of Utah Press, 1986.

———. "On Justice, the Common Good, and the Priority of Liberty," In *Dimensions of Radical Democracy,* edited by Chantal Mouffe. London: Verso, 1992.

Smith, Adam. *An Inquiry into the Nature and Causes of the Wealth of Nations*. Oxford: Oxford University Press, 1976.

———. *Lecture on Jurisprudence*. Oxford: Oxford University Press, 1978.

———. *The Theory of Moral Sentiments*, edited by D. Raphael and A. L. Macfie. Oxford: Oxford University Press, 1976.
Smith, Bruce. *Politics of Remembrance*. Princeton: Princeton University Press, 1985.
Smith, Rogers. "Beyond Tocqueville, Myrdal, and Hartz: The Multiple Traditions in America." *American Political Science Review* 87 (1993): 549–66.
Spragens, Thomas. *The Irony of Liberal Reason*. Chicago: University of Chicago Press, 1981.
Storing, Herbert J. *What the Antifederalists Were For.* Chicago: University of Chicago Press, 1981.
Strauss, Barry. "On Aristotle's Critique of Athenian Democracy." In *Essays on the Foundations of Aristotelian Political Science,* edited by Carnes Lord and David O'Connor. Berkeley: University of California Press, 1991.
Strauss, Leo. *The City and Man*. Chicago: University of Chicago Press, 1964.
———. *Natural Right and History*. Chicago: University of Chicago Press, 1953.
Sullivan, Vickie. "Machiavelli's Momentary 'Machiavellian Moment.'" *Political Theory* 20 (1992): 309–18.
Sullivan, William. *Reconstructing Political Philosophy*. Berkeley: University of California Press, 1982.
Swanson, Judith A. *The Public and the Private in Aristotle's Political Philosophy*. Ithaca: Cornell University Press, 1982.
Talmon, J. L. *The Rise of Totalitarian Democracy*. London: Seckler & Warburg, 1952.
Tarcov, Nathan. *Locke's Education for Liberty*. Chicago: University of Chicago Press, 1984.
Taylor, Charles. *Hegel*. New York: Cambridge University Press, 1975.
———. *Sources of the Self*. Cambridge: Harvard University Press, 1989.
———. "Cross Purposes: The Liberal-Communitarian Debate." In *Liberalism and the Moral Life* edited by Nancy Rosenblum. Cambridge: Harvard University Press, 1989.
———. *Multiculturalism and the Politics of Recognition*. Princeton: Princeton University Press, 1992.
Terchek, Ronald J. "The Fruits of Success and the Crisis of Liberalism." In *Liberals on Liberalism,* edited by Alfonso J. Damico. Totowa, N. J.: Rowman & Littlefield, 1986.
———. "Gandhi and Moral Autonomy." *Gandhi Marg*. 13, 4 (1992): 454–65.

Thompson, Dennis. *John Stuart Mill and Representative Government.* Princeton: Princeton University Press, 1976.
Tocqueville, Alexis de. *Democracy in America.* Translated by Henry Reeve. New York: Vintage, 1957.
Toennies, Ferdinand. *Community and Society.* East Lansing: Michigan State University Press, 1957.
Truman, David. *The Governmental Process.* New York: Knopf, 1951.
Turner, Stephen. *Social Theory of Practice.* Chicago: University of Chicago Press, 1994.
Unger, Roberto. *Knowledge and Politics.* New York: Free Press, 1975.
Vaughan, Frederick. *The Tradition of Political Hedonism from Hobbes to Mill.* New York: Fordham University Press, 1982.
Voegelin, Eric. *From Enlightenment to Revolution.* Durham: Duke University Press, 1975.
Wallach, John R. "Liberals, Communitarians and the Task of Political Theory." *Political Theory* 15 (1987): 581–611.
Walzer, Michael. *Spheres of Justice: A Defense of Pluralism and Equality.* New York: Basic Books, 1983.
———. "Liberalism and the Art of Separation." *Political Theory.* 12 (1984): 315–30.
———. "The Communitarian Critique of Liberalism." *Political Theory* 18 (1990): 6–23.
Warren, Howard. *A History of Associational Psychology.* New York: Scribners, 1921.
Weber, Max. *From Max Weber,* edited by H. H. Gerth and C. Wright Mills. New York: Oxford University Press, 1958.
Wills, Garry. *Inventing America: Jefferson's Declaration of Independence.* Garden City: Doubleday, 1978.
Winch, Donald. *Adam Smith's Politics.* Cambridge: Cambridge University Press, 1978.
Wolin, Sheldon. *Politics and Vision.* Boston: Little, Brown, and Company, 1960.
———. "The Liberal/Democratic Divide." *Political Theory* 24 (1996): 97–142.
Wood, Gordon. *The Creation of the American Republic.* New York: W. W. Norton, 1969.
———. *The Radicalism of the American Revolution.* New York: Knopf, 1992.
Wood, Neal. *John Locke and Agrarian Capitalism.* Berkeley: University of California Press, 1984.

Woolhouse, R. S. *Locke*. Minneapolis: University of Minnesota Press, 1983.

Yolton, John. *Locke and the Compass of Human Understanding*. Cambridge: Cambridge University Press, 1983.

Zastoupil, Lynn. "J. S. Mill and India." *Victorian Studies* 32 (1988): 31–54.

Zilles, Michael. "Universalism and Communitarianism: A Bibliography." *Philosophy and Social Criticism* 14, ns. 3 & 4 (1988): 441–67.

Zuckert, Michael. *Natural Rights and the New Republicanism*. Princeton: Princeton University Press, 1994.

Index

Ackerman, Bruce, as a procedural liberal, 5, 38n7
Adams, John, 77, 209, 212
agrarian society, 81. *See also* Aristotle
American political languages, 205–30
anxious liberalism, 4, 5, 11, 21, 121–203, 231–32, 236–39, 242 and abstracted persons, 124; and autonomy, 125–27, 163, 164; compared with strong republicans, 33; contrasted with procedural liberals, 21, 37; and corruption, 121, 124; as critics of contemporary culture, 162–63; and education, 139; and freedom, 126; and Hobbes, 128; identified, 8–10, 121–24; and interests, 164; and poverty, 123; and procedural liberals, 164; and Rawls, 123; and religion, 164; and responsibility, 123, 126–27; and secular fall, 125; and standards, 124, 139, 141n8, 163–64, 236–39; and virtue, 162, 164. *See also* autonomy; civil society; Locke; Mill; Smith
Appleby, Joyce, 46n106, 209–10, 227n17, 228n33
Arendt, Hannah, 24, 46n105, 46n107

Aristotle, 21, 22, 34, 69, 83; and agrarian society, 59–60; and autonomy, 63; biology, 35; and Booth, 59, 62; and civic decay, 60–62; and civic education, 61–62; and civil society, 63; and civic time, 62–64; and commerce, 60; and Dahl, 62; and diversity, 54; and economy, 55–60, 63; and education, 59, 61; and equality, 62; and equilibrium, 61; and the family, 55–56, 57–58, 63; and founding, 115n6; and the household, 54–64; and inequalities, 60; and leisure, 62, 63–64; and Machiavelli, 70; and money, 54–64, 86n41, 87n54; and multiple needs, 48–49, 54–55, 58, 63, 64; and noisy republicans, 114n1; and poverty, 86n41; and private property, 49, 51–53, 57–59, 63–64, 80; and Salkever, 28, 54–55, 63; and slavery, 35, 62; and Socrates, 57–58; and stakes, 54–64; as strong republican, 4, 6–8, 20, 34, 47, 49, 50, 54–64; and Swanson, 60; and telos, 55–56; and virtue, 54, 55, 56, 61–62; and wealth 59–60. *See also* communitarians; Galston; MacIntyre; Mill; Pocock; Skinner

267

Ashcraft, Richard, 23, 143n35
Augustine, St., 19–20, 70, 217, 224. *See also* MacIntyre
autonomy, 16, 211, 215, 230, 231, 246, 247; and anxious liberals, 125–27, 236–39; and J. S. Mill, 33, 147, 148, 149, 154, 161, 164; and Pocock, 52–53, 215; and property, 81, 215; and Rousseau, 73, 74, 112. *See also* Locke; Mill; Smith

Bailyn, Bernard, 206, 207, 208, 209, 211, 228n39
Barber, Benjamin, 5, 16, 21, 167n38, 226n2, 228n34, 239
Baumgold, Deborah, 23
Beiner, Ronald, 16, 44n85
Bell, Daniel, 153
Bellah, Robert, 17, 52, 96; and American revolution, 16, 21, 22; and civil religion, 46n107, 116n14
Bentley, Arthur, 172, 196n2, 197n8
Berlin, Isaiah, 241–42, 243
Bloom, Alan, 16, 17
Bobbio, Norberto, 248n2
Bock, Gisela, 117n36
Booth, William, 59, 62
Brint, Michael, 92n117

Carlyle, Thomas, 155
children: and anxious liberals, 242. *See also* family; household; Machiavelli; Mill
Christianity. *See* Lincoln; Locke
Cicero, 13n6, 40n31, 40n35, 54
citizens, 63; and property, 51–54; and stakes, 80; and strong republicans, 6–8, 29, 50; and substantive stakes, 82. *See also* citizenship; Machiavelli
citizenship, 47–93; and communitarians, 47–48; and property, 49, 51–54. *See also* Aristotle; Machiavelli; property; Rousseau

citizen-soldier, 65
civic decay. *See* Aristotle
civic duty, 47, 83; and Skinner, 42n62. *See also* Smith
civic education, 8, 79; and communitarians, 62. *See also* Aristotle
civic memory, 103
civic time. *See* Aristotle
civic virtue, 21, 25, 30, 25, 79, 89n81, 97, 206, 207, 225; and communitarians, 52–53. *See also* Machiavelli; Pocock; Skinner; Smith; strong republicans
civil society, 216, 241; and anxious liberals, 125; and strong republicans, 47, 79, 241. *See also* Locke; Mill; Smith
civilization, Mill on, 154–55
class, 77–79
Coleridge, Samuel, 155
Colman, John, 28
commerce, 60, 81, 171, 182. *See also* Aristotle; commercial society; Mill; money; property; Smith
communitarians, 25, 35, 37, 52, 83, 97, 205, 210, 226, 231, 246; agreements among, 16; and Aristotle, 47, 64, 87n63; and autonomy, 3, 16; challenges to, 62–63, 78, 83; and civic education, 62; and civic virtue, 16, 64; and conflict, 96–97, 113, 114; contrast with strong republicans, 8, 14n18, 20, 47–48, 50–51, 53, 235–36; as critics of liberalism, 1, 2, 15–17, 47, 51, 136; debate with liberals, 4–5, 41–45, 30, 33, 213–33; debates among communitarians, 4, 16, 239–41; identified, 3–5; as latest expression of republicanism, 1; and leisure, 62; and Machiavelli, 22, 77, 78, 99, 104, 107; and Mill, 158, 163, 164; nostalgic, 36, 233, 235, 241; problems with critique, 18,

19, 48; retrieving community, 16; and tradition, 22, 31–37, 48, 50–51
conflict, 96
conformity. *See* Mill
Connelly, William, 29, 118n45
conscience. *See* Mill
Corlett, William, 217
corruption, 29, 52, 206, 207, 208, 223, 225, 246; in America, 205. *See also* Machiavelli; Mill; Rousseau; Smith
Crick, Bernard, 24, 42n55

Dahl, Robert, 62, 196n1, 197n3, 197n5
decay, 31. *See also* civic decay, Machiavelli; Rousseau
deception. *See* Smith
Declaration of Independence. *See* Lincoln
deference, 187–89, 194, 206, 207, 212–14, 216, 228n39. *See also* Pocock; Smith
dependencies. *See* Machiavelli; Smith
Diggins, John, 217–18, 229n48
diversity, 1, 64, 96, 115n2. *See also* Aristotle; Mill
Donner, Wendy, 28
Downing, Lyle, 248n3
Downs, Anthony, 197n8
Dunn, John, 28, 136, 138
Dworetz, Steven, 211, 228n30
Dworkin, Ronald, as procedural liberal, 5, 17–18

economy. *See* Aristotle; Locke; Machiavelli; money; property; Rousseau; Smith; wealth
education, 98. *See also* Aristotle; Locke; Mill
Elster, Jon, 196n1
equality of opportunity, 82, 205–7, 211. *See also* Lincoln
equilibrium, 211, 224, 225, 235; and interest-group pluralists, 172, 197n8; and republicans, 113, 234. *See also* Aristotle; Machiavelli; one-class society; Smith
Euben, Peter, 22

factions, 50, 207. *See also* Machiavelli; Rousseau
family, 214, 237, 246; as attachment, 19, 20; and communitarians, 240; and liberals, 242. *See also* Aristotle; Locke; Machiavelli; Mill; Rousseau
fixed property. *See* Smith
founding, 95–115, 206; American, 5, 11, 21, 217–22; in republicanism, 233, 234. *See also* Lincoln; Machiavelli; Rousseau
Fowler, Robert, 13n14
fragments, 27, 28, 33, 35–37, 52, 171, 174, 231, 234; in American rhetorics, 205, 214–16. *See also* Lincoln
Frankfurter, Harry, 126

Galston, William, 18, 248n10; and Aristotle, 21, 28; and Kant, 21; and neutrality, 140n5; and Rawls, 123
Gandhi, Mahatma, 32
Glendon, Mary, 44n78
good despot. *See* Mill
Gordon, Thomas, 208
Gramsci, Antonio, 44n88
Grant, Ruth, 28
Gray, John, 44n89, 168n44
Green, T. H., 32
Greenstone, J. David, 13n11; and Lincoln, 218–19, 224
growth, economic. *See* Smith
Gunnell, John, 24, 41n50
Gutmann, Amy, 39n19, 248n10

Harrington, James, 16, 22, 77; Isaac on, 27
Hartz, Louis, 36, 41n41, 210

Haworth, Alan, 198n16
Hayek, Friedrich, 6; and interest-group liberals, 198n19; and minimal state, 198n14; and Nozick, 202n88. *See also* Smith
Hegel, G. W. F., 246
Himmelfarb, Gertrude, 28, 168n44
Hirsch, Fred, 153
Hirschman, Albert, 236
Hobbes, Thomas, 124, 127–28. *See also* Mill; Smith
Hollowell, John, 23
Holmes, Sherlock, 34
Holmes, Stephen, 39n22
honor, 99, 119n59
household, 6, 7, 19, 20, 52, 234, 237, 240, 246. *See also* Aristotle; Machiavelli; Rousseau
Houston, Alan, 37, 43n72; on Sidney, 27
Hume, David, 1, 33, 237
Huyler, Jerome, 247n1

individualism, 3, 28, 51, 206, 208, 210, 214, 219, 224, 225, 232; and Hobbes, 128. *See also* Mill; Smith
inequality, 234, 235, 238. *See also* Aristotle; Machiavelli; Mill; private property; Rousseau; strong republicans
interest-group liberals, 5, 10, 15, 17; 96–97. *See also* Smith
interests, 19, 96, 97, 208, 210, 212, 213, 233, 234. *See also* Mill; Smith
invisible hand. *See* Smith
Isaac, Jeffrey, 27, 53

Jefferson, Thomas, 28, 81, 219, 220
Justman, Stewart, 161, 168n44

Kant, Immanuel, 1, 21, 33, 123; and Rawls, 21, 22, 122
Kloppenberg, James, 248n1
Kramnick, Isaac, 209–10, 227n13

Kress, Paul, 44n82
Kymlicka, Will, 17, 38n5, 45n102; and Mill, 21

Lasche, Christopher, 17
leisure. *See* Aristotle; Rousseau
liberalism. *See* liberals
liberals, 1, 3, 21, 25, 29, 35, 37, 214; in America, 208–16; criticism of communitarians, 27; criticized by communitarians, 2–3, 15–17; debates with communitarians, 18, 30, 205; enlarging the debate for, 241–45; excesses of, 29; identifying liberalism, 5–6, 10; procedural liberals, 5, 9, 10, 21, 31, 114, 138, 241, 244–46; and standards, 17–18; and two-language paradigm, 28; varieties of liberalism, 17–18. *See also* anxious liberals; Lincoln; Locke; Mill; Smith
libertarians, 1, 5, 17; debts, 173–74; goals, 17, 31, 40n32. *See also* Hayek; Locke; Nozick; property; Smith
Lienesch, Michael, 207
Lincoln, Abraham: and Christianity, 217–19; and Corlett, 217, 219; and Declaration of Independence, 217, 218, 220, 225; and Diggins, 217–18, 219; and Stephen Douglas, 219, 221, 222; and equality, 220, 221; and equality of opportunity, 219; and fragments, 224; and Greenstone, 218–19, 224; his liberalism, 218–19, 229n50; and Machiavelli, 216, 220, 222, 224; and Madison, 218; and noisy republicans, 224; his paradox, 223; and republicanism, 217–18; and Rousseau, 216, 220, 222, 224; and slavery, 216, 220–22, 230n56
Locke, John, 1, 3, 4, 22, 27, 31; in America, 207, 210–11, 228n8,

228n30; as anxious liberal, 4, 5, 8–10, 20, 121–43, 237–39, 241, 242; and autonomy, 33, 126, 129, 134, 138–39; and Christianity, 134–37; and civil society, 10, 32, 132, 134; and Colman, 28; and communitarian critics, 136; and contemporary controversies, 129; and Dunn, 28, 136, 138; and Dworetz, 211; and economy, 124, 133; and education, 130, 134, 136; and equality, 124; and eternal self-preservation, 135; and family, 239; and hedonism, 129, 133, 142n25; and influence on Anglo-American thought, 129; and interests, 129, 139; and liberty, 130; and Mill, 148, 149, 158, 163, 164; and money, 124, 125, 132, 133, 238; and moral standards, 121, 130, 132, 134, 136–39; and neutrality, 129; and Pocock, 142n21; and procedural liberals, 137–39; and property, 125, 138–39; and reason, 124, 128, 129–32, 133, 135, 136; and responsibility, 126, 133, 137, 138; and secular fall, 124, 132–34, 144n41; and self-reflection, 130, 131 32; and Sidney, 27; and simple self, 124; and Smith, 173, 176; and state of nature, 124, 132–34, 238; and Tarcov, 28; and time, 131, 132–34; and tradition, 239; as universalizer, 29, and virtue, 33. *See also* Nozick; proceduralism

Lowi, Theodore, 200n68, 203n96
Lutz, Donald, 228n30

MacDonald, Forest, 247n1
Machiavelli, Niccolo, 22, 77, 83, 95, 97, 107, 108, 109, 111, 113, 114; and Augustine, 70; and children, 66; and citizenship, 64–70; and citizen-soldier, 65; and civic memory, 103; and civic virtue, 33, 64, 66, 67, 99, 102, 103, 105, 107; and class, 78; and corruption, 67, 68, 69–70, 89n77, 90n92, 97, 98, 105, 107, 113; and decay, 64, 70, 103–4, 107, 114; and dependency, 68; and Diggins, 229n48; and economy, 32, 66, 77–78; and equilibrium, 68, 99–100, 104, 105, 106; and equity, 68; and factions, 68, 96; and families, 65, 100; and Florence, 105–6; and foundational principles, 68, 69, 100–102, 106, 113; and household, 64–70; and inequalities, 68; and justice, 68, 89n83, 102–4; and MacIntyre, 16; and noisy republicans, 99–107; and his paradox, 53, 66–69, 113–14; and participation, 65, 66, 99–107, 113–14; and peace, 66; and poverty, 69; and power, 99; and private property, 66, 67, 78, 80, 99, 100; and religion, 64, 99, 100–102, 106, 116n14, 116n15; and Rome, 101, 104–5; and Rousseau, 118n50; and self-interest, 64; and shame, 101; and Adam Smith, 68; as strong republican, 4, 6, 7, 20, 64–70; and tumult, 104, 106; and wealth, 66, 68–69, 78, 99. *See also* Aristotle; communitarians; Lincoln; Pocock; Rawls; Skinner; stakes; tradition; virtue

MacIntyre, Alasdair, 16, 17, 27, 31, 32, 45n98, 96, 239; and Aristotle, 21, 22, 28, 34–35, 54; and Augustine, 21; and Hume, 1, 33; as critic of liberalism, 17, 23, 34; and Machiavelli, 16; and moral reasoning, 26, 32; and sociology, 34–35; and St. Thomas, 21. *See also* Skinner

Macpherson, C. B., 23, 143n35, 210
Madison, James, 218

Mansbridge, Jane, 168n42, 197n11
markets, 236. *See also* Hayek; interest-group liberals; libertarians; Smith
McWilliams, Wilson Carey, 45n103
merchants. *See* Smith
Meyers, Marvin, 13n11
Michelman, Frank, 85n19
Mill, John Stuart, 5, 22, 27, 50, 124, 125, 241; as anxious liberal, 4, 5, 8–11, 20, 28, 121, 127, 147–69, 237–39; and Aristotle, 152, 163; and autonomy, 33, 147, 148, 149, 154, 161, 162, 164, 238; and Carlyle, 155; and children, 160, 163; and civil society, 32; and civilization, 154–55, 238; and Coleridge, 155; and commercial society, 151–55; and commercialism, 151, 162; and communitarians, 158, 161, 163, 164; and conformity, 152, 162; and conscience, 149, 150–51, 158, 161; and corruption, 162; and countertendencies, 154; and decay, 153; and diversity, 161; and education, 160; and equipoise, 152–53; and family, 160, 163, 237, 239, 248n9; and good despot, 162; and higher pleasures, 165n12; and Himmelfarb, 28, 168n44; and Hobbes, 149; and individualism, 162; and inequality, 154; and interests, 157, 164; and Justman, 161; and Kymlicka, 21; and mobility, 156; and money, 151, 152, 156; and moral facts, 155; and natural self, 148, 238; and nature, 148–51, 155, 165n8; and participation, 155–59, 167n38, 168n41, 238; and procedural liberals, 161, 164; and reason, 149; and relativism, 162, 164; and religion, 163, 164; as republican, 159–62; and "savage," 149, 154; and slavery, 148, 155; and Smith, 173, 190; and stakes, 163; and standards, 121, 149–56; 158, 159, 162; and strong republicans, 162, 164; and tolerance, 164; and tradition, 153–55, 162, 163, 169n52, 238; and utilitarianism, 161; and virtue, 149, 160, 164; and wealth, 154, 162, 166n20. *See also* Locke
Milton, John, 22
money, 237. *See also* Aristotle; Locke; Mill; property; wealth
Moon, Donald, 22
Moore, Margaret, 141n8
moral sentiments. *See* Smith
multiple languages, 11
multiple needs, 31, 54, 233, 239, 247. *See also* Aristotle

natural jurisprudence. *See* Smith
neutrality, 5, 16, 18, 29n24, 128, 129, 245, 246; and Galston, 18; and Rawls, 122. *See also* procedural liberals; Smith
Niebuhr, Reinhold, 24
Nisbet, Robert, 17
noisy republicans, 95–119; and Lincoln, 224; and Machiavelli, 99–107; and Rousseau, 107–13
Norton, Anne, 249n11
Nozick. *See* Hayek; Locke; Smith
Nussbaum, Martha, 22

Oakeshott, Michael, 22, 24
Offe, Claus, 81
Okin, Susan, 31, 35
one-class society, 78–79, 93n130. *See also* Rousseau
opportunity society, 214–16

Pangle, Thomas, 210–11
paradox, 4, 8, 11, 30, 51, 53, 95, 113; liberal paradox, 178; Lincoln's paradox, 223; Machiavel-

li's, 53, 66–69, 113–14; republican paradox, 231–34, 247
participation, 16, 30, 64, 64, 66, 99–107, 113–14. *See also* Machiavelli; Mill; Pocock; Rousseau; Smith
Pateman, Carole, 167n38
peace, 95. *See also* Machiavelli
Pocock, J. G. A., 30, 225; and American republicanism, 206–15, 227n14; and Aristotle, 16, 27, 28, 63; and autonomy, 52–54; and civic humanism, 16; and civic virtue, 30; and credit, 227n13; as critic of liberalism, 23; criticized by Isaac, 27; and deference, 228n36; and Locke, 142n21; and Machiavelli, 16, 21, 23, 52–53, 69, 107; and private property, 52–53, 215; and tradition, 25, 26; two-language paradigm, 25–26; and virtue, 229n45
poverty, 181–82, 192. *See also* Machiavelli; Rousseau
Preus, J. Samuel, 116n15
proceduralism, 16, 21, 29, 31, 82, 83, 114; and autonomy, 137–38; and Dworkin, 17–18; and Locke, 137; and responsibility, 137, 138. *See also* liberals procedural; Mill; neutrality
property, 3, 5, 7, 8, 17, 19, 27, 33, 49, 206, 207; as attachment, 19; and autonomy, 81, 215; and citizenship, 51–54; fixed property, 124, 237; and inequality, 49–50, and libertarians, 17; and stakes, 49–51, 47–93; and strong republicans, 47–93. *See also* Aristotle; money; Locke; Pocock; Skinner; Smith; stakes; Wood

Raphael, D. D., 28
Rawls, John, 17, 21, 22, 27, 44n81, 128, 241; and anxious liberals, 123; and Kant, 21, 22, 123; and Machiavelli, 100; as procedural liberal, 5, 38n7, 122–23, 140n2; and responsibility, 122–23; and standards, 122; and two-language paradigm, 26; and wealth, 122. *See also* liberals; proceduralism; Skinner
reason, 137. *See also* Locke; Mill; Smith
Reich, Charles, 249n12
relativism, Mill on, 162, 164
religion, 210–11. *See also* Lincoln; Locke; Machiavelli; Mill; Rousseau; Smith
republicanism, strong, 4, 6, 11, 12, 16, 18, 19, 206–7, 214, 231–35; identified, 6–8; and Smith, 191, 193. *See also* Aristotle; Machiavelli, Rousseau
responsibility. *See* Locke
rights, acquired, 178–79, 191, 196; rights in conflict, 242–45
Rogers, Daniel, 210, 226n3, 227n23
Rome. *See* Machiavelli; Smith
Rorty, Richard, 42n52
Rousseau, Jean-Jacques, 4, 6, 7, 22, 47, 83, 95, 97, 98, 113–14; and autonomy, 73, 74, 112; and Barber, 21; and civic duty, 108, 111; and civic virtue, 71; and civil society, 75, 110; and civilization, 71; communitarians on, 28; and conflict, 111; and corruption, 76, 97, 110, 112, 113; and decay, 108, 109, 114; and economy, 32; and equality, 71, 73, 76, 77, 91n108, 110, 111; and factions, 96, 112; and the family, 109, 111; and the founding, 75, 91n112, 108–11, 112, 113; and general will, 74–75, 108, 112; and honor, 111; and household, 70; and inequality, 74, 76, 79, 110–11, 119n57; and leisure, 72, 73–75; and Lincoln, 216, 220,

222, 224; and Machiavelli, 118n50; and mobility, 74; and multiple needs, 74, 110; and noisy republicanism, 107–13; and one-class society, 73, 78–79, 110, 111; his paradox, 75, 113–14; and participation, 70, 73, 74–75, 76, 77, 107–13; and peace, 75–77; and property, 73–75, 76, 77, 79, 80, 108, 109, 111; and poverty, 73, 74, 78; and reason, 109; and religion, 109; and Smith, 192; and stability, 74, 76; and stakes, 70–77, 109; as strong republican, 4, 6, 7, 20, 49–51, 70–77, 108, 206, 233–34; and Sullivan, 21; and taxes, 119n54; and traditions, 108, 111, 113; and wealth, 73–74, 110, 111. *See also* Machiavelli

Ryan, Alan, 28, 41n44

Said, Edward, 41n43
Salkever, Stephen, 28, 54–55, 63, 86n27, 114n1
Sandel, Michael, 17, 38n14, 96, 115n6, 239, 248n6; on Kant, 1, 33; and Rawls, 140n2
savage. *See* Mill; Smith
Schumpeter, Joseph, 153, 196n1
secular fall. *See* Locke
Semmel, Bernard, 28
Sidney, Algernon, 22, 27
Sinopoli, Richard, 13n15
Skinner, Quentin, 23, 27; and Aristotle, 16, 54, 63; and Cicero, 13n16, 40n35, 54; and Machiavelli, 16, 21, 26, 40n35, 52–53, 106; and MacIntyre, 38n12; and property, 52–53, 215; and Rawls, 42n62; and republican paradox, 53; and republican tradition, 16
slavery. *See* Aristotle; Lincoln; Mill; Smith
Smith, Adam, 4, 22, 27, 124, 125, 126, 171–203, 241, 242; and acquired rights, 178, 179, 191, 196; and American revolution, 229n41; as anxious liberal, 4, 5, 8–11, 20, 28, 121, 127, 171–203, 237; and autonomy, 33, 126, 182, 193, 194, 196; and civic duty, 180, 186, 191–93; and civic virtue, 187, 190, 191; and civil society, 10, 32, 55, 177; and commerce, 171, 182, 183, 237; and corruption, 187, 190–91; and deception, 85, 87, 171, 185–89, 196, 237; and deference, 187–89, 194; and democracy, 190, 195; and dependencies, 179–83, 185–87; and equality, 185; and equilibrium, 172, 190; and family, 239; and fixed property, 124, 177–78; and Greece, 190; and growth, economic, 190, 192; and Hayek, 21, 173–74, 193–94, 198n17; and Hobbes, 177; and individualism, 187; and inequality, 178, 193; and innocent self, 124; and interest-group liberals, 171, 172–73, 191; and interests, 174, 175, 180, 183–86, 188–91, 194–95; and invisible hand, 180, 184, 185, 188, 194–95; and libertarians, 1, 10, 19, 171, 173–74, 194; and luxury, 180, 186–87, 193; and Machiavelli, 68, 190; and markets, 10, 171, 172, 173, 183–85, 188–89, 193–95, 200n63; and merchants, 189–90, 200n66, 200n85, 202n95; and Mill, 173, 190; and moral sentiments, 171, 175, 176, 183, 187–88, 192, 198n24, 238; and natural jurisprudence, 183, 189, 195, 196; and neutrality, 178; and Nozick, 173, 191; his paradox, 178, 186; and participation, 178, 192; and poverty, 181–82,

191, 192, 202n94; and property, 176–79, 180, 191 192, 199n39; and rationality, 173, 184, 185, 189, 191; and reason, 200n64; and religion, 201n80; and republicans, 191, 193; and responsibility, 126; and Romans, 186–87, 190; and Rousseau, 192; and savages, 181–82; and scarcity, 181, 182, 196; and slavery, 190–91, 192, 200n54, 200n87; and standards, 121, 175–76, 188; and strong republicans, 190; and taxes, 191–93; and tradition, 239; and virtue, 175, 185; and wealth, 11, 178, 179, 183, 185–87, 190, 192; and Winch, 28. *See also* Locke

Socrates, 19, 22, 127. *See also* Aristotle

stakes, 47–93, 95, 246; and agrarian society, 81; and equality of opportunity, 82; and Hobbes, 48–49; and modern citizenship, 80–83, 235, 239; and procedures, 82. *See also* Aristotle; Machiavelli; Mill; property; Rousseau

Strauss, Leo, 38, 39, 40

strong republicans, 47–93, 95, 233–36; and civil society, 79; and distributional issues, 79–80; and multiple needs, 49. *See also* Aristotle; communitarians; Machiavelli; Mill; property; Rousseau; Smith

Sullivan, William, 21, 27; and republican tradition, 16

Swanson, Judith, 60

Tarcov, Nathan, 28

taxes. *See* Rousseau; Smith

Taylor, Charles, 5, 12n8, 17, 27, 36, 39n25, 52, 239; and diversity 16; and Hegel, 21

telos, 35, 55–56

Terchek, Ronald, 249n13

Thigpen, Robert, 248n3

Tocqueville, Alexis de, 50, 93n130, 115n7

Toennies, Ferdinand, 46n104

tolerance. *See* Mill

tradition, 25, 36, 47, 51; constructing traditions, 21–25; liberalism as opposed to, 141n8; in political theory, 15–46; problematizing elements, 23; rich traditions, 30–34; and strong republicans, 50, 83, 95, 97, 98. *See also* Machiavelli; Mill; Rousseau

Trenchard, John, 208

Truman, David, 196n2, 197n8

tumult, 104, 106

two-language paradigm, 25–30, 232–33

usable past, 37

Vaughan, Frederick, 17

virtue. *See* Aristotle; civic virtue; Locke; Machiavelli; Mill; Pocock; Smith

Voegelin, Eric, 23

Walzer, Michael, 16, 18, 31, 36, 44n80; and liberal excesses, 29

wealth. *See* Aristotle; economy; inequality; Machiavelli; money; poverty; property; Rousseau; Smith

Wills, Gary, 28

Winch, Donald, 28, 201n25

Wolin, Sheldon, 89n71, 116n11

Wood, Gordon, 209, 226n27; and American Revolution, 21, 23, 206, 208, 213; and property, 215; and republican tradition, 16, 207, 210, 211

Zastoupil, Lynn, 169n53

About the Author

Ronald J. Terchek is associate professor of government and politics at the University of Maryland at College Park. In addition to his work on liberal and republican theory, he has published numerous articles and lectured extensively on liberal-democratic theory, theories of autonomy, and the political theory of Mahatma Gandhi in the United States and abroad.